*Servants and
Masters in
Eighteenth-Century
France*

Servants and Masters in Eighteenth-Century France

∽

THE USES OF LOYALTY

Sarah C. Maza

PRINCETON UNIVERSITY PRESS

PRINCETON, NEW JERSEY

Library of Congress Cataloging in Publication Data will be
found on the last printed page of this book

ISBN 0-691-05394-4

This book has been composed in Linotron Garamond

Clothbound editions of Princeton University Press books
are printed on acid-free paper, and binding materials
are chosen for strength and durability.
Paperbacks, although satisfactory for personal collections,
are not usually suitable for library rebinding.

Printed in the United States of America by
Princeton University Press
Princeton, New Jersey

TO MY PARENTS

Contents

Contents

List of Tables and Figures

TABLES

List of Illustrations

All illustrations except no. 9 are from the Cabinet des Estampes
of the Bibliothèque Nationale. No. 9 is in the Louvre Museum,
Paris. Reprinted with permission.

Abbreviations and Note on Translations

A.D.A.   Archives Départementales des Bouches-du-Rhône, Dépôt d'Aix-en-Provence
A.D.C.   Archives Départementales du Calvados, Dépôt de Caen
A.D.M.   Archives Départementales des Bouches-du-Rhône, Dépôt de Marseille
A.M.A.   Archives Municipales, Aix-en-Provence
A.M.B.   Archives Municipales, Bayeux
A.M.M.   Archives Municipales, Marseille
B.M.   Bibliothèque Méjanes, Aix-en-Provence
M.A.   Musée Arbaud, Aix-en-Provence

Unless otherwise indicated, all translations are my own. Quotations in verse have been left in the original in the text and are translated in the notes.

Acknowledgments

Despite the seemingly endless succession of drafts that eventually yielded this book, this project has almost invariably been a pleasure to work on, not least because of the people and places that have been associated with it since its inception. I wish first of all to thank Robert Darnton of Princeton University, who supervised this work in its earlier stages, for his criticisms, his kind encouragement back then and since then, and for the example of his own writings. I am also pleased to have this chance to acknowledge a long-standing debt to Michel Vovelle of the University of Provence, who introduced me in my undergraduate years to the social history of the Ancien Régime and first guided me through the maze of the French archives. His expertise and kindness have helped on countless occasions over the last decade.

The research I carried out in Normandy and part of the writing were funded by Northwestern University and by a Shelby Cullom Davis Grant from Princeton University. In France the staffs of several libraries and provincial archives went out of their way to help me locate sources and make the best use of my time. I am especially grateful to M. Auguste Villion of the Archives Municipales of Aix; to M. Charles Foucquart, Melle Elizabeth Martinez, and the rest of the staff of the Archives Départementales in Aix; and to M. Christian Bernard and Melle Odile Jurbert in Caen. My trips to France have been facilitated and enlivened by the hospitality and friendship of Bérénice Grissolange in Bayeux and Chérine Gébara in Aix.

As I was writing, I benefited from helpful comments on different chapters from Bernadette Fort, David Joravsky, and Robert

Acknowledgments

Lerner. Jeff Lipkis and Michael Sherry assisted in eradicating semicolons, gallicisms, and assorted stylistic atrocities from my prose. Joan Stahl typed the final draft with skill, patience, and good cheer. The entire manuscript was read at different stages by Natalie Davis, Cissie Fairchilds, Theodore Koditschek, William Reddy, and William H. Sewell, all of whom contributed greatly to its improvement. I am most particularly grateful to my colleagues Karen Halttunen, T. William Heyck, and Robert Wiebe, whose intellectual contributions and moral support were equally crucial as I recast an unwieldy dissertation into the book it has become.

I will not name all of the friends who, in the past few years, have demonstrated some of the better uses of loyalty. They know who they are and, I hope, how much I owe them. My mother's love of literature and my father's curiosity about the varieties of culture no doubt contributed long ago to shaping my own interests. For this, and much else, the book is dedicated to them.

Evanston, Illinois
October 1982

*Servants and
Masters in
Eighteenth-Century
France*

Introduction

This book is about domestic servants and domestic service in France from the late seventeenth to the early nineteenth century. It concerns first of all the servants themselves, the thousands of men and women who embraced this occupation for all or part of their working lives and made up the single largest category of workers in French towns under the Old Regime. It also explores the many facets of an institution which in the eighteenth century cast a bridge between country and town, threw the very poor into intimate contact with the very rich, and allowed the social elites to define, both in theory and in practice, their understanding of the means and ends of personal authority.

More than any other category of workers, domestic servants are familiar figures to anybody acquainted with the great literary works of seventeenth- and eighteenth-century France. Valets and maids argue loudly with their masters in the comedies of Molière; they flirt and scheme their ways through the plays of Marivaux and Lesage; Diderot's Jacques the Fatalist exhausts his employer in endless metaphysical debate; Beaumarchais's Figaro challenges the unscrupulous Count Almaviva to a duel of wits and willpower. Yet despite the conspicuousness of such characters in contemporary plays and novels, and despite the sheer numerical weight of a group that made up one-tenth or more of the urban population, domestic servants in France and elsewhere are a category of workers whose history has long been neglected.[1]

[1] Domestic servants are not mentioned at all in such standard recent syntheses on Ancien Régime society as Pierre Goubert, *L'Ancien Régime*, vol. I or Camille

This neglect is no doubt partly due to the fact that since the nineteenth century domestic service has been categorized as women's work, and that the latter subject itself has not received much attention until very recently. In more recent years, practitioners of the "new social history" which has flourished in the last two decades at first gravitated spontaneously toward the study of workers who asserted their autonomy from their masters and employers either economically, culturally, or politically. They have been interested primarily in peasants, artisans, and factory hands, in groups that engaged in productive activities, participated in strikes and rebellions, and left traces of autonomous cultures. Household servants were by definition unproductive, never openly or collectively protested their fate, and were reputed to identify with those who employed and often exploited them.

Although some older monographs on domestic service in Europe do exist, it is the recent reawakening of interest in the history of women and the family which has done most to rescue domestic workers of past centuries from oblivion. But as a result most recent works on the subject concern the era in which service was most typically a woman's occupation: the nineteenth and early twentieth centuries. While a number of recent works deal with servants in nineteenth-century France and Britain, only two monographs in the last several decades concern their counterparts in earlier times.[2]

Ernest Labrousse et al., *Histoire économique et sociale de la France*, vol. II. Only a few references to servants are to be found in Roland Mousnier, *Les Institutions de la France sous la monarchie absolue.*

[2] Recent works on nineteenth- and twentieth-century service include Pamela Horn, *The Rise and Fall of the Victorian Servant*; Theresa McBride, *The Domestic Revolution: The Modernisation of Household Service in England and France, 1820–1920*; Pierre Guiral and Guy Thuillier, *La Vie quotidienne des domestiques en France au XIXe siècle*; Anne Martin-Fugier, *La Place des bonnes: La domesticité féminine à Paris en 1900*; David Katzman, *Seven Days a Week: Women and Domestic Service in Industrializing America*. On eighteenth-century service besides the much older study by Albert Babeau, *Les Artisans et les domestiques d'autrefois*, see J. Jean

The purpose of this study is therefore in part to explore a central and neglected aspect of the history of French society in the century before the Revolution. But more importantly, perhaps, it is also intended to suggest a new approach to the subject. To date most studies of domestic service have tended to fall into one of two categories. To an earlier generation of scholars especially, domestic service was a particular aspect of the history of upper-class life in past centuries. Older studies rely heavily on sources emanating from the elites such as letters, diaries, and books on household management.[3] By largely confining the experience of service to the masters' households, these works implicitly define service within the terms set by employers.

More recently, historians have turned the question inside-out by approaching domestic service from the point of view of servants rather than from that of their masters. Where did domestic workers come from in the eighteenth and nineteenth centuries? What were their hopes, fears, and expectations as they entered and pursued a career in service? What were their working and living conditions? And what chances of economic or social promotion were offered to them by domestic service? These and other questions have been explored in the last few years as increasingly sophisticated approaches to labor history have come to complement earlier traditions of social history. Thus, Leonore Davidoff has written of service as a stage in the working-class life cycle, and Theresa McBride has discussed it as a "bridging occupation"

Hecht, *The Domestic Servant Class in Eighteenth-Century England*, and Jean-Pierre Gutton, *Domestiques et serviteurs dans la France de l'Ancien Régime*. Gutton's book appeared in print as this study was almost completed, and therefore is not systematically cited in the notes. It is a useful but succinct overview, based mostly on published material, which includes a discussion of rural as well as urban servants. Cissie Fairchilds's book on the same subject is forthcoming.

[3] Hecht, *The Domestic Servant Class*, is most representative of this approach. But it is also adopted in more recent works such as Horn, *The Victorian Servant*, and Guiral and Thuillier, *La Vie quotidienne des domestiques*.

that facilitated a young woman's transition, in the nineteenth century, from country to city life and from the values of the rural or working classes to those of the middle class.[4]

There can be no denying the necessity or legitimacy of this recent shift in emphasis: domestic service in past centuries was even more important, no doubt, as a means of survival for the poor than as a practical necessity or a sign of status for the rich. Yet either one of these approaches alone fails to highlight what playwrights, novelists, and their readers have long known: that domestic service is first and foremost a relationship. The complex appeal of such different fictional characters as Caliban, Pamela Andrews, and Figaro has to do mainly with the fact that they define and assert themselves in opposition to and in symbiosis with a Prospero, a Mr. B., or a Count Almaviva. And the same can be said of domestic service as a historical reality. The men and women who, in eighteenth-century France, left home to seek employment in town in the houses of the wealthy did so with specific goals in mind. The men and women who employed them had their own views of the purposes of service, which very often were at odds with those of their employees. The characteristic features of domestic service in France under the Old Regime were therefore determined by a perpetual process of negotiation, conflict, and compromise between master and servant. One of the central purposes of this book is to show the ways in which the view of service "from above" and that "from below" were organically related within the social and cultural context of eighteenth-century France.

The nature of the bond between master and servant therefore lies at the heart of the matter. Although, as the following chapters

---

[4] Lenore Davidoff, "Domestic Service and the Working-Class Life-Cycle," *Society for the Study of Labour History Bulletin* 26 (Spring 1973): 10–13. (Davidoff has elsewhere discussed the in-house relationship between master and servant in Victorian England.) See also McBride, *The Domestic Revolution*, and Gutton, *Domestiques et serviteurs*, which is also weighted toward a discussion of the servants themselves.

will show, the tenor of such relationships varied widely in practice, contemporaries did have a clear idea of how in theory masters and servants should act with one another. A whole body of prescriptive literature published in the seventeenth and eighteenth centuries offered readers an ideal of master-servant relations which I have termed "aristocratic paternalism." The main features, and indeed the very existence of such an ideal, offer clues and raise questions about the meaning of the master-servant relationship in society at large.

Eighteenth-century employers could find advice on how to conduct themselves with their servants in handbooks for masters, in confessional guides and religious tracts, and in books on household management. The authors of most prescriptive literature published from the late seventeenth to the late eighteenth century were members of the first two estates or lived in the entourage of the rich and powerful. They were ecclesiastics such as Fénelon, Fleury, Blanchard, or Collet; high-ranking servants such as Audiger, a former steward at Versailles; or aristocrats, such as the Prince de Conty or the Duchesse de Liancourt.[5] All of these writers assumed that their readers would have to contend with a large staff of domestics, most of them menservants. According to Audiger in *La Maison Réglée* (1688), the staff of a *grand seigneur* should comprise thirty to thirty-six menservants, ranging from the steward, chaplain, secretary, and equerry down to the six lackeys, two pages, four grooms, and two postilions. The only female servant listed is a scullery maid. The lord's wife, *la dame*

---

[5] Claude Fleury, *Les Devoirs des maîtres et des domestiques* and Audiger, *La Maison réglée*, both reprinted in Alfred Franklin, *La Vie de Paris sous Louis XIV: Tenue de maison et domesticité*; Prince de Conty, *Mémoires de Monseigneur le Prince de Conty touchant les obligations d'un gouverneur de province et la conduite de sa maison*; François de la Mothe-Fénelon, *De l'Education des filles* (reprint ed., Paris, 1881); Antoine Blanchard, *Essai d'exhortation pour les états différens des malades*; Abbé Pierre Collet, *Traîté des devoirs des gens du monde et surtout des chefs de famille*; Duchesse de Liancourt, *Règlement donné par une dame de qualité à M*** sa petite-fille pour sa conduite et celle de sa maison*.

1. An aristocratic mistress and her servants, late seventeenth century. (Phot. Bibl. nat. Paris)

de qualité, should have her own retinue of fourteen, only three of whom were to be female.[6] Audiger himself admitted that this ideal staff of fifty-odd retainers was out of reach of all but a few very wealthy employers. But he and most other writers on such matters aimed their handbooks at the upper crust of employers, at the aristocracy and those who emulated it. The prescriptive literature published in the last century of the Ancien Régime discusses lackeys and pages, valets and chambermaids, coaches and liveries. Hardly anywhere in this body of literature are there references to the merchant employing a couple of servants or to the artisan family served by a single maid. The standards for domestic service were set, throughout most of the Old Regime, by and for the aristocracy.

The relationship described in these texts can be termed paternalistic because masters and mistresses were encouraged to look upon their servants as child-like, dependent beings. Employers were held responsible, in theory, for every aspect of the material and moral welfare of their domestics. A good master would provide his servants with adequate clothes and nourishment, and would take good care of them if they were sick, sparing neither food nor medicine.[7] He would see to their future as well as present needs, apprentice them to respectable craftsmen if they wanted to learn a trade, or bestow a generous dowry on them if they wished to get married with his consent.[8]

In this best of all possible domestic worlds, employers would take charge of the secular and religious education of their menials. Audiger and Fleury both recommended that all servants in the household be taught reading, writing, and arithmetic, and that good books be made available to lackeys and valets.[9] But the

---

[6] Audiger, *La Maison réglée*, pp. 11–12, 68–69.

[7] Fleury, *Devoirs des maîtres*, pp. 214–215, 237; Audiger, *La Maison réglée*, p. 8; Liancourt, *Règlement*, pp. 108–109, 116.

[8] Fleury, *Devoirs des maîtres*, p. 237.

[9] Ibid., pp. 217–218, 319, 323–324; Audiger, *La Maison réglée*, pp. 24, 30.

master's primary duty was to oversee the religious instruction of his servants. He should see to it that they attend services and religious instruction, provide them with prayer books, and make sure that they took communion at least four times a year.[10] In a more general way, prescriptive texts made it clear that the real justification of domestic service lay in the master's endeavors at reforming his servants: "God only gives you servants that they may find help and refuge in your charity, an example in your piety, enlightenment in your teachings, and in your zeal and dedication a powerful exhortation to salvation."[11] The master, wrote Fleury, "must consider it inevitable that every one of [his servants] has a fault, and must charitably endeavor to correct it."[12] If no such reform was possible, the relationship between master and servant had no meaning.

Material responsibility and moral guidance would enable masters to establish control over their staffs. But these were not the only means of control advocated to employers. By definition, paternalism invests the dominant party with a great deal of untrammeled authority, and the ethos that pervades seventeenth- and eighteenth-century handbooks is nothing if not authoritarian. The texts from the Scriptures most often quoted to explain and justify the master's power within the household are the fifth and sixth chapters of Saint Paul's Epistles to the Ephesians: "Servants, be obedient to them that are your masters according to the flesh, with fear and trembling, in singleness of your heart, as unto Christ" (VI: 5). The Epistles of Paul invest the patriarch with absolute dominion over wife, children, and servants. They stress obedience as the cardinal virtue within the household, whose members must submit themselves "one to another in the fear of

[10] Audiger, *La Maison réglée*, pp. 21–22; Fleury, *Devoirs des maîtres*, p. 222; Conty, *Mémoires*, pp. 79–80; Collet, *Traîté des devoirs*, p. 212; Benigne Lordelot, *Les Devoirs de la vie domestique par un père de famille*, pp. 120–121.

[11] Jacques-Joseph Duguet, *Conduite d'une dame chrétienne pour vivre saintement dans le monde*, p. 231.

[12] Fleury, *Devoirs des maîtres*, p. 219.

God." The Abbé Fleury, also quoting from the Bible, wrote that the master owed his servant "bread, work, and punishment." The servant in return was held to his own triad of duties, "to suffer, to work, and to be silent."[13]

The master was not only expected but encouraged to resort to corporal punishment in order to assert his fatherly role: "You must serve as a father to them, and act with them as would a reasonable father. And the Scriptures tell fathers not to spare the rod with their children."[14] Such precepts may seem brutal to the modern reader, but in fact most of these writers explicitly denounced random and overly cruel punishments. Floggings were permissible if meted out deliberately, for the purpose of reforming servants, but random or gratuitous violence was frowned upon.

Where the general demeanor of masters was concerned, authors insistently reminded their readers to behave with humility and compassion. These texts are laced with reminders, drawn from the Bible, of the natural equality that exists between Christians. The Apostle Paul himself had admonished masters that they were no better than their bondsmen in the eyes of their Maker: "Your master also is in heaven; neither is there respect of persons with him" (VI: 9). The same litany runs through the writings of Fleury and Fénelon in the seventeenth century, Madame de Lambert and the Abbé Collet in the eighteenth: servants are our equals, drawn from the same earth and redeemed by the blood of Christ; death, the great leveler, will turn us all back to dust; only fate and necessity determine our station in life; servants, in the end, are superior to their masters, for Christians are born to serve, not to be served.[15] "Nothing is further from the spirit of Christianity," wrote Fleury, "than that tyrannical spirit that makes us look

[13] Ibid., pp. 214–215.

[14] Ibid., pp. 230–231.

[15] Ibid., pp. 207–209; Fénelon, *Education des filles*, p. 71; Lordelot, *Devoirs de la vie domestique*, pp. 113–116; Liancourt, *Règlement*, pp. 106–107; Anne-Thérèse de Lambert, *Avis d'une mère à son fils et à sa fille*, p. 203; Collet, *Traîté des devoirs*, pp. 207–208.

upon our servants as a different sort of animal, born to serve us and to satisfy our every whim."[16] The overall message of prescriptive literature was that the relationship between master and servant should not be tyrannical but reciprocal. For all of their acknowledged power to control and coerce, masters did not have rights over their servants, but duties toward them. Authority had to be mitigated with compassionate concern, for only then could the servant live up to his side of the covenant and obey his master in his heart as well as in his actions.

The relationship as presented in prescriptive literature was not a contractual arrangement: master and servant were not bound to one another by an exchange of work for money. Employers were not urged to pay their servants regularly, but were encouraged to reward outstanding demonstrations of diligence and loyalty with occasional largesse or by providing for their servants' futures. Servants were expected to work very hard, but for broad ethical reasons, rather than to fulfill their part in a monetary transaction: "Work is the occupation of mankind, the penance of Christians, and the duty of servants," wrote one author.[17] Writers freely acknowledged that a servant's job often entailed long stretches of idleness: lackeys spent hours waiting for their masters in the antechamber or the kitchen, and a valet had little to do once his master was dressed in the morning. But servants should do their best to occupy themselves, not because their time was precious but because idleness was unchristian and could breed mischief.[18]

Just as the master's main responsibilities were moral rather than material, a servant's character and disposition were more important, in theory, than his or her competence at work. Among the many qualities a good servant should possess were diligence,

[16] Fleury, *Devoirs des maîtres*, p. 210.

[17] *Devoirs généraux des domestiques de l'un et l'autre sexe envers Dieu et leurs maîtres et maîtresses*, p. 20; see also Fleury, *Devoirs des maîtres*, pp. 216, 269.

[18] Fleury, *Devoirs des maîtres*, pp. 319, 324; Duguet, *Conduite d'une dame chrétienne*, p. 234.

honesty, and discretion; but these were less important than the cardinal virtues of obedience and loyalty. Though the Bible proclaimed the equality of all men before God, servants should submit to their masters because authority and deference were the glue that cemented the social order: "There must necessarily be subordination in the world, superiors and inferiors, masters and servants, so as to maintain the harmony of the universe and of civil society."[19] But it was not enough that servants obey their masters in appearances only. They should internalize obedience and be faithful in their hearts as well. They should submit themselves, in the words of Saint Paul, "not with eyeservice as men-pleasers; but as servants of Christ doing the will of God from the heart" (VI: 6).

The most important quality a servant could demonstrate was that of loyalty, *fidélité*. Loyalty, like obedience, was crucial not just to the domestic sphere but to the proper functioning of the world beyond the household. It was loyalty from the heart, not just simple deference, that ensured the cohesion of the social order:

> [Loyalty] is the servant's first duty. It is the bedrock of human society, and particularly of domestic society, which depends on the trust that the father places in his wife, his children, and his servants. Take away that trust, and man's existence will sink into crime and horrible confusion, will be worse than the life of the wildest beasts.[20]

Fidélité, then, was a principle essential not just to harmony of the household, but indeed to the whole social order. The family, wrote Fleury, was but a microcosm of the state, itself a family writ large. Without *fidélité*, family and society would dissolve into chaos.[21]

Such were the norms governing domestic service under the

[19] Fleury, *Devoirs des maîtres*, pp. 255–257.
[20] Ibid., p. 258.
[21] Ibid., pp. 208–209.

Old Regime. The ideal was that of a reciprocal relationship that revolved around notions of responsibility and compassion on the part of the master and loyalty on that of the servant. Those who set the norms in writing associated domestic service with the aristocracy, to the exclusion of any other social group. And they insisted that the bond between master and servant was essential not just to the household, but to the very fabric of society: only if the relationship were symbiotic and reciprocal could it fulfill its role as a link in the chain of *fidélités* that united mankind in society.

These texts were, of course, prescriptive. They were written by moralists whose purpose was to inform their readers of what ought to be—not to describe things as they actually were. But historians have tended to take these writings at face value and to assume that on the whole the relationship between master and servant was indeed paternalistic and reciprocal throughout most of the Ancien Régime. This, at least, is the assumption that underlies recent discussions of the subject by Cissie Fairchilds and Jean-Pierre Gutton.

Both Fairchilds and Gutton have argued that over the course of the eighteenth century the relationship between master and servant shifted from a paternalistic to a contractual mode. Before 1750, writes Fairchilds, master and servant were bound to one another by "intangible ties of duty and loyalty, rather than a cash-nexus."[22] After mid-century these bonds slackened as "patriarchalism" gave way to more starkly monetary employer-employee relations. Gutton's recent work on the same subject also chronicles an eighteenth-century shift in the status of the servant from *domestique*, a nonsalaried worker considered a member of the household, to *serviteur*, an employee who worked for wages.[23]

It is not my intention to deny that such a change did take

[22] Cissie Fairchilds, "Masters and Servants in Eighteenth-Century Toulouse," *Journal of Social History* 12:372.

[23] Gutton, *Domestiques et serviteurs*, pp. 217–219 and passim.

place over the long run. There can be no question that the relationship between master and servant was fundamentally transformed between the seventeenth and the nineteenth century: one need only compare the masters and servants in Molière to those portrayed in television's recent "Upstairs, Downstairs" to sense the magnitude of that change. But, as the following chapters will show, I doubt that under the Old Regime very many masters and servants were ever bound to one another by ties that were primarily moral or psychological. Most of the evidence suggests that no matter how irregularly or arbitrarily wages were doled out to servants, they were always a crucial factor in the relationship. And except where a few very wealthy and powerful households were concerned, this was probably as true in the sixteenth and seventeenth centuries as it was in the eighteenth. Nor do I believe that the shift to a more nakedly "contractual" relationship occurred as early or as decisively as these writers suggest. Significant changes in the tenor of domestic relations did take place in the second half of the eighteenth century, as masters and servants grew increasingly independent and diffident of one another. But whether the "cash nexus" loomed much larger in the 1770s than it did in the 1720s is open to debate.

Framing the problem at the outset around the question of the "decline of paternalism" in the eighteenth century amounts to hitching up the proverbial cart before its horses. What is at first most intriguing about the set of values outlined above is not that they eventually became obsolete, as indeed they did, but that they endured for so long. There is little difference between the underlying assumptions of Claude Fleury, whose handbook was published in 1688, and those of Abbé Collet, who wrote in the 1750s and '60s. Both of them extol loyalty, compassion, and a sense of reciprocal duty as cardinal virtues in domestic relations. How can we explain the social and ideological atavism implicit in the survival of an ideal of patriarchal authority and personal bonding well into an age of demographic explosion, social mobility, and enlightened reform? Where did these ideas come from, and why did they prove so resilient?

It is easy enough to point to the ideological roots of aristocratic paternalism. The central idea of the servant's loyalty to his master no doubt derived from the oath of allegiance that bound the vassal to his lord in the Middle Ages.[24] This notion was integrated to the authoritarian ethos that characterized family life among the European middle and upper classes under the Old Regime. This "patriarchal" stage in the evolution of the western family, which began in the sixteenth century and flourished in the seventeenth, has been convincingly linked by its recent historians to the enforcement of stricter moral and religious standards in the wake of the Reformation and Counter-Reformation, and to the consolidation of absolute monarchies. Contemporaries themselves readily drew analogies between the head of the household, the ruler, and God.[25]

In France specifically this ideal of reciprocal loyalty between master and man derived from aristocratic and monarchical institutions that were central to early modern French society. Under the Old Regime the basic social unit was the household, *la maison*. And the households that stood out as models for society at large were those of rich and powerful noblemen whose establishments, in the seventeenth century, sometimes included over a hundred retainers and dependents. Towering over these great aristocratic *maisons* was the household par excellence, that of the king himself.[26] The king's household numbered over one thousand servants in the late sixteenth century, and over four thousand under Louis XIV. Other members of the royal family were surrounded by

[24] See Marc Bloch, *La Société féodale*, I:223–250; Marcel Cusenier, *Les Domestiques en France*, pp. 10–11.

[25] Jean-Louis Flandrin, *Familles: Parenté, maison, sexualité dans l'ancienne société*, pp. 117–142; Lawrence Stone, *The Family, Sex, and Marriage in England, 1500–1800*, chap. 5.

[26] Mousnier, *Institutions de la France*, I:78–82; Gutton, *Domestiques et serviteurs*, chap. 1.

retinues of lesser but comparable size, and noblemen all over the realm attempted to emulate in their own domestic arrangements the size and organization of these *maisons royales*. Within the royal households, domestic and political functions were often confused since the lines between upper servants, courtiers, and political agents (*créatures*) were easily blurred.[27] The ideal of *fidélité*, of a reciprocal bond between master and man, was therefore central to the institutions of Early Modern France, since it governed relationships in royal and aristocratic households that served as models for society at large. "From top to bottom of the social scale," writes Roland Mousnier, "men were linked to one another by the ties of *fidélité* that bound man to man, master to *fidèle*."[28]

The survival of feudal notions in a postfeudal society, the cultural hegemony of the old aristocracy, the diffusion of stricter religious and moral norms in the seventeenth century, and the strengthening of the absolutist state—all of these can be invoked in order to explain the tone and content of "classic" domestic handbooks. But if one is interested in realities as well as ideals, explaining one ideological system—that which pertained to domestic relations—by analogy with others that governed religion, politics, or the social order merely begs the question—or rather, several questions. Why did aristocratic paternalism survive so late into the eighteenth century as an ideal? How could eighteenth-century masters expect to command the loyalty of men and women who were neither kin nor vassals but, for the most part, total strangers who worked for wages? Why was the idea of domestic service associated with the aristocracy, to the exclusion of any other social group? Why did writers insist that the bond between master and servant was essential not just to the household but to the whole of society? The answers to these questions do not lie in religious tracts or in treatises on the social order. They are to be found in the street, the marketplace, and the household,

[27] Gutton, *Domestiques et serviteurs*, pp. 28–38.
[28] Mousnier, *Institutions de la France*, I:85.

in antechambers and bedrooms, in the very texture of life inside and outside of the household. This book proposes to examine the lives of eighteenth-century domestics and their masters in order to explain the very concrete meaning and uses of the loyalty that was demanded and expected of servants.

The archival research for this study was carried out in two provincial towns—one northern, Bayeux, and one southern, Aix-en-Provence. Both of these towns can be considered typical of Ancien Régime provincial society. Their economies were stagnant: neither was important as a commercial or manufacturing town. Both were residential, administrative, and ecclesiastical centers. Aix was the seat of a *Parlement* and an archbishopric, Bayeux of a *Bailliage* court and a wealthy bishopric. In both towns the nobility, clergy, and royal administration were prominent and their servants numerous.[29] I have used Aix and Bayeux as representative examples of provincial society under the Ancien Régime. But rather than treat these towns as case studies I have integrated the material from their archives (and accessory material from the larger neighboring towns of Marseille and Caen) into a broader discussion that also draws on published material pertaining to other French towns such as Paris, Lyon, Bordeaux, Nantes, and Toulouse.

The context of this study is exclusively urban for it focuses on a specific category of servants. In eighteenth-century France the terms *servante* and *valet* were widely applied to most menial workers who resided with the family that employed them. Female silkworkers in Lyon were called *servantes*; women who worked in taverns and inns were known as *servantes de cabaret* or *servantes*

---

[29] On the history of these towns under the Old Regime, see Jean-Paul Coste, *La Ville d'Aix-en-Provence en 1695: Structure urbaine et société*; Michel Vovelle et al., *Histoire d'Aix-en-Provence*, chaps. 5–6; Mohammed El Kordi, *Bayeux aux 17e et 18e siècles*; Olwen Hufton, *Bayeux in the Late Eighteenth Century: A Social Study*.

d'hôtellerie; servantes, valets, and *domestiques* were also the terms used to designate rural laborers who resided with the farmer's family. The category of workers discussed in this book is that of urban household servants. The group therefore excludes rural servants as well as those who officially engaged in trade or productive economic activities as part of their job. The servants discussed here made up a group which contemporaries recognized as distinctive and referred to as *les domestiques* or *la livrée*.

The first part of the book (chapters 1 through 3) describes the world of the servants. Although they worked in an urban environment, a great majority of eighteenth-century domestics were rural immigrants who had moved from their native villages and hamlets to town with specific goals in mind. This first section examines the social and geographic origins of servants, their attitudes toward their occupation, and the perils and rewards of the life that they led in town. The second part also concerns the lives and behavior of servants, but this time as they were defined and controlled by their employers. Chapter 4 analyzes the ways in which masters established ascendance over their servants within the household, and chapter 5 describes the uses to which that authority was put outside of the home.

In the last section of the book, the focus shifts from stasis to change. Prescriptive literature suggests that a sea change of sorts affected the nature of the master-servant relationship in the last decades of the eighteenth century and the early decades of the nineteenth. The ideals and standards described above remained standard fare in handbooks well into the 1760s. But by the time the next spate of handbooks appeared in the early nineteenth century, the genre had been completely transformed. Handbooks published in the 1810s, '20s, and '30s were written for middle-class households that employed no more than three or four servants; they were aimed at mistresses rather than masters. Their authors ignored earlier ideals of compassion and reciprocity, and merely advised employers on how to control their servants so as to obtain disciplined and efficient work from them. The bond between master and servant was no longer presented as central to the social order, but as an anomaly and a problem. In order to explain how this change came about, the last two chapters follow the gradual transformation of ideals and realities that began early in the eighteenth century and gained momentum after 1750. The final chapter sketches the outcome of these changes in the revolutionary and postrevolutionary eras.

Although the views of service "from above" and "from below" have been separated for the sake of clarity, I have tried to suggest throughout the text the ways in which they were in fact organically related. The identities and origins of servants and their own views of their occupation may explain why, in certain circumstances, domestic workers were indeed loyal to their employers. But masters and mistresses were also aware that their servants had needs and expectations different from their own. This in turn accounts for the particular blend of coercion, contempt, and closeness that characterized the attitudes of eighteenth-century employers in their dealings with their servants.

To these two approaches to service, from above and from below, I have added another one that is particularly germane to preindustrial service, namely, a discussion of domestic service as a public occupation. Many of the tasks and roles assigned to servants in the eighteenth century were carried out and acted out in public, in the street, in the marketplace, and on the doorstep. Central to the argument of this book is the contention that under the Old Regime the nature of domestic service was determined not just by the interaction between master and servant, but by a three-way relationship involving masters, servants, and "the public." The conspicuousness of fictional servants on the seventeenth- and eighteenth-century French stage and the importance of the roles they played in dramatic fiction are not merely of anecdotal or illustrative value. Rather, the ubiquity of servants on stage reflects the importance of domestic service in public as well as private life. Only by exploring the role of servants not only in the household but in the street and on stage as well, may we begin to understand the ways in which the intimate relationship between master and servant was shaped by and in turn reverberated upon society at large.

Part One

THE WORLD OF THE SERVANTS

CHAPTER I

Jobs of Necessity

Domestic servants were conspicuous and familiar figures in the towns of France under the Old Regime. If one were to travel back in time into one of the streets of eighteenth-century Paris, Lyon, or Bordeaux, or even a smaller town such as Aix or Bayeux, one could not fail to notice them: young lackeys dressed in colorful liveries adorned with gold braid and shoulder knots, playing, idling, and taunting one another; chambermaids decked out in ill-fitting and faded hand-me-downs from their mistresses, chatting in the street; doormen and sedan-chair carriers assembled at the doorsteps of wealthy houses; and the more numerous cooks, scullery maids, and maids-of-all-work of bourgeois households, dressed in the coarse garments of the laboring poor, ambling endlessly to and fro on errands. The visibility of domestic workers derived in part from the conspicuousness of their clothing and in part, as we shall see, from the nature of an occupation that put many of them in constant contact with the urban public. But it had mostly to do with the sheer weight of their numbers.

In many of the towns of eighteenth-century France, and in fact of other European countries as well, household workers made up a full tenth of the urban population and as much as one-fifth of the adult workforce.[1] On this point the estimates of contempo-

---

[1] Carlo Cipolla, *Before the Industrial Revolution*, pp. 77–78. Cipolla estimates that in European cities of the fifteenth, sixteenth, and seventeenth centuries, servants made up 17 percent of the population over age fifteen.

raries and the work of recent historians corroborate each other. The size of the group nationwide is difficult to determine precisely, because contemporaries usually included live-in workers, apprentices, and farmhands in the category of *domestiques*. But their calculations do indicate that a substantial proportion of the population of Ancien-Régime France engaged in "service" of one sort or another. In his *Projet d'une dîme royale*, published in 1707, Vauban claimed that there were one and a half million domestics in the realm, 7.5 percent of a population of about twenty million.[2] A century later, the Abbé Grégoire advanced exactly the same proportion, one-thirteenth of the total population.[3] The great French demographers of the later eighteenth century, Expilly, Messance, and Moheau, estimated the servant population at around 8 percent in the small provincial towns of Auvergne and Normandy, 6 to 12 percent in Provence, and 9 or 10 percent in larger towns such as Rouen, Tours, Lyon, and Paris.[4]

Recent estimates based on sources such as tax rolls and parish registers do confirm that on the whole the proportion of servants was most substantial in the largest and wealthiest towns in the realm. But the size of the servant population also varied according to the nature of the local economy and social structure. In small towns and villages, servants made up only 5 to 7 percent of the population.[5] They were also less conspicuous as a group in large commercial or manufacturing centers such as Caen, Lyon, or Marseille. In Caen, the largest textile center in Normandy, 2,300 persons out of a total of 32,000 were listed as household employees

[2] Sébastien le Prestre de Vauban, *Projet d'une dixme royale*, p. 82.

[3] Henri Grégoire, *De la Domesticité chez les peuples anciens et modernes*, pp. 72–74.

[4] Expilly, *Dictionnaire géographique, historique et politique des Gaules et de la France*, IV:962. Messance, *Recherches sur la population des généralités d'Auvergne, de Lyon, de Rouen, et de quelques provinces et villes du royaume*, pp. 13–15, 31–32, 73. Moheau, *Recherches et considérations sur la population de France*, p. 116.

[5] Noel Biraben, "A Southern French Village: The Inhabitants of Montplaisant in 1644," in Peter Laslett, ed., *Household and Family in Past Times*, pp. 239–242. Peter Laslett, *Family Life and Illicit Love in Earlier Generations*, p. 32.

at mid-century, or 7 percent of the population. The much larger textile-manufacturing town of Lyon numbered some 6,000 domestic servants in 1791, making up about 6 percent of the population. The ratio of servants to population was smaller still in the busy seaport of Marseille, where they added up to a mere 4 percent of the population at century's end.[6]

Larger proportions of servants were usually found in those towns typical of provincial urban society under the Old Regime— administrative and residential centers where aristocrats, clergymen, and *rentiers* rather than merchants and manufacturers made up the core of high society. Some towns, of course, combined both sorts of functions. The Atlantic seaport of Bordeaux was about the same size as Marseille, yet the proportion of servants there amounted to a full tenth of the population because the town combined the activity of an increasingly wealthy commercial center with its traditional role as an aristocratic residential center and as the seat of one of France's thirteen courts of high justice, the Parlements.[7] In the south of France two other such courts were located in Aix-en-Provence and Toulouse, both of them important residential and administrative centers. In Aix a servant population of about 2,000 staffed mainly the elegant townhouses of the old Provençal aristocracy, many of whom were members of the Parlement of Provence or the Cour des Comptes. Servants in Aix accounted for 8 percent of a population of 27,000 in 1695, and the proportion rose to 12 percent in the course of the next century.[8] In Toulouse, several hundred miles west of Aix, many

---

[6] Jean-Claude Perrot, *Genèse d'une ville moderne: Caen au XVIIIe siècle*, I:334. Maurice Garden, *Lyon et les lyonnais au XVIIIe siècle*, p. 249. Thérèse Reynaud-Lefaucheur, "Les Femmes dans la population marseillaise en 1793" (Mémoire de Maîtrise, Univ. de Provence, 1975), pp. 15, 36.

[7] François Pariset, ed., *Bordeaux au XVIIIe siècle*, pp. 325–367.

[8] Jacqueline Carrière, *La Population d'Aix-en-Provence à la fin du XVIIe siècle*, pp. 33, 85–86. Jean-Paul Coste, *La Ville d'Aix-en-Provence en 1695: Structure urbaine et société*, I:61–64, 712. The figures for the eighteenth century are my own calculations from the *Capitation* lists in A.M.A. CC 13, CC 52–59, CC 68–69 for 1701, 1715–1719, and 1755–1756, respectively. The *Capitation* lists

of the town's 4,400 domestics were also in the employ of officers of the Parlement.[9] Elsewhere in the realm substantial numbers of servants could be found even in sleepy provincial centers like Bayeux, where they numbered 700 among a population of 9,200 in 1768.[10]

It was in Paris, of course, that the largest number of servants in the country was concentrated, but the continual flow of migrants in and out of the capital city made it very difficult to determine their numbers. The demographer Messance cited a figure of 37,400 on the basis of a 1754 tax roll, but added that the servant population of Paris was in fact much larger than this, at least 50,000 out of a total population of nearly half a million. One Parisian family in four, he claimed, employed some sort of domestic help.[11] If Parisian servants cannot be numbered with precision, at least their visibility is beyond doubt. In 1749, 16 percent of all marriage contracts settled before Parisian notaries were drawn up by male servants. Even during the Revolution, when one might expect their numbers to have been depleted by the emigration of wealthy masters, menservants still accounted for one-third to nearly half of the adult male population of elegant

---

1,621 servants in 1701 (7.4 percent of the total population), and 2,131 in 1715–1719 (11.3 percent). The tax rolls for 1755–1756 are incomplete, but list 1,527 servants, or 13.4 percent of the population listed. The two latter figures are minimal estimates, since in about one hundred cases the tax collectors merely noted "ses domestiques" opposite the name of the head of household. Since in all of these cases the masters clearly belonged to the topmost stratum of society, I have counted 3 servants for each notation. The actual number of servants in Aix may very well have been larger by two or three hundred persons. According to Expilly, there were 3,069 servants in Aix in 1765, or 11.7 percent of the population. Expilly, *Dictionnaire*, IV:926.

[9] Cissie Fairchilds, "Masters and Servants in Eighteenth-Century Toulouse," *Journal of Social History* 12:369. The proportion of servants apparently dropped to 7 percent under the Revolution. Jean Sentou, *Fortunes et groupes sociaux à Toulouse sous la Révolution*, p. 437.

[10] Mohammed El Kordi, *Bayeux aux 17e et 18e siècles*, p. 69.

[11] Messance, *Recherches sur la population*, pp. 186–187.

districts such as the Place des Vosges or the Faubourg Saint-Germain.[12]

For all of these variations in the size of the servant population, there can be no doubt that in every large town in France domestics made up a substantial proportion of the population. And yet despite a recent proliferation of monographs dealing with urban society under the Old Regime,[13] we know very little about them beyond the numbers recorded in tax rolls.

One of the reasons for our ignorance is that the most obvious sources for the study of urban society reflect the prejudices of contemporaries for whom domestic servants did not legally "exist" as a group. As Pierre Goubert has pointed out, up to the end of the Old Regime urban society still defined itself within the framework of the traditional corporate bodies—guilds, associations, confraternities—which provided the legal basis for social recognition in town.[14] Servants were never legally integrated into urban society for there was never any such corporate framework to their occupation. Numerous as they were, domestic servants did not really "belong" in the towns where they worked, for a vast majority of them came from the countryside and were immigrants drawn from pure rural stock. Even they themselves, perhaps, sought no such integration, for many viewed their occupation as a temporary necessity rather than a lifelong career.

[12] Adeline Daumard and François Furet, *Structures et relations sociales à Paris au milieu du XVIIIe siècle*, pp. 18–19. Maurice Reinhard, ed., *Contributions à l'histoire démographique de la Révolution Française*, I:92, II:53, III:30, 128, 143. Under the Revolution, servants formed 36 percent of the population of the aristocratic Place des Vosges, 27 percent of that of the Faubourg Saint-Germain, 40 percent of that of the Section Grange-Batellière, but only 4 percent of a poorer section like Popincourt.

[13] Those of Garden and Perrot, cited earlier, are the most important. But see also Pierre Deyon, *Amiens, capitale provinciale* (Paris, 1967), and Olwen Hufton, *Bayeux in the Late Eighteenth Century: A Social Study*.

[14] Pierre Goubert, *L'Ancien Régime*, I:199–203.

In the late eighteenth century, the author of a Parisian police handbook summed up the motives behind migration and service in these unflattering terms:

> Hatred of work, the desire to enjoy the pleasures of the cities, a taste for laziness, the habit of vice, indifference to the ties most dear to the heart of men, the hope of getting rich, and lastly, the most decided and most shocking egotism, are the motives which cause domestic work to be cherished; it is they which cause men to prefer the baseness of this state to the honorable and useful fatigue of the farmer. One may thus correctly conclude that the class of servants is composed exclusively of the scum of the countryside.[15]

Our man obviously had an axe to grind, as would presumably anyone saddled with the unrewarding task of maintaining order among bands of boisterous Parisian lackeys. In assuming that it was the glamor of service that lured peasants out of their villages and that this occupation was especially attractive to the riff-raff of rural society, he was echoing mostly the prejudices of his contemporaries. But he was not at all unjustified in associating servants with immigrants: in every large town in France, the bulk of domestic workers was supplied by traditional patterns of migration from the countryside.

In Aix and Marseille, eight or nine out of ten female servants who came before notaries in the eighteenth century were of rural origin (see table 1.1). Not all of these rural-born women came from purely agricultural families. Notarial documents in Toulouse and illegitimate pregnancy records in Aix show that only one-half to two-thirds of them were the offspring of farmers and agricultural laborers.[16] Many others were daughters of village weavers or rural artisans. But most of them came from the world beyond the city walls. Only a tenth of the servants who reported

---

[15] Quoted in Jeffry Kaplow, *The Names of Kings: The Parisian Laboring Poor in the Eighteenth Century*, p. 51.

[16] Fairchilds, "Masters and Servants," pp. 371, 382.

TABLE 1.1.
Origins of Female Servants in Aix and Marseille

	1715–33	1749–52	1764–87
Urban	11%	16%	16.5%
Rural	89%	78%	82.0%
Abandoned children	—	6%	1.5%
Total number in sample	66	64	77

Source: Notarial Records, A.D.A. 301E to 309E; A.D.M. 351E, 363E, 364E

pregnancies in Aix between 1695 and 1765 were native Aixoises. The others had come from as close as a few miles away, or as far as the northernmost Alpine regions.[17] In Bayeux a mere 7 percent of the maidservants listed in the census of 1796 had been born in that town, and over a third of them had migrated there within the preceding five years.[18]

The social and geographic origins of menservants, while more varied, were similar. In the first half of the century, 35 percent in Toulouse, 45 percent in Paris, and 75 percent in Lyon were from peasant families. Whether or not they were sons of peasants, a large majority had left their native fields, vineyards, or villages to try their luck or wits out in town. In Paris, at least eight out of ten menservants had converged to the capital from the provinces (see appendix 1.b). Only 6 percent in Lyon were natives of the town in which they worked.[19] From whatever occupational group they were drawn, a majority of servants were sons and daughters of the countryside. Even when their origins were not purely rural, most servants did come from impoverished backgrounds. Outside

[17] A.D.A. XXH G26, 28, 29, 32, 33. I have information on the geographic origin of 383 servants who reported illegitimate pregnancies between 1695 and 1765; only 30 were natives of Aix.

[18] A.M.B. 1F 27, "Dénombrement de l'an IV." Twenty-seven out of a total of 489 maidservants are listed as natives of Bayeux.

[19] Fairchilds, "Masters and Servants," p. 371; Garden, *Lyon*, p. 251. For Paris see appendix 1b.

of the rural world, one-fifth or more of the women, both in Toulouse and in Aix, were daughters of wage laborers or petty craftsmen, and a small percentage had fathers in service (see appendix 1.a).[20]

The most wretched of these women, without doubt, were those for whom service was an unavoidable fate, those who had been illegitimate and abandoned children. By a sad irony, they were likely to be the offspring of ill-fated unions between masters and servants, and thus perpetuated the vicious cycle that had linked illegitimate sex and domestic service for centuries. Throughout the eighteenth century, an estimated 4 percent of all servants in Aix and Marseille were recruited among the girls whose mothers had left them on the steps of the Hôtel-Dieu, sometimes attaching a ribbon, Bible, or small trinket around their children's necks in the hopes of recognizing them some day.[21] In 1749 and 1750, four of these girls came to sign marriage contracts before notaries in Marseille. All of them bore the same surname, and none could sign her name: Marie Blanc, Catherine Blanc, Louise Blanc, and Jeanne-Marie Blanc. All four had been in service, and all four married peasants—strangers to Marseille—who must have seen in the meager dowry allotted by the Hôtel-Dieu some sort of compensation for the disreputable backgrounds of their fiancées.[22] And these, of course, were the lucky ones. Most of those who

---

[20] See appendix 1a.

[21] For vivid examples of the connection between bastardy and service in the fourteenth century, see Emmanuel Le Roy Ladurie, *Montaillou, village occitan* (Paris, 1975), pp. 74–78. François-Paul Blanc, "Les Enfants abandonnés à Marseille au XVIIIe siècle" (Thèse de Droit, Univ. de Provence, 1972), pp. 610, 626–640. Details on the careers of these women, who were identified by their first name only or by notations such as "Marie-Madeleine de l'évangile à la sangle" or "Catherine de l'entrepôt," can be found in the records of the Hôtel-Dieu of Marseille, A.D.M. XXH IVG 103, 104, 106, 108.

[22] A.D.M. 363 E 322, fol. 1460; 364E 380, fol. 419; 364E 381, fol. 1034; 364E 383, fol. 419.

managed to survive past age fifteen remained in service, turned to prostitution, or returned to the hospital as paupers.[23]

The picture of servants' origins is, overall, a bleak one, and one may well wonder where novelists and playwrights found models for those dapper valets and chambermaids who could, on occasion, masquerade as their masters and mistresses as the twists and turns of the plot demanded. These fictional servants were perhaps modeled on the small minority of domestics who did in fact come from more prosperous families. In Aix, 7 to 10 percent of the women, and still a smaller proportion in Toulouse, had come into domestic service from apparently comfortable backgrounds (see appendix 1.a).[24] The fathers of these women belonged to those ambiguous groups which, in the social taxonomy of the Old Regime, implied a modicum of status but not necessarily a great deal of wealth: bourgeois, merchants, master-surgeons, and so on. Sudden turns of fate no doubt accounted for their presence among the ranks of the destitute. The Abbé Collet, in a handbook for masters published in 1764, specifically asked employers to show consideration for those girls who had been "reduced into service by one of those sudden blows of fate that changes the fortune of an honest family."[25] Some women of middling background were compelled to spend a few years gathering or supplementing a dowry in order to regain some sort of status through marriage. Sometimes they entered the service of a relative or a friend in order to mitigate the dishonor attached to their occupation.

The ambiguities, tensions, and animosities inherent in such an arrangement are well illustrated in the case which in 1751 opposed one Agnès Monoyer to her employer and former friend, Thérèse Laborel. In the course of the trial, Monoyer bitterly asked

[23] Blanc, "Les Enfants abandonnés," p. 640.
[24] Fairchilds, "Masters and Servants," p. 371.
[25] Pierre Collet, *Traité des devoirs des gens du monde et surtout des chefs de famille*, p. 219.

her mistress whether *she* would have accepted insults in lieu of wages when she was in service, before she inherited her brother's money:

> She is therefore ill-advised in refusing, under false and friv-
> olous pretexts, the wages owed to mistress Monoyer, who,
> though her father is a bourgeois, is forced to work in order
> to feed and keep herself. And it behooves mistress Laborel
> less than any other to make light of the subject because,
> although her family is one of the most distinguished in these
> parts, it has not been very long since she herself was in the
> same condition as mistress Monoyer, and forced to go work
> for others.[26]

No doubt, members of the upper classes would prefer to choose their closest personal servants among these unfortunate victims of fate.

The social origins of male servants, while also heavily skewed toward the lower end of the social scale, were more varied than those of women. Outside of the rural world, the scope of social strata from which they were drawn was surprisingly wide, or so it appears from the figures we have on Paris and Toulouse. Some allowances must be made for the specificity of the capital city, for in other towns servants were probably of a less varied and humbler extraction. In Paris a full quarter of the male servants who came before notaries in 1749 were sons of skilled workers, master artisans, and merchants, another 5 percent were of middle-class origin, and the rest were drawn from a wide range of other social strata. Surprisingly, though, the unskilled urban working classes are underrepresented, with sons of workers and journeymen adding up to only 3.6 percent.[27] Paris, of course, was an atypical city, and one can easily guess that the high quality of skills demanded and the level of wages offered made service in the

[26] A.D.A. IVB 358, 1751.
[27] See appendix 1b.

richest Parisian households attractive to men of good social standing. But a similar pattern of recruitment has been found in Toulouse. At the beginning of the century, 12.8 percent of Toulousain menservants came from the petite bourgeoisie, while only 2.6 percent were sons of textile workers and wage laborers.[28] This disparity in recruitment no doubt reflects different attitudes toward service among different sorts of men who engaged in the occupation. Furet and Daumard, whose work on Paris I have been quoting, suggest that this curious pattern speaks to a disparity between popular rural and urban mentalities. Large numbers of rural youths were driven into service by necessity or tradition, and may have found it easy to enter a situation of personal bondage if they came from areas where strong seigneurial ties still conditioned social relations. But the urban working classes may have balked at the idea of jeopardizing their independence and looked down on workers, even secretaries and clerks, who eked out their living as parasites. Finally, for a minority of young men from middling backgrounds whose families had hit upon hard times, a spell of time as a well-paid valet in a wealthy household was no doubt the best choice. The ranks of Parisian domesticity comprised many provincial *déclassés* whose lack of training and wealth drove them to the capital and into service.[29]

A majority of servants of both sexes, then, belonged by birth to the rural world, as did eight out of ten Frenchmen under the Old Regime. Many others came from destitute families of petty craftsmen and traders; still others had no family at all. But unlike any other unskilled occupation, domestic service also drew from a small pool of young men and women from the middle ranks of society. This disparate assortment says much about the originality of an occupation whose structure reflected the demands of masters. Most employers wanted unskilled and inexpensive employees, but the wealthiest also needed a few educated, well-groomed and

[28] Fairchilds, "Masters and Servants," p. 371.

[29] Daumard and Furet, *Structures et relations sociales*, pp. 59, 66. Yves Castan, *Honnêteté et relations sociales en Languedoc, 1715–1780*, p. 181.

presentable men and women to serve as valets and chambermaids or even tutors and governesses. What all of these servants had in common, though, was that nine out of ten had migrated to the towns in which they worked. One would like to know what fears, what hopes, or simply what unrecorded traditions drove them out of the farms and villages where they were born onto the road to town. Unfortunately only an atypical few ever consigned their motives to paper, and one is left to infer the reasons for their departure from their patterns of migration. The question, Why did they come? is inseparable from another question, Where did they come from?

Widespread patterns of seasonal and permanent migration among the rural poor were not new to the eighteenth century. Emmanuel Le Roy Ladurie has given us vivid descriptions of the paupers who in the sixteenth century flocked down from the north to the south of the country or from barren mountains to richer coastal regions in quest of subsistence and warmer weather.[30] Throughout the Old Regime, large segments of the rural poor were forced to leave their homes in order to survive. In a recent work, Olwen Hufton has demonstrated how vital this mobility was to the survival of peasant families in the eighteenth century, since one-half to nine-tenths of all rural households lacked the resources to support themselves on the land, and most were forced to resort to temporary or permanent expatriation in order to support a faltering family economy.[31] The eighteenth century witnessed an exacerbation of the problems inherent to an economy based on traditional, inelastic forms of agriculture. The early decades of the century saw the disappearance of great local plagues and famines, those "malthusian scissors" that sliced through the population and kept a check on demographic expansion throughout the "tragic" seventeenth century. As a result the population of

---

[30] Emmanuel Le Roy Ladurie, *Paysans de Languedoc*, I:93–110.
[31] Olwen Hufton, *The Poor of Eighteenth-Century France*, chap. 2, esp. pp. 36–48.

the realm jumped from twenty to twenty-six million on the eve of the Revolution. In the eighteenth century, the roads of France were swarming with a surplus population that would have been wiped out by hunger or pestilence just a few decades before. Instead of cemeteries, the eighteenth century had paupers. This resulted in an intensification of the traditional patterns of mobility that had existed for centuries independently of demographic pressure.[32]

Throughout the eighteenth century, and well into the nineteenth, the same regions spilled out their inhabitants. The great poles of rejection were the vast "desert" of Brittany and all of the mountainous zones—the Massif Central, the Pyrenees, and the Alpine regions stretching from Savoy in the north to the Dauphiné in the south.[33] Migrants from the mountains, with their husky builds, often employed as sedan-chair carriers, were familiar figures in Paris and in the large towns of the south to which they flocked. In Montpellier in 1768, an observer noted: "A prodigious number of peasants from the mountains, whose disposition is sturdy by nature, are hired for this arduous task."[34] Sixty years later, very little had changed: "Every year, as winter approaches, the mountains of Savoy and Auvergne send great numbers of their inhabitants to Paris."[35] The *gavots* and *gavottes*, migrants from the Alpine regions, were familiar figures in Paris and the large towns of the south. In one of his stories, Restif de La Bretonne described these strange creatures who made their way to Paris in their ancestral costumes, congregating in tight-

---

[32] Hufton, *The Poor*, pp. 18–19. Pierre Guillaume and Jean-Pierre Poussou, *Démographie historique*, pp. 205–217. Emmanuel Le Roy Ladurie, in Georges Duby and Armand Wallon, eds., *Histoire de la France rurale*, II:359–391.

[33] Hufton, *The Poor*, pp. 69–95. Jean-Pierre Poussou, "Les Mouvements migratoires en France de la fin du XVe siècle au début du XIXe siècle," *Annales de démographie historique* (1970), pp. 11–78.

[34] Joseph Berthélé, ed., *Montpellier en 1768 et 1836, d'après deux documents inédits*, p. 69.

[35] *Les Domestiques chrétiens ou la morale en action des domestiques*, p. 36.

TABLE 1.2.

Geographic Origins of Servants in Aix and Marseille

	1715–52		1764–87	
	Male	Female	Male	Female
Born in town	15%	9.0%	4.5%	1.5%
Lower Provence*	30%	22.0%	24.5%	35.0%
Upper Provence**	10%	27.0%	13.0%	27.5%
Dauphiné and Northern Alps	43%	37.0%	40.0%	17.5%
Other	2%	1.5%	18.0%	5.0%
Unknown	—	3.5%	—	13.5%
Total number in sample	*47*	*140*	*45*	*80*

* Departments of the Gard, Var, and Bouches-du-Rhône
** Department of the Basses-Alpes
Source: Notarial Records A.D.A. 301E to 309E; A.D.M. 351E, 363E, 364E

knit networks in the Faubourg Saint-Marceau, playing the hurdy-gurdy on the boulevards in order to earn a few coins.[36] It was from the ranks of such people that most servants were drawn.

In the south of France especially, mobility had always been intense because of the stark juxtaposition of high mountains, where year-long subsistence was difficult, and the plains and coasts of Provence, Languedoc, and Gironde, where wheat and vine grew easily and where large seaports and towns were located.[37] Little wonder, then, that throughout the century, half or more of the servants who came before the notaries of Aix and Marseille had been born in the barren areas north of the Verdon river, Upper Provence, and the Alps (see table 1.2).

Seasonal migration had been a way of life for the inhabitants

[36] Nicolas-Edmé Restif de La Bretonne, "La Jolie Vielleuse" in *Les Contemporaines.*

[37] Le Roy Ladurie, *Paysans de Languedoc,* I:96–99. Hufton, *The Poor,* p. 72. For a more general discussion, see Fernand Braudel, *The Mediterranean and the Mediterranean World in the Age of Philip II,* 2 vols. (New York, 1976), I:41–47.

of the Alpine foothills throughout the Old Regime. Men traveled south in the early summer months to hire themselves out at harvest time in the wheat fields around Arles and the vineyards along the banks of the Rhône. Whole families uprooted themselves during the bitter winter months to go beg for a living in the low country. Traditionally, most migrants would return after a few months or a few years. But in the eighteenth century the population of these areas declined as seasonal migrations turned into permanent departures.[38] "This population would be much more numerous," wrote a local scholar in 1784, "if all those who are forced to expatriate themselves to earn a living came back to their homeland; but out of five or six hundred who leave the valley [of Barcelonette] each year, one fourth never returns."[39]

Migrants did not come back because very often there was nothing to return to. In these areas of the Alps, from the north of Provence to the Dauphiné, the effects of the demographic upsurge that began early in the century resulted in a widening at the base of the social pyramid. As landholdings dwindled in the Dauphiné, the Velay, and along the eastern bank of the Rhône valley, small peasant proprietors became increasingly vulnerable to the predatory efforts of an elite of dynamic landlords. For many peasant families the further fragmentation of plots that had never really sufficed to keep them alive meant poverty, indebtedness, and ultimately departure.[40] The most perfunctory look at the social and economic crisis which, from the early eighteenth century on, affected this part of the Alps is enough to explain why many of the lackeys who worked in the households of Aix and Marseille were nicknamed Dauphiné after the large Alpine province that lay to the southeast of Lyon.

[38] Raoul Blanchard, *Les Alpes occidentales*, vol. IV, *Les Préalpes françaises du sud*, pp. 452–475.

[39] Darluc, *Histoire naturelle de la Provence* (Paris, 1784), quoted in Raymond Collier, *La Vie en Haute-Provence de 1650 à 1800* (Digne, 1973), p. 70.

[40] Pierre Léon, ed., *Structures économiques et problèmes sociaux du monde rural dans la France du sud-est*, pp. 20–21, 49–60, 74–78, 53–120, 311–313.

In other parts of France, servants were drawn from areas in which peasant property was subjected to the same sorts of pressure. Menservants in Lyon were also likely to come from the Dauphiné, but the town drew equal numbers of domestics from Savoy to the east, the Jura mountains to the north, and the regions of the Massif Central that lay to the west just across the Rhône valley.[41] In Bordeaux, many of them came from the northern and western provinces of the Massif Central, the Perigord, Quercy, and Limousin, while others had traveled north from the Pyrenees.[42] Many of the male servants who worked in Toulouse had originated from the southwestern fringes of the Massif Central around Albi, Rodez, and Castres, others from the foothills of the Pyrenees.[43] Typically, then, many servants, but especially males, migrated to towns like Bordeaux, Lyon, Toulouse, Aix, and Marseille from the *pays de petite culture* in and around the great mountain ranges of the realm. These areas were traditional reservoirs of manpower from which the wealthier regions had always drawn a destitute workforce. The pressure of increased population on limited resources in the eighteenth century resulted in the dwindling of landholdings and reinforced much older patterns of migration by setting ever larger numbers of migrants on the road to town. Whatever hopes or dreams may have been harbored by the young men and women who left the Dauphiné for Marseille or the Limousin for Bordeaux, the main reason for their departure was tradition, a tradition always and increasingly compounded by necessity.

It is true that not all servants had traveled this far in search of a livelihood. In all of these towns, many servants had trickled in, quite predictably, from the surrounding countryside. One-quarter to one-third of the servants in Aix and Marseille were from Lower Provence; as many or more in Toulouse came from

[41] Garden, *Lyon*, pp. 251, 713.
[42] Pariset, *Bordeaux*, p. 338.
[43] Fairchilds, "Masters and Servants," pp. 370, 383.

the very diocese of that town (see table 1.2).[44] Those servants who migrated from the town's immediate hinterland were usually women rather than men. This sex differentiation held true for all migrants, regardless of their occupation. In Bordeaux, three-quarters of the migrants from more distant areas were male, whereas two-thirds of those who had moved within a thirty-mile radius around the city were female. Servants were no exception to this rule.[45] In Toulouse early in the century, less than a tenth of all male domestics came from the same diocese, as opposed to well over a third of the females. The typical female servant, Olwen Hufton tells us, traveled only twenty or thirty miles from her native village, usually to find work in the nearest town.[46] If these women did not come from areas that were especially poverty stricken, why did they choose to leave their villages?

Some women who were questioned by the police told of specific misfortunes that had determined their departure. In Marseille, Claire Martelly claimed that she left her mother's house because of repeated beatings; Marie-Anne Lafarge, who worked in Aix, was rejected by parents who "did not show much affection for her, all of their predilections, on the contrary, being for her brother and sister"; Anne Auvray in Bayeux cryptically declared that she was forced to leave "because of her sister's behavior."[47] But most women apparently felt no need to explain their departure, nor did the officials who questioned them seem to expect an explanation. Leaving one's family and village to seek employment in town was a normal and necessary step for many young country girls to take. If the long-range migration more characteristic of male servants reveals the economic vulnerability of whole segments of the peasantry in certain parts of the realm,

[44] Ibid.

[45] Pariset, *Bordeaux*, p. 335.

[46] Fairchilds, "Masters and Servants," pp. 370, 383; Hufton, *The Poor*, p. 28.

[47] A.D.A. IVB 1275, June 16, 1790; A.D.A. IVB 1269, July 1, 1786; A.D.C. 2B 863, September 1718.

2. The drudgery of lower service: *A Woman Sweeping*, by Edmé Bouchardon. (Phot. Bibl. nat. Paris)

the constant influx of single women into the nearest town says more about the position of all women within a fragile family economy.

Given the level of female wages in the eighteenth century, no woman could expect to support herself on an independent footing into old age, nor could a country girl blessed with male siblings ever hope for much of an inheritance. Whatever its other attractions might be, marriage was above all a necessary precondition to survival for most women. Since settlement could not be envisioned without a dowry, and few families had money to spare for their daughters, most country girls began working toward marriage while in their early teens. Because few rural areas had much to offer by way of employment to a large workforce of single females, departure was the only solution, and some sort of service was the most likely choice.[48]

Very often the death of a parent served as a catalyst for departure. Eight out of ten of the female servants who drew up marriage contracts in Aix and Marseille had lost one or both of their parents. In both Marseille and Lille, 70 percent of the maidservants who reported illegitimate pregnancies were orphans or half orphans.[49] The death of a father was the single most decisive factor in the matter. Whereas a girl might be expected to replace her mother if the latter died, the disappearance of the crucial male breadwinner in a family that survived at subsistence level could jeopardize the whole family economy and force the children to go out and earn their keep.

It could be argued that under the demographic conditions of

[48] Hufton, *The Poor*, pp. 25–29.

[49] One hundred seventy-two, or 80 percent, of the 213 women who gave such information before notaries in Aix and Marseille had lost one or both parents. Of the 172, 77 had lost their fathers only. For Marseille, see Marie-Claire Ollivier, "Grossesses illégitimes à Marseille" (Mémoire de Maîtrise, Univ. de Provence, 1974), p. 14. For Lille, see Alain Lottin, "Naissances illégitimes et filles-mères à Lille," *Revue d'histoire moderne et contemporaine* 17 (April–June 1970): 305.

the Old Regime, most women, regardless of social class or occupation, would have lost at least one parent by the time they
reached their twenties. This may be true, but the causal link
between death, departure, and service is evident in the sad le-
galistic litany that appears in a third of the marriage contracts
of these Provençal servants: the bride, it is stated, gathered this
dowry "since she came to this town to work as a servant upon
the death of her father." Whether their families were ruined or
whether they simply needed a dowry, single women had to work.
And very often the only work available was domestic service in
the nearest farm, village, or town.

Traveling either long or short distances, the men and women
who took the road to town were heading off toward an uncertain
future, but the bleakness of the prospects they faced on the land
made the gamble worthwhile. Most of them had to leave to avoid
pure and simple misery, but others were running away from more
immediate threats. For men, domestic service was a good loophole
for evading the dreaded *milice*, the drawing of lots for military
service, since any master with a bit of pull could get the draft
waived for his servants. This practice was made official in February
of 1743, much to the annoyance of the Parisian lawyer Barbier,
who wrote angrily in his journal that

> They are not making *la livrée* [male servants] draw lots, and
> there are great numbers of these people in Paris who have
> left the country in order to avoid the militia, which has
> resulted in depopulation of the countryside.[50]

For any emigrant, leaving the countryside meant escaping the
many forms of seigneurial and communal fiscality that crushed
the peasantry. But servants in town were specifically privileged
with regard to royal taxation as well. In Aix in 1715 a servant,

[50] Edmond Barbier, *Chronique de la régence et du règne de Louis XV*, III:442.
On servants and the militia see also André Corvisier, "Service militaire et
mobilité géographique au dix-huitième siècle," *Annales de démographie historique*
(1970), p. 189.

male or female, paid one livre a year for the *Capitation*, a town-dwelling peasant paid two livres, and an artisan, skilled or un-skilled, upwards of three.[51]

Service provided relief not just from structural types of misery but from conjunctural accidents as well. In 1709, one of the most calamitous years of famine and plague that the Old Regime ever knew, the number of servants in Lyon swelled to inordinate proportions: the guarantee of a roof and subsistence was enough to drive hundreds of workers to offer their services for little or no pay. In more respects than one, domestic service constituted, as one historian has put it, a "shelter profession."[52] It was also the only option available to most women and to young men fresh from the countryside who had neither money nor skills that could be put to use within an urban environment. Jean-Joseph Esmieu, a young migrant from the Alps who arrived in Marseille in the 1770s with the firm determination to avoid service, was thus discouraged by a compatriot:

> My friend, I know of no trade for which you will not need at least four or five hundred francs as your guarantee; after that they will ask you for over two hundred more to teach you the skills. . . . You have no choice, since you have no money, but to get some clothes, and I will take care of getting you placed. You will be well provided with a bed and food, and I can assure you of six francs a month.[53]

By dint of obstinacy and large amounts of hubris, Esmieu even-tually became a peddler. For countless others, there really was no choice.

[51] A.M.A. CC52-59.

[52] Henri Muheim, "Une Source exceptionnelle: Le recensement de la popu-lation lyonnaise en 1709, les domestiques dans la société," in *Actes du 89e congrès des sociétés savantes, section histoire moderne et contemporaine*, p. 216.

[53] Pierre Dubois, ed., *La Vie pénible et laborieuse de Jean-Joseph Esmieu, marchand-colporteur en Provence sous la Révolution Française* (Toulon, 1967), p. 17.

The evidence surveyed up to this point suggests very strongly that domestic service was a job of necessity; that those who engaged in this occupation were born destitute or had fallen upon hard times; that fear and poverty rather than ambition or idleness drove men and women into temporary servitude; in short, that the "push" factor overrode the "pull" factor by far in the choices that most servants had made. This argument may surprise anyone who thinks of mythical or literary stereotypes of emigrants like Dick Whittington or Rastignac, or of ambitious servants like Figaro or Julien Sorel. It raises questions that are legitimate, if difficult to answer. Did not some of these men and women leave their villages in the hopes of striking it rich? Were they not more able and enterprising than those who remained in their native villages? Had they perhaps consciously chosen and accepted the role that they were to play?

Undoubtedly, some migrants must have regarded domestic service as a steppingstone to fortune and social promotion. It did allow one to rub elbows with the high and mighty, and, as we shall see in a later chapter, the financial rewards could be considerable if one played one's cards right. Marivaux's literary success of 1731, *Le Paysan Parvenu*, which traces the career of an amoral young peasant named Jacob who forces his way into Parisian respectability via domestic service, is only the best-known of a whole spate of eighteenth-century novels that revolve around similar plots.[54] One may well wonder in what reality these literary clichés were grounded.

Direct evidence on such matters is not only scarce, but most likely biased and atypical to boot. Legrain, a young man from Picardy who was to achieve fortune as valet to the Comte de Mirabeau of revolutionary fame, left a surprisingly candid and articulate autobiography. For him, service was clearly a dramatic promotion out of his rural background. "I was brought up the

---

[54] Simon Davies, "L'Idée de Paris dans le roman au XVIIIe siècle," in *La Ville au XVIIIe siècle* (Aix-en-Provence, 1975), pp. 14–17.

way country folks are raised," he wrote. He left home at age seventeen, was a coachman for two different monasteries, worked for an aristocractic household and as a courier for the post, and finally secured a place as valet to a local priest.

> I stayed five years with him. I had acquired good enough knowledge of everything to do with service. I was about twenty-eight when I left to come to Paris. My master was quite vexed that I should leave him. I can say that I was very good, and well considered by all his friends. But at last my idea was to go to Paris. I believe I can say that when I left I was no longer a novice.[55]

In order to fight one's way into the coveted upper echelons of Parisian service, one needed skills and connections. And for all his apparent innocence, young Legrain was keenly aware of this.

Another servant, whose memoirs antedate Legrain's by about a hundred years, was even more blunt about his motivations. Gourville, who soared up to wealth and power as the personal servant and confidante of the Prince de Conti in the late seventeenth century, began his career in his native village as a valet to the Abbé de La Rouchefoucault. The Abbé's brother, the Prince de Marillac, pleaded to secure the services of Gourville for the military campaign of 1646. Despite the entreaties of his master and his own brother, Gourville followed Marillac off to war: "My desire for promotion prevailed."[56] Men like Gourville and Legrain must have not been very different from Marivaux's fictional Jacob. But it would be rash to consider either one as typical of the occupation as a whole. For one thing, the tone of their memoirs is understandably self-congratulatory, and their recollections are most certainly biased. And obviously, the very act of consigning their autobiographies to paper implies a high degree of literacy

---

[55] Legrain, "Souvenirs de Legrain, valet de chambre de Mirabeau," *Nouvelle revue rétrospective* 1 (1901):1–2.

[56] Gourville, *Mémoires de Monsieur de Gourville concernant les affaires auxquelles il a été employé par la cour depuis 1642 jusqu'en 1698*, I:6–8.

and self-consciousness, and above all an uncommon measure of success.

There is little in the sources to suggest that for most women domestic service could have been anything but an unpleasant necessity. But the attitudes of Gourville and Legrain may be extreme examples of a careerist mentality that was shared by a certain number of male servants. Not all of the men employed as valets and footmen in the towns of the Old Regime came from predictable areas of recruitment, the surrounding countryside or the nearest mountain range. A minority, which increased as the century progressed, had traveled very long distances. In Toulouse, 5 percent at the beginning of the century and 16 percent at the end came from areas other than the southwest.[57] In Aix and Marseille, the proportion of male servants from beyond Provence and the Alps grew from 2 to 18 percent (see table 1.2). One cannot extrapolate very much from this information alone. After all, the "foreign" servants of Aix and Toulouse probably came from equally poor areas of northern and western France, and their presence in these towns may have been due more to accident than to design. One would like to know, for instance, what curious set of circumstances brought the servant Thirisiau Mingam from his native village of Landirisiau in lower Brittany to Aix, where he drew up his will in 1784. We do know, however, that life was no easier for the poor in the heart of Brittany than it was on the slopes of the Alps and the Pyrenees in the eighteenth century.[58]

In comparative perspective, though, some evidence does in fact suggest that male servants were more footloose and enterprising than the average unskilled migrant. From Maurice Garden's study of Lyon in the eighteenth century, we know the geographic origins of the various socioprofessional groups in that town, which can

[57] Fairchilds, "Masters and Servants," pp. 370, 383.

[58] A.D.A. 305E 195, fol. 148, February 15, 1784. Le Roy Ladurie, *Histoire de la France rurale*, II:417; Hufton, *The Poor*, pp. 15–16; Goubert, *L'Ancien Régime*, I:107.

be compared easily on the maps he has constructed. It comes as no surprise to discover that skilled artisans such as wigmakers, hatmakers, and masons often came from distant provinces: the tradition of the tramping artisan was alive and well in the eighteenth century. But among unskilled workers, servants definitely had the widest area of recruitment. The *affaneurs* and *journaliers* of Lyon who sold their labor in the fields and on the docks for a daily wage came almost exclusively from southeastern France, especially the Lyonnais and the Dauphiné. The areas of recruitment of servants, while also located predominantly in the southeast, fan out all over northern and western France, stretching to Burgundy and Normandy in the north, almost to Brittany in the west, and over the eastern border to Switzerland.[59] This disparity no doubt reflects different attitudes toward occupational migration among *journaliers* and servants. Unskilled day laborers invariably gravitated toward the nearest urban center that could use their services, whereas some servants at least had traveled inordinately long distances, maybe heading deliberately for the larger and wealthier towns which offered better opportunities for employment and social mobility.

Servants may have been poor and vulnerable, but they also had a cultural headstart over unskilled workers in other occupations. In any town in France, a male servant was more likely to know how to sign his name than was a gardener or a docker. Both Gourville and Legrain indicated in their memoirs that they had received some elementary education before leaving their native villages. In fact, both men considered this early contact with the written word so important in shaping their destinies that they mentioned it in the very first sentences of their memoirs. Gourville begins his autobiography: "I was born in La Rochefoucault on July 11, 1625. After my father's death, my mother taught me how to write."[60] Legrain also indicated within the first three

[59] Garden, *Lyon*, pp. 237, 243, 251, 711–713, 731–736.
[60] Gourville, *Mémoires*, p. 6.

TABLE 1.3.
Literacy Rates among the Laboring Poor in Lyon (in percentages)

		1728–30	1749–51	1786–88	Whole Century
Servants:	Male	51	56	64	58
	Female	26	37	35	33
Day laborers:	M	20	21	37	27
	F	11	7	19	13
Cobblers:	M	64	68	70	68
	F	31	28	29	29
Bakers:	M	65	72	75	71
	F	62	61	76	68

Source: Maurice Garden, *Lyon et les lyonnais*, pp. 242, 254, 351

sentences of his memoirs that he attended school in the winter until his early teens.[61] In retrospect, learning to read and write represented an important turning point since it determined the shape of what both men considered to be exceptional careers.

Reading and writing skills were not confined to the aristocracy of service alone. In Lyon, throughout the century, half or more of the male servants, and a third of the females, could append their signatures to notarial documents (see table 1.3). The rates of literacy of servants in Lyon are consistently lower than those of artisans like cobblers or bakers, and *a fortiori* of elite artisanal groups like master silkworkers. Artisans and their wives strove to acquire even rudimentary writing skills since their trades often made the keeping of account books vital.[62] But if one compares servants to day laborers (*journaliers*) or to the *affaneurs* who carried loads on the docks of the city, the balance tips the other way: throughout the century, only 20 to 30 percent of these unskilled workers, whose backgrounds were similar to those of servants,

[61] Legrain, "Souvenirs," p. 1.
[62] Garden, *Lyon*, pp. 459–460; Roger Chartier, M. Compère, and D. Julia, *L'Education en France du XVIe au XVIIIe siècle*, pp. 103–104.

TABLE 1.4.
Literacy Rates of Servants in Aix and Marseille

	1715–52		1765–84	
	Male	Female	Male	Female
Aix	44%	6%	81%	17%
Marseille	72%	6%	80%	10%
Total number in sample:				
Aix	39	69	64	76
Marseille	18	80	10	48

Source: Notarial Records A.D.A. 301E to 309E; A.D.M. 351E, 364E

could sign their names. The same was true in the towns of the diocese of Rouen in Normandy, where at the end of the eighteenth century 55 percent of the male servants were literate, as opposed to 79 percent of the artisans and only 42 percent of the day laborers.[63] In a wealthier, more aristocratic town such as Aix, male servants achieved even more impressive rates, with 60 to 80 percent of them able to sign their names, as compared to 75 percent among skilled workers (see table 1.4).[64] In sharp contrast, among the *travailleurs*, unskilled day laborers who often worked the town's gardens or plots of land just outside the city walls,

[63] François Furet and Jacques Ozouf, *Lire et écrire: L'Alphabétisation des français de Calvin à Jules Ferry*, p. 144.

[64] Two different sources have been used to measure literacy in Aix. The parish registers of the Paroisse Saint-Sauveur, which indicate that 40 percent of the male servants could sign their names in the first half of the century, 60 percent in the 1770s. In contrast, 75 percent of all artisans could sign their names in the 1740s, a proportion that changed little in later decades. Thirty to 40 percent of the overall male population could sign in the first half of the century, just over 50 percent could do so on the eve of the Revolution. See Michèle Siméoni and Joseph Siméoni, "L'Alphabétisation à Aix au XVIIIe siècle" (Mémoire de Maîtrise, Univ. de Provence, 1975), pp. 26–27, 36–39. The Siméoni study does not record the literacy rates of women and rests on a thin numerical basis where servants are concerned, which is why I have cited my own calculations from the notarial records in the text.

less than a tenth could even scrawl the letters of their name.[65] Female servants remained for the most part illiterate, with literacy rates of 30 percent at most in both Provence and Normandy.[66]

Unskilled workers, be they *affaneurs, journaliers,* or *travailleurs,* were drawn, on the whole, from the same provinces as servants. Both categories were made up essentially of migrants of rural extraction, and not even the presence of *déclassés* among the ranks of domestics can account for the gap in levels of literacy between the two groups. Perhaps the prevailing paternalistic ethos encouraged masters and mistresses to force a smattering of education upon their employees. There is, however, little evidence to suggest that this was in fact the case.[67] It is more likely that, as Maurice Garden argues, the high rates of literacy among servants derived from a choice on the part of masters, many of whom hired employees who already knew how to read and write.[68] No doubt any immigrant equipped with those skills would prefer placing himself in service for the sake of protection and in the hopes of some sort of promotion to the unstable work of a day laborer, which was unquestionably a dead end.

Domestic service was not the worst of the alternatives open to penniless male immigrants. At the very least, it assured them of bed, board, and sometimes clothing, which working as a day

---

[65] Siméoni and Siméoni, "L'Alphabétisation à Aix," p. 39; Michel Vovelle, "Y a-t-il eu une Révolution culturelle en Provence au XVIIIe siècle? À propos de l'éducation populaire en Provence," *Revue d'histoire moderne et contemporaine* 22 (January–March 1975):11–114.

[66] Furet and Ozouf, *Lire et écrire,* p. 144.

[67] The standard handbooks for masters recommended that all servants be taught to read and write. See for instance Audiger, *La Maison réglée,* and Claude Fleury, *Devoirs des maîtres et des domestiques,* both reprinted in Alfred Franklin, *La Vie de Paris sous Louis XIV: Tenue de maison et domesticité,* pp. 24, 30, 33–34, 218. The only example I have encountered of this precept being followed is the enrollment of a servant in a school in Sens in 1712, probably at his master's instigation. See Chartier, Compère, and Julia, *L'Education en France,* p. 103.

[68] Garden, *Lyon,* p. 255.

laborer certainly did not. As a result, the occupation attracted the more educated and probably the more resourceful among migrant workers. It also drew men from distant provinces and even from abroad. All of this does indeed suggest that domestic service was attractive to some people, or at least that it was preferable to other types of employment—in other words, that a "pull" factor did influence both departure and choice of occupation for some servants. The most extreme and classic case of this sort of attraction operating in full occurred in the countryside, where powerful landlords still held sway over the rural population, and could easily draw the ablest among the local youths into their households. This was how young men like Gourville and Legrain began their careers before turning their footsteps toward the Parisian eldorado. Examples such as these are rare, however, and for the most part are confined to the world of the rural nobility.[69] The high turnover rate of urban servants makes it hard to believe that many of them sought employment in town out of loyalty to the *notables* of their native villages.

If it is difficult to sort out the motivations of those who surround us, let alone our own, in those crucial decisions that shape our life histories, it is that much more awkward to presume to do so for anonymous workers who lived two centuries ago. To evaluate the decision to leave one's village and become a servant in terms of an either-or distinction between "push" and "pull" means overlooking the many instances in which both factors must have operated at once. Overall, it cannot be denied that many rural youths did want to sell their services as valets or footmen, and consciously chose this occupation over other types of work. These men were willing to travel long distances to where the best opportunities awaited them. But evidence of careerism does not account for the fate of thousands of women, nor in all probability does it reflect the average male servant's experience. In-

---

[69] Perrot, *Genèse d'une ville moderne*, II:1028.

stances of nomadism and ambition are outweighed by far by evidence that points to tradition and penury.

The defenselessness of servants derived in great part from their social origins. If masters could expect to command the loyalty of their servants and often did coerce and manipulate them, it was in large part because most domestics were immigrants driven into service out of necessity rather than choice. Their identity as aliens and migrants explains their vulnerability. As strangers living and working in an unfamiliar environment, servants were continually exposed to the suspicions and sometimes even the hostilities of native town dwellers.

Servants had always been distrusted by the judicial authorities, who looked upon them as potentially dangerous elements. Special vigilance was recommended in police handbooks and legal dictionaries.[70] A whole battery of laws, royal ordinances, and local police regulations issued over three centuries were aimed at establishing the identitites and whereabouts of servants in the larger towns. The terms that recur insistently in these documents are *sans aveu, inconnus, mal famés*—rootless unknown, disreputable. As early as the sixteenth century, several royal edicts were issued prohibiting the hiring of unknown persons and requiring that servants provide information as to their origins and previous employment.[71] Eighteenth-century police regulations elaborated on these laws in tones that varied in urgency, depending on time and place. The statutes issued in the 1720s in Aix and Marseille contained perfunctory requirements that a servant decline his or her identity to prospective employers.[72] A contemporary Parisian regulation explained in much more strident tones that the mo-

[70] Jean-Pierre Gutton, *La Société et les pauvres: L'Exemple de la généralité de Lyon* (Paris, 1971), p. 81; idem, *La Société et les pauvres en Europe* (Paris, 1974), pp. 78–85; Richard Cobb, *The Police and the People*, pp. 15–17.

[71] François-André Isambert el al., *Recueil général des anciennes lois françaises*, XIV:178–179. Bibliothèque Nationale, Ms. 21800, fol. 19. Philippe-Antoine Merlin, *Répertoire universel et raisonné de jurisprudence*, IV:2.

[72] A.M.M. FF 191, pp. 35–36; A.M.A. FF 98, fol. 90.

bility and anonymity of Parisian servants contributed to "the great number of vagabonds and licentious people that are to be found in this town." It went on to establish that any servant who remained in Paris for a week without finding a new place would be considered a vagrant, and would be dealt with accordingly.[73]

By the end of the century, population growth and increased mobility had infused the same fears into Parisians and provincials alike. A new lengthy regulation was issued in Paris in November of 1778, once again requiring full biographical details of all prospective employees, and upping the fine on masters who hired unknown persons from twenty to two hundred livres; but this time jobless servants were allowed a month of unemployment before the authorities clamped down on them for *vagabondage*. Seven months later the Parlement of Provence parroted the law, down to the last detail.[74] Servants provoked the same suspicions as other migrants in a society fearful of anonymity and individual mobility. A sixteenth-century jurist, commenting on one of the edicts aimed at controlling the mobility of servants, explained that they were "lazy and idle people, rootless people, abandoned people, people with no dwelling, no trade or vocation . . . they are a weight useless to the world."[75] Such fears were not new but did not abide in the century preceding the Revolution.

The extent to which town dwellers shared the distrust of legislators toward servants as migrants is hard to gauge. Police records do offer an occasional glimpse of the visceral resentment of foreign elements that could surface among native workers when they came into conflict with servants. In 1762 a maidservant in

---

[73] Edmé de Poix de Fréminville, *Dictionnaire ou traité de la police générale des villes, bourgs, paroisses et seigneuries de la campagne*, pp. 216–218. Jean-Baptiste Denisart, *Collection de décisions nouvelles et de notes relatives à la jurisprudence actuelle*, II:7.

[74] Isambert, *Recueil général*, XXV:446–448. A.M.A. FF 1, fol. 58.

[75] Bronislaw Geremek, "Criminalité, vagabondage, paupérisme: La Marginalité à l'aube des temps modernes," *Revue d'histoire moderne et contemporaine* 21:348–349.

Aix was abused by an irate neighbor who screamed at her that "she was a whore, a bitch, a slut; she'd been banished from her homeland."[76] When the innkeeper Paul Amy venomously accused Françoise Richard of sleeping with her master, he pointedly added that "it was not too difficult for her, since she was from Savoy and a trooper's mattress [*une paillasse de corps de garde*]."[77]

It is difficult to determine just how pervasive this sort of hostility really was. But whatever the attitudes of others, the servants themselves had a strong sense of their own foreignness. Acculturation was a long process for many of these migrants who spoke only their native *patois*. Esmieu gives us an idea of what the problems could be when he tells us in his memoirs that he learned neither to read nor to write because "the idiom of the mountains differs a good bit from that of lower Provence, which is the only written language." Upon arrival in Marseille he deliberately contacted at least five people from his native region, the first of whom was a servant to the wealthy Forresta-Collongue family in Marseille.[78] Servants sought each other out, and strong regional monopolies would develop among chair carriers from the Lyonnais, cooks from Picardy, Savoyard errand boys, Swiss doormen, and valets from Gascony.[79] Pages and lackeys felt close enough to their rural backgrounds to beat up the *chasse-coquins* who harassed tramps from the mountains; whole households of domestics in Paris would show up in the courtroom to testify on behalf of compatriots who had been arrested and hauled before the police.[80] The most mundane, but also the most telling, evidence of the enduring identification of servants with the world beyond the city walls comes from their marriage contracts. Out of twenty-six male domestics born outside of Aix who married

[76] A.D.A. IVB 1228, August 11, 1762.

[77] A.D.A. IVB 1180, August 14, 1721.

[78] Dubois, ed., *Jean-Joseph Esmieu*, pp. 1, 17.

[79] Hufton, *The Poor*, p. 101; Cobb, *The Police and the People*, pp. 228–230.

[80] Gutton, *La Société et les pauvres*, p. 139. Le Roy Ladurie, *Paysans de Languedoc*, I:94; Hufton, *The Poor*, pp. 102–103.

there in the eighteenth century, only six took native Aixoises as their brides; and of ninety-two immigrant female servants, only twenty-four were wed to men born in Aix.[81] Barely a quarter of these men and women finally married natives of the town in which they worked. Most of them chose their spouses among migrants from the same areas as they, not infrequently from the same village. Servants were not easily absorbed into the urban environment in which they worked.

There were many reasons for the suspicions that servants encountered in the towns to which they migrated. Much of the hostility to which they were exposed arose from the peculiarities of their occupation, which will be discussed in a later chapter. But the fundamental characteristics common to nearly all domestic workers were poverty and foreignness, and these traits go a long way toward explaining both the behavior of servants themselves and the attitudes of others toward them. Often penniless, cut off from kith and kin and suddenly plunged in a foreign environment, servants could be malleable matter in the hands of their employers. They easily provoked the ire of poorer townsfolk who resented the defensive arrogance of young peasants dressed in silk and lace. Servants themselves, finally, must have felt ambivalent toward an occupation which in theory implied commitment to household and masters, but which few had embraced for positive reasons. For all but the most skilled and ambitious among them, domestic service was not a career but an expedient, not an end in itself but a bridge to better things. How servants themselves viewed their occupation, how they pursued their own goals in households and towns in which they were strangers, is the subject of the next chapter.

[81] Sampling of marriage contracts drawn up in Aix between 1715 and 1787. Notarial records, A.D.A. 301E to 309E.

CHAPTER 2

Love and Money

In the closing scene of Molière's *Dom Juan*, the legendary rake and libertine is struck down by lightning and sucked into a fiery furnace that opens in the ground beneath his feet. As he disappears, his chilling cry is echoed by the shrieks of his manservant. Sganarelle, a weak-willed and greedy man who has applauded his master and toadied to him throughout the play, drops down on his knees and wails: "My wages, my wages!" This ugly scene probably shocked seventeenth-century audiences much less than it does us, because in the comedies of France's classical age the venality and greed of servants were conventional traits that were used to provide comic relief, or served as foils to the nobler demeanor of upper-class protagonists.[1] But Sganarelle and the hundreds of other coarse and grasping valets and maids who kept theater audiences laughing in the seventeenth and eighteenth centuries did not owe their existence entirely to literary convention.

One real servant, Mirabeau's valet Legrain, admitted with disarming candor in his memoirs to motives and behavior no more commendable than those of Molière's most rascally creations. In the course of his years in service, Legrain perfected to a hilt the art of self-debasement, with the conscious goal of furthering his

[1] Molière, *Dom Juan*, act V, scene 6; on this aspect of the dramatic role of servants, see Jean Emelina, *Les Valets et les servantes dans le théâtre comique en France de 1610 à 1700*, pp. 289–295.

own interests. "If a master," he advised a fellow servant, "dismisses us after having been satisfied with our services, if he speaks ill of us, let us speak well of him, and take the blame upon ourselves, and you'll see that you will do well."[2] Following his own maxims, Legrain spent most of his life in service scurrying around officiously, blowing his own trumpet whenever a member of the master class was around to listen to him. He did not even bat an eyelid when Mirabeau momentarily swiped his *bonne amie* from him. But he also developed an intimate relationship with his master, a curious mixture of love, dependency, and rivalry, which he maintained by shows of meekness and loyalty and the occasional display of wounded pride.

Oddly enough, the memoirs end with the death of the count, as if the reason for Legrain's own existence disappeared with his master. Strangest of all is his callous description of his master's agony:

> It was my wife who kept him during his illness, without a moment's rest, and with that she was pregnant and tired; and watching a man waste away who should not have failed to provide us with at least enough to live sparely. He had not forgotten us, but where there is nothing, the King himself loses his rights.[3]

The memoirs end there, on the final triumph of self-interest over whatever affection and mutual dependency had bound the two men for years. Without a trace of self-consciousness, Legrain admitted that in the end financial considerations overrode his attachment to the count. Yet playwrights invariably presented the servant's obsession with material rewards as comical and contemptible. The portrayal of fictional servants as grasping and venal characters may well reflect a tension between the expecta-

---

[2] Legrain, "Souvenirs de Legrain, valet de chambre de Mirabeau," *Nouvelle Revue rétrospective* 1:80.

[3] Ibid., p. 120.

tions of masters, which were shared by much of their society, and the real needs of domestic servants.

It is not my intention to deny in this chapter the strength of the bonds that united most servants to their employers. Indeed, it would be simplistic to assume that loyalty and self-interest were mutually exclusive. The complexities inherent to the relationship between master and servant and the ambiguities of their feelings toward one another will be the subject of a later chapter. My purpose here is to show that certain attitudes and patterns of behavior characteristic of servants, which masters and others saw as cupidity or debauchery, were in fact conditioned by the servants' very legitimate concern with marriage, settlement, autonomy, or even mere survival. What were the aims and expectations of eighteenth-century servants? How difficult was it for them to attain their goals? How vulnerable were they? And what could happen to them if their quest for security and independence went awry? These considerations bear directly upon the quality of the relationship between master and servant. Both the dangers and the rewards of service must be taken into account if we wish to understand why Legrain's attachment to his master apparently broke down in the face of financial disappointment. This in turn will help explain why, notwithstanding the admonitions in their handbooks, masters could recognize their servants in the unsavory traits of a Sganarelle.

The expectations of men and women differed significantly, as did the range of possibilities open to them. The hopes of women focused on marriage. This was, after all, why they had entered service in the first place, and their minds could never stray very far from the event that would allow them to put an end to a life of drudgery and settle down as mistress in their own household, no matter how poor. Most menservants worked for wealthier masters in multiservant households, but women were more likely to find employment as maids-of-all-work in more modest establishments where they were paid less and worked harder.[4] The incentive for women to accumulate enough money to buy their way out of service and into marital life was consequently all the more pressing.

In the popular literature of the Old Regime, chambermaids and serving girls were always counting their pennies and dreaming of the man who was to wed them. Sixteenth-century poems recorded the lament of *la chambrière en mal d'amour*:

> Mais bien à l'heure qu'il viendra
> Puis quelque mignon surviendra
> De village ou varlet d'hostel
> Qui à espouse me prendra.[5]

In another poem, the *chambrière* is seen proudly counting the hundred livres she has just won at the lottery: "C'est pour celuy lequel m'épousera/Et quy amy mon cueur réclamera."[6] In these verses, economic considerations are bound up with yearnings for emotional security, sexual satisfaction, and establishment in society. In other texts, as in the seventeenth-century *Cacquets de l'accouchée*, marriage is crudely equated with a mercantile transaction. In the *Cacquets*, three women—mistress, chambermaid,

---

[4] Jeffry Kaplow, *The Names of Kings: The Parisian Laboring Poor in the Eighteenth Century*, pp. 47–48. In Aix in 1701, out of 1,043 female servants, 589 or 56 percent worked in households employing only one servant; for men, the proportion is 47 out of 900, or only 5 percent. In addition, Aix was a wealthy town with many multiservant households. The contrast probably would be greater in most other French towns. As regards social distribution of servants of either sex, here is an example: nobles of the sword in 1701 employed 72 male servants and 151 females, or a staff that was 67 percent female; by contrast, 94 percent of the servants who worked for professional men—doctors, apothecaries, and so forth—were women (113 out of 120). A.M.A. CC 13.

[5] *Recueil de pièces rares et facétieuses anciennes et modernes*, p. 5. The verse translates to: "But he will come in good time/ Some sweet young man will arrive/ A village boy or an innkeeper's valet/ To take me as his wife."

[6] Ibid. "It is for he who will marry me/ For the friend who will claim my heart."

TABLE 2.1.
Length of Women's Careers in Service,
Aix and Marseille, 1730–1787

	Number of Cases	Average Time in Service (years)	Average Earnings (livres per year)
1730–33	6	9	42
1749–52	9	11	58
1764–67	9	11	48
1784–87	15	11	65

Source: Notarial Records A.D.A. 301E to 309E; A.D.M. 351E, 363E, 364E

and young servant—are seen earnestly discussing the problem of dowry-inflation. The little maid assures them that she suffers the most from the sorry state of the market:

I deserve more pity than you do, because it used to be that when we had served for eight or nine years and gathered a belt of silver and a hundred *écus* in cash, we could find a good sergeant or a haberdasher to marry. But now for our money the best we can get is a coachman or a stableboy, who will make us three or four children in a row. And since they cannot feed them on the paltry wages they earn, we have to go back and serve as before.[7]

Marriage did not always solve the problem of survival, nor did it put an end to a woman's working life *a fortiori*. But the dowry that a young girl earned over long years of menial work was the only means that she had of buying her way into some sort of economic and emotional security. For this reason, most women went through their years in service with their eyes fixed on a dowry and their hearts set on betrothal.

Gathering a dowry was a lengthy proposition. In Aix and

[7] *Les Cacquets de l'accouchée* (n.p., 1623), as quoted in Jean-Louis Flandrin, *Les Amours paysannes* (Paris, 1975), pp. 61–62.

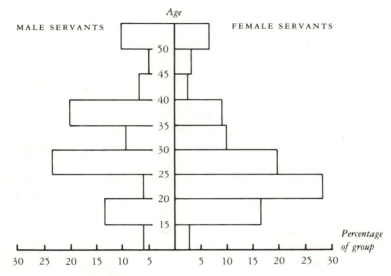

Figure 2.1. Age Distribution of Male and Female Servants in Bayeux, 1796

Marseille, the few women who recorded the time spent in service in their marriage contracts had worked a decade or more on the average collecting the few hundred livres which they presented to their fiancés (see table 2.1.).

That domestic service was a premarital occupation for most women, one in which they engaged at a certain point in their life cycle, is evident from the age structure of the occupation. Fiscal documents under the Old Regime do not record the ages of the persons surveyed, but revolutionary censuses do include such information. In 1796 in Bayeux, for instance, a great majority of female servants were less than thirty years old (see figure 2.1.). Sixty-seven percent of the 354 servants listed in the 1796 census were aged fifteen to thirty, with the largest proportion in the twenty to twenty-five age bracket. The pyramid tapers off progressively in the higher age groups, swelling only in the over-fifty age bracket, which presumably includes widows as well as spinsters and devoted retainers.

Careers in service could be interrupted by bouts of work in other occupations, a course often dictated by personal vicissitudes and the nature of local opportunities. Suzanne Reboul, suspected of domestic theft in Marseille, had no recourse but to seek employment in the countryside as a field hand.[8] In Normandy, by contrast, where textile manufacturing was strongly implanted, some women alternated between work as domestics and spinning, sewing, or lace making. Anne Auvray, who was cross-examined by the police in Bayeux in 1718, worked alternatively as a seamstress and as a servant; seventy years later, Marie Anne Loiselleur described a similarly erratic pattern of employment in the same town: she began as a lacemaker servant, then worked as a cook, and finally rented a room where she spun and sewed.[9] These women could not afford to stop working, if only because they had to keep themselves alive. For all the restrictions, drudgery, and occasional humiliations attendant to domestic service, women were likely to choose it over other occupations because it offered the best opportunities for saving up the meager earnings that were to become a dowry.[10]

In the eighteenth century, servants' dowries usually ranged from one hundred to five hundred livres, depending on time and place.[11] In Aix and Marseille, women gathered sums of two to three hundred livres in the 1730s, and five to six hundred in the 1780s (see table 2.3, *infra*). Though the value of these dowries was reckoned down to the last sou when a couple drew up a marriage contract, few women kept all of their possessions in cash. In two out of three cases at least, the contract indicates that only part of the dowry consisted of money. Over half was made

---

[8] A.D.A. 208U 29/279, October 20, 1813.
[9] A.D.C. 2B 863, September 1718; A.D.C. 2L 241/3, 6 Ventôse, Year VII.
[10] Olwen Hufton, *The Poor of Eighteenth-Century France*, pp. 28–29.
[11] Ibid., p. 29.

up of possessions in kind, variously described as "hardes, robes et proviments," or "coffres, robes, bagues et ameublements."

These formulas refer to the strange medleys of clothes, jewelry, linen, and small sticks of furniture known as *hardes* on which female servants usually spent substantial parts of their earnings. These were disparate collections of objects, seemingly purchased at random or acquired by accident. Marie Jacob's trousseau in 1705 included three dresses, seven shirts, fifteen palatines, and nine bonnets. A few years later another servant described a more balanced wardrobe made up of three corsets, two aprons, six shirts, and four petticoats. Not infrequently the *hardes* included gold earrings, chains and crosses, or small pieces of furniture. Gabrielle Ausselet's whole fortune in 1706 consisted of a chair, a candlestick, a sheet, a serge petticoat, and two shirts.[12] Servants who engaged in domestic theft would as often as not walk off with sheets, napkins, pillowcases, and shirts, instead of or as well as money.[13] The reflex that made women convert the money they acquired, whether legally or not, into hard goods was a long-lived one. In Marseille as late as 1812, Marie Anne Seguin made off with eight hundred francs belonging to her employer; instead of stashing the proceeds of her theft, she immediately acquired two mattresses, a complete wardrobe, and some gold and silver trinkets.[14] None of these objects, even the least functional, were considered frivolous acquisitions. One woman described the calico housecoat and gold chain she purchased as "des objets nécessaires."[15]

[12] A.M.A. FF 65, July 30, 1705; A.M.A. FF 72, March 12, 1722; A.M.A. FF 66, December 16, 1706.

[13] An exemplary case would be that of Marie Borel, accused of stealing from her employer a long list of garments, including one pair of sheets, several towels, shirts, skirts, handkerchiefs, scarves, pillowcases, jackets, yarn, and several lengths of cloth, plus 450 francs in cash. A.D.C. 2L 224/2, 22 Brumaire, Year VIII.

[14] A.D.A. 208U 29/225, January 25, 1812.

[15] A.D.A. 208U 28/200, December 11, 1811.

Why were these objects necessary? Why did servants insist on burdening themselves with these cumbersome possessions instead of carrying their savings around in cash? No doubt hard goods were easier to protect, if not to store, than money. Whenever possible, women would entrust their belongings to a friend or acquaintance, and made no mystery of why they did so. Marie Larmette, for instance, "entrusted her *hardes* to the woman Delphine, the servant of sieur Burel, for fear of their being withheld if she gave in her notice to the son of mistress Roquière."[16] In Marseille at the turn of the century, a whole nexus of unmarried women, servants, seamstresses, and unemployed *journalières* helped each other out by finding shelter and work for one another, and providing storage for each other's *hardes*. Of course even good friends could prove unreliable, and endless haggling often took place when the *hardes* were retrieved.[17] But sheets and mattresses were evidently easier to protect from both masters and fickle friends than were gold and silver coins.

Linens and household goods were valuable capital assets before the advent of mass-produced goods lowered their price. In Paris between 1750 and 1790 there were five times as many thefts of linen and clothing as of money or jewels.[18] But their importance to these women was psychological as well as economic, as the composition of a sampling of dowries in Aix and Marseille may suggest (see table 2.2).

Even in the mixed dowries, possessions in kind represented, on the average, half or more of the total value of the woman's

[16] A.M.A. FF 66, October 22, 1708.

[17] For instance, A.D.A. 208U 29/305 and 208U 29/279. Four women, Catin Jouve, Baptistine Fabre, Marianne Creillon, and Suzanne Reboul were implicated in a theft committed by the latter. Baptistine Fabre testified: "These napkins belong to Marianne Creillon, with whom I have been living for the last ten years . . . this Marianne Creillon is in service right now, but she thought it was best to leave all her belongings with me, except what she needed for daily use."

[18] Arlette Farge, *Le Vol d'aliments à Paris au XVIIIe siècle*, p. 114.

TABLE 2.2.

Composition of Servant Dowries, Aix and Marseille, 1715–1787

	Aix		Marseille	
	Number	Average Value (in livres)	Number	Average Value (in livres)
Mixed dowries (money + *hardes*)	56	431	56	508
Hardes only	37	207	25	361
Unspecified	6	355	13	368
Total	99		94	

Source: Notarial Records A.D.A. 301E to 309E; A.D.M. 351E, 363E, 364E

assets. The disparity in wealth between the women who contributed both cash and belongings to the financial settlement and their poorer sisters who had only their *hardes* to offer is quite noticeable. The ages of the spouses are not recorded in the marriage contracts, but this may very well mean that women invested in a trousseau before they started to save money, and that, on the whole, the poorer brides are merely the younger ones. Among the laboring poor, a man might look favorably on a woman who could present him with clothes, jewels, and a bit of furniture, for these were the first trappings of marital establishment.

Whether the main value of these objects was economic, sentimental, or both, their importance is evident from the frantic attempts that servants made to retrieve them if they were lost or fell into the hands of unscrupulous masters. In Marseille, Claire Achard got into a fight with her mistress in the course of which she was bitten, beaten with a candlestick, and narrowly escaped strangulation. She was thrown out into the street on Christmas Eve. The next morning at eight she was back hammering at the door, demanding her *hardes*. In 1721, the terrible year of the last great plague in Provence, a servant named Anne Farruelle returned to a farmhouse where seven people had just died, in the hope of recovering her possessions.[19]

Trunks and mattresses, trinkets, sheets, and coins represented far more to these women than just the sum of money they would fetch on the market or would one day be recorded on a notary's log. The belongings that were lovingly assembled and fiercely guarded by domestics were no doubt invested with greater value because they stood for a servant's future status as a married woman. These mundane symbols of a future life, of an identity separate from one's occupation, bear eloquent testimony to the female servant's tension about marriage.

Nowhere, perhaps, is this preoccupation with marriage more visible than in the female servants' attitudes toward the men who bestowed attentions on them. Evidence from police blotters and illegitimate pregnancy records strongly suggests that the relations that most servants had with men were conditioned by their eligibility as potential spouses. A contrario proof of this attitude can be detected, for instance, in the protestations of Elizabeth Arnaud, who admitted to having had with her master des liaisons particulières: "I did not have much affection for Noreda. He was a married man, and it was for money rather than anything else that I endured his attentions."[20]

Among the unfortunate women who came to report extramarital pregnancies before the police or religious authorities, a minority had been raped or psychologically coerced by their masters or other men of superior status. Others were manifestly the victims of rakes or rapists of a social station comparable to their own. All of this speaks to the sexual vulnerability of servants, and we shall return to this subject later in more detail. But most of the women—servants and others—who got pregnant out of wedlock in the eighteenth century had been misled by the promises of marriage of eligible men who had subsequently abandoned

[19] A.M.A. FF 72, November 20, 1721; see also A.M.A. FF 72, March 12, 1722.
[20] A.D.A. 208U 29/65, 21 Floréal, Year X.

them for one reason or another.[21] "He said he would marry me" is the refrain that comes up time and time again in the stories that these women told the authorities. In Aix, fifty-eight women out of eighty who in the earlier years of the century described the circumstances leading to their pregnancy, claimed that such promises had been spoken. If one looks only at sexual encounters between men and women of similar social class, the proportion that took place under promises of marriage ranges, over the century, from 66 to 80 percent in Aix, and 63 to 89 percent in Nantes.[22] Of course some women, in the presence of the severe officials who cross-questioned them, must have lied about how they got into their sorry state. But the proportions of women who told this tale are so high that it is hard to believe that there was not a kernel of truth to most of these stories. As Cissie

---

[21] These patterns have transpired in several good studies of illegitimate pregnancy records, or *déclarations de grossesse*, that have been published over the last decade. I have drawn extensively on them in the discussion below. The *déclarations de grossesse* were made compulsory by an edict of Henri II in 1556. Their original intent was to prevent unwed mothers from committing infanticide; but this law was also part of the post-Tridentine effort to control morality, especially among the lower classes, by making unwed mothers admit publicly to their condition. There were also good economic reasons for the institution: if the community could track down the presumed father, he could be forced to contribute to the upkeep of a child whose needs might otherwise have to be met by the community, hence the careful cross-examination of the mother. *Déclarations* were received by different authorities in different parts of France, ecclesiastical courts, judges, hospital administrators, or municipal officials. For institutional aspects of the *déclarations*, see Marie-Claude Phan, "Les Déclarations de Grossesse en France: Essai institutionnel," *Revue d'histoire moderne et contemporaine* 22:61–88. The best studies of these documents to date are: Alain Lottin, "Naissances illégitimes et filles-mères à Lille," *Revue d'histoire moderne et contemporaine* 17:278–322; Jacques Depaw, "Illicit Sexual Activity and Society in Eighteenth-Century Nantes," trans. Elborg Forster, in Robert Forster and Orest Ranum, eds., *Family and Society* (Baltimore, 1976), pp. 145–191; Cissie Fairchilds, "Female Sexual Attitudes and the Rise of Illegitimacy: A Case Study," *Journal of Interdisciplinary History* 8:627–667.

[22] Fairchilds, "Female Sexual Attitudes," pp. 641, 663, 666; Depaw, "Nantes," p. 163.

Fairchilds has pointed out, few of the eighteenth-century working women who engaged in premarital sex did so because they were promiscuous, romantically inclined, or on the lookout for physical fulfillment. Most of them yielded to the men who harassed them because they sincerely believed that this was a first step toward securing a marriage partner.[23]

What Fairchilds has argued with regard to working women in general certainly applies to servants, who accounted for large proportions of these hapless unwed mothers. Like other working women, servants were more likely to give in to seduction, persuasion or even sheer brutality when it was accompanied by the promise of an engagement that would begin to legitimize the situation. Servants often tried to extract a commitment from the men who pursued them. When the cook Etienne Girard told Jeanne James that he loved her, she bluntly responded that "if he wanted to look upon her as a mistress, he was wrong, and that she would only listen to him if he intended to marry her." This is almost word for word what another servant, Magdeleine Jourdan, said as she tried to wrest a commitment from her suitor: "If he wanted to treat her as a whore, he was mistaken; he would never get anything from her but through marriage."[24] Another cook, Gayetan Laurens, pursued Marguerite Poncet for several months, and was sent packing at every visit with orders to go talk to her masters and to her father.[25]

Some women admitted that they once liked and trusted the men with whom they had slept. Marie Chailhan, for one, had been courted for a whole year by a young servant who swore eternal love and promised marriage: "When he saw that he was loved, he asked her for her favors, which she long refused, but at last she gave in because of his promises." He left her eight months pregnant.[26] Charlotte Chaud, a chambermaid, kept com-

[23] Fairchilds, "Female Sexual Attitudes," pp. 654–659.
[24] A.D.A. IVB 1250, March 1774; A.D.A. IVB 1245, February 1771.
[25] A.D.A. IVB 1274, February 8, 1789.
[26] A.D.A. IVB 1269, May 22, 1786.

pany with a man named Jouve for six months, and resisted his "pressing solicitations," begging him to go talk to her parents. But one day as they were walking in the countryside she gave in to him, "and since then they lived together freely." Charlotte's reputation was destroyed, but she clung to her hopes of marriage until Jouve dashed them with the crushing lie that he could not marry until he turned thirty.[27]

Even when they were taken in by good looks and flowery compliments, even when they did fall in love, these women always had an eye to wages and employment. This is the chambermaid Magdeleine Cotton's account of how she fell for a womanizer named Blondin who worked as a valet:

> He held forth to her as seducers ordinarily do, praised her appearance and her character, and repeatedly told her that he would be only too happy if he could have a wife like her. These utterances seduced the plaintiff, who knew that Blondin worked in one of the best houses in town, where he was making excellent wages.[28]

Even when men forced themselves brutally on servants, they also got their way more easily by mentioning the magic word, marriage. Marguerite Barbier had the misfortune to be employed in the same house as Claude Ollivier, who pursued her relentlessly. One night, as she was entering her room, he sprang out from a hiding place and forced his way in with her. "She said, 'Alas what do you want with me, you know that you want to be my ruin, and that you will be,' to which Ollivier replied, 'Don't be afraid, I will marry you.'"[29] Catherine Martel was raped by a lackey who kept protesting that "whatever happened, even if she hadn't a penny, she would be his wife." Rose Hermitte was assaulted late at night in the countryside by a farmhand who had

[27] A.D.A. IVB 1248, January 13, 1774.
[28] A.D.A. IVB 1239, April 19, 1768.
[29] A.D.A. IVB 1173, January 25, 1718.

been coveting her: "He tried to know her carnally, telling her that she had nothing to fear because he intended to marry her."[30]

The same story crops up again and again with minor circumstantial variants, in pregnancy records and *procès en rapt*. The sad irony behind these women's fates was that they violated codes of safe and acceptable behavior precisely because they wanted security and respectability. Inasmuch as we can judge from the stories that they told, their downfall was the direct result of their preoccupation with marriage.

All of this does not mean, of course, that servants were much different from working women in other occupations. Whatever their work might be, women all over France toiled, saved, gathered a dowry, and, with some luck, got married.[31] Seamstresses and spinners were no doubt equally concerned with finding a husband, were courted in much the same way, and ran the same risks as servants. Domestic service was in some ways the archetypal female occupation because it involved more women than any other work. It was different, though, in that it occupied them for only part of their lives. The wives of laboring men certainly worked, since their wages were indispensable to the family economy. In the countryside they assisted their husbands on the land, hired themselves out as field hands, or became domestic textile workers. In town they helped in their husbands' craft or retail shops, peddled goods, nursed other people's children, sewed, or spun.[32] None, or very few, continued in or returned to service.

The unique character of domestic service can be clearly seen if one compares the ages of servants to those of female workers in another occupation. Lace making was the other major type of work available to women in Bayeux in the late eighteenth century. But whereas, as we saw, a large proportion of female servants was aged fifteen to thirty, *dentellières* were evenly distributed in

---

[30] A.D.A. IVB 1180, March 18, 1726; A.D.A. IVB 1250, January 30, 1774.

[31] Joan Scott and Louise Tilly, *Women, Work, and Family*, pp. 31–42.

[32] Ibid., pp. 44–51.

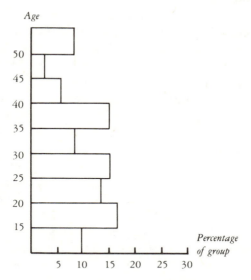

Figure 2.2. Age Distribution of Female
Lacemakers in Bayeux, 1796

all age brackets except between the ages of forty and fifty (see figure 2.2). More very young girls could work at this occupation at home, under the supervision of their mothers, and older women continued to make lace at home after they were married.

Most women employed as domestics must have been anxious to get out of service as soon as they possibly could. A servant was cut off from her family, and her work placed her at the mercy of employers who would normally demand that she perform the hardest and dirtiest chores in the household.[33] No wonder that these women strove for the independence that only marriage or other skills could bring them—for a price. Marie Jeanne Auvray of Bayeux was talked into robbing her masters by the woman Bidot who offered to sell the booty for her, assuring her that "with your share of the profits you can learn to work as a seam-

[33] Ibid., pp. 35–36.

stress."[34] Another woman, Félicité Gance, was hauled before the police on charges of infanticide. The young man who had made her pregnant was called up for military service. She claimed, "He promised to marry me. He wanted to learn to bleach thread, and we could have worked at the same trade together."[35]

Domestic service was a necessary ordeal for most of the thousands of women who, in every French town, engaged in it for a decade or so before marriage. They could not afford to invest their identities in it, even if they wanted to. Their hopes and dreams, which usually crystallized around the prospect of finding a husband, were set aside to be gazed at and protected just as were the *hardes* that were stored with friends. This divorce between self and occupation in some cases resulted in resistance to the will of employers, and in greed, disobedience, or petty larceny. More often it seems to have had the opposite effect, to have made female servants, who were isolated, poor, and vulnerable to begin with, into docile and tractable workers. The hardships of service were perhaps more easily complied to because the women knew, or hoped, they were temporary.

The careers of women in service tended to fall into very similar patterns, with savings and marriage as the principal goals. But similarities between the fates of men who engaged in this occupation are much harder to discern. The problem may come simply from a lack of information: even in the eighteenth century, male servants were much less numerous than females and we have no systematic series of documents relating to them comparable to the pregnancy records or *procès en rapt*. But even the scraps of information that can be culled from police records and memoirs suggest that there was, in fact, no typical route followed by menservants.

This derives in part from the extremely hierarchical nature of

34 A.D.C. 2L 281/5, Year XIII.
35 A.D.C. 2L 302/8, 1809.

male service, as opposed to its female counterpart. The most a woman could aspire to, if she were skilled or ambitious, was to work as a chambermaid or a governess. The stratifications of male service were, by contrast, almost infinite. A skilled valet, a cook, or a steward no doubt looked very differently upon his occupation than did the lackey or stableboy who stayed a few months with the household before trying out his luck elsewhere. The options available to unskilled men were far more numerous than those open to women. As a result, male servants were and remain elusive creatures. One can, however, try to sketch out the routes followed by a few of them.

At the summit of the pyramid were the high-ranking careerists whom we have already met in the persons of Gourville and Legrain. These men were probably more numerous in Paris than elsewhere, and they certainly aroused an uncommon measure of resentment. In the *Persian Letters*, Montesquieu wrote scathingly of their sort:

> The profession of lackey deserves more respect in France than elsewhere, for it is a nursery of noble lords: it fills up the gaps left by other classes. Its members replace great men who have come to grief, legal officials who have been ruined, gentlemen killed in the paroxysms of war; and when they cannot take their places themselves, they restore great families by means of their daughters, who are a sort of manure for fertilizing land that is both high and dry.[36]

In Paris, especially at court, male servants could hope for the most drastic sort of financial and social promotion. According to Sébastien Mercier, whose testimony was admittedly biased by his hatred of Versailles, valets at court could even engage in games of power politics. "At Versailles," he wrote, "valets who gain favor can buy their way into office holding, so that the households

---

[36] Montesquieu, *Persian Letters*, trans. C. J. Betts (London, 1973), p. 183.

of Princes are really in the hands of servants who transmit posts to one another as if this were a guaranteed succession."[37]

As we saw in the last chapter, young men who hoped to make a career out of service were ready to attach themselves to one master, to uproot themselves, and to travel long distances as the job demanded. Many first gravitated from the provinces to Paris, where the busiest market for servants was located. Joseph Blanchet, arrested in Aix in 1790 on charges of counterrevolutionary utterances, had traveled from his native Lorraine to Paris, where he was hired by the master who brought him to Aix. Julien Binet, the maître d'hôtel of the Président d'Entrecasteaux in 1784, was a native of Normandy whose services had been secured in Paris thirty-seven years earlier.[38]

If some men attached themselves to a household out of ambition or loyalty, others apparently did so because they knew of no other course to take. Joseph Limousin, a lackey to the Charleval household in Aix, had been dispatched directly to his masters by the *curé* of his native village; Joseph Blacas, another of the d'Entrecasteaux servants, said that "since his earliest years he had frequented the château in Entrecasteaux, where he comes from. His father serves in the country."[39]

Overall, male servants fall into two very different categories: an elite of faithful retainers who, out of loyalty or self-interest, remained for years with the same employers, and the far more numerous ranks of unskilled transients who often made no more than a cameo appearance in the houses where they worked. The account books of aristocratic households bear witness to this dichotomy. In the twenty-nine years between 1746 and 1775, the Gosselin de Manneville family in Caen employed two valets, Du Parc for twenty years and Michel for six. They had one steward, Vergeon, over the entire period, but hired fifteen young lackeys,

[37] Louis-Sébastien Mercier, *Le Tableau de Paris*, IX:9.
[38] A.D.A. IVB 1275, July 3, 1790; A.D.A. B 6270.
[39] A.D.A. IVB 1245, March 6, 1775; A.D.A. B 6270.

two or three of whom usually overlapped.[40] For all this turnover, the Mannevilles were luckier with their lower staff than the Mazenods in Aix who, in the twenty-one years between 1769 and 1790, were blessed with only one valet and seven cooks, but had to cope with the hiring of twenty-five different lackeys.[41]

Male service was not, like its female counterpart, an occupation characteristic of a specific stage of life. Either one devoted one's life to it or, more frequently, one drifted in and out of it as different opportunities presented themselves. The irregular age structure of the male side of the occupation in Bayeux appears to confirm this, though the concentration of servants in the higher age brackets is no doubt best explained by the draining of younger men into the armies of the Republic in the last years of the century (see figure 2.1). But impressionistic evidence does suggest that the careers of men were far more varied than those of women. One of the most enduring stereotypes in the fiction of the age was that of the valet as freewheeling jack-of-all-trades. Such was the hero of Lesage's monumental picaresque novel, *Gil Blas de Santillane*. Gil Blas had many a famous brother on the stage. In Regnard's *Les Folies amoureuses*, for instance, Crispin introduced himself with these words:

> J'ay fait tant de métiers d'après le naturel
> Que je puis m'appeler homme universel.
> J'ay couru l'univers, le monde est ma patrie,
> Faute de revenu, je vis de l'industrie.[42]

Eighty years later, the most celebrated fictional servant of the century treated the audience to an autobiographical avalanche that began with the question: "Could anything be stranger than

[40] A.D.C. 2E 2810, Fonds Gosselin de Manneville.

[41] B.M., Ms. 1652, "Livre de Raison de Charles-Alexandre de Mazenod."

[42] Jean-François Regnard, *Théâtre*, I:35. "I have had so many trades according to my nature/ That I might well be called a universal man./ I've roamed the universe, the whole world is my nation/ When I have no income, expedients will do."

a fate like mine?"[43] Figaro's account of his years of wheeling and dealing links him, via the picaresque literary tradition, to another great fictional servant, the Spanish Lazarillo de Tormes.

But are these literary clichés really that removed from reality? There were plenty of real menservants whose lives resembled those of Gil Blas and Figaro, and they may even have been a majority. Thirty-three-year-old François Borelly, a servant in Aix, was arrested in 1771 for selling meat on the black market. He turned out to have connections with the underworld of prostitution and pimping, and reeled off an account of his last fifteen years that nearly matches Figaro's: one year as a carter, two as a coachman, four years in the army, seven places in Provence and Paris in the course of the following eight years, including a couple of long spells of unemployment *sur le pavé*.[44] Nor is this typical of only the servants who rubbed elbows with the "dangerous classes." Auguste Reynaud, who was subjected to routine interrogations because a murder was committed in the house where he worked, rattled off a similar story: he had started out—like Figaro—as a barber's apprentice, and in between spells in service had put in time in the army and worked in the fields.[45]

Unlike female servants, some men embraced the occupation for the duration of their working lives. Marriage did not necessarily interrupt their careers. Most employers disapproved of servants marrying, or prohibited it outright; but this rule seems to have been applied far more rigorously to women than to men, whose work would not be interrupted by child bearing and nursing.[46] It remains to be seen whether these men really invested

[43] Beaumarchais, *Le Mariage de Figaro*, act V.

[44] A.D.A. IVB 1245, June 4, 1771.

[45] A.D.A. B 6270.

[46] This is at least what normative texts suggest. A law of 1567 prohibited servants from marrying without their masters' consent under penalty of dismissal and loss of wages. See Philippe-Antoine Merlin, *Répertoire universel et raisonné de jurisprudence*, IV:3; some handbooks advised masters to keep only unmarried servants, while others deplored the fact that they did. See for instance Duchesse

their personalities into the lives they had chosen. For every faithful steward or valet, there were a dozen lackeys and stableboys who switched households or even occupations every six months or every year. Their view of household, masters, and occupation must have been, if anything, more detached than that of their female counterparts.

The typical servant, male or female, was legitimately concerned with money, marriage, and old age. The extent of this concern is better understood with some knowledge of how the odds were stacked in the complex game of love, luck, and money that led them through and out of service. How much money did servants need or want, and how much could they earn? How vulnerable were they—economically, legally, and sexually? And what tactics could they and did they adopt to put the best chances on their side?

The answer to the first question is relatively easy to provide where female servants are concerned. The drawing-up of marriage contracts was practiced by a majority of the urban population under the Old Regime. In large cities such as Paris and Lyon and smaller urban centers such as Toulouse and Agen, 60 to 95 percent of all town dwellers drew up contracts before notaries.[47]

---

de Liancourt, *Règlement donné par une dame de qualité à M*** sa petite-fille, pour sa conduite et celle de sa maison*, p. 114; Claude Fleury, *Les Devoirs des maîtres et des domestiques*, reprinted in Alfred Franklin, *La Vie de Paris sous Louis XIV: Tenue de maison et domesticité*, p. 241. In police records and other contemporary documents, it is extremely rare to find mention of married women working as domestics, but married menservants appear quite frequently.

[47] In Lyon, 95 percent of the population, on the average, drew up marriage contracts, in Paris 60 percent, in Agen late in the century 76 to 96 percent, and in Toulouse in 1785, 93 percent. Maurice Garden, *Lyon et les lyonnais au XVIIIe siècle*, pp. 213–223; Adeline Daumard and François Furet, *Structures et relations sociales à Paris au milieu du XVIIIe siècle*, pp. 8–11; Anne-Marie Petit, "Mariages et contrats de mariage à Agen en 1785 et 1786," *Annales du midi* 72 (April 1960): 223; Adeline Daumard, "Structures sociales et classement socio-professionel: L'Apport des archives notariales aux 18e et 19e siècles," *Revue historique* 227 (January–March 1962):139–154.

TABLE 2.3.
Average Dowries of Female Servants, Aix and Marseille, 1715–1787
(in livres tournois)

	Aix		Marseille	
	Earnings	Total Dowry*	Earnings	Total Dowry*
1715–18	229	251	—	313
1730–33	253	280	257	377
1749–52	312	357	541	565
1764–67	415	442	528	567
1784–87	501	554	680	862
Total number in sample	115		110	

* Earnings plus gifts and bequests to the bride
Source: Notarial Records A.D.A. 301E to 309E; A.D.M. 351E,
363E, 364E

Nearly always the sum of money cited in the contract consisted
solely of the bride's fortune. The amounts that servants in Aix
and Marseille brought their future husbands are shown in table
2.3.

The dowries of female servants, rarely less than two hundred
and fifty livres, and sometimes amounting to more than eight
hundred, were more substantial than those of other servants in
other regions of France. According to Olwen Hufton, dowries of
working women in excess of five hundred livres were rare anywhere
in the realm. Very few exceeded two hundred livres in Bayeux,
and in Lyon they were closer to one hundred.[48] Given the level
of contemporary wages, these dowries represented a tremendous
sacrifice for most women (see table 2.4).

The sums of money that these servants brought to their marriage settlements were consistently equal to about ten times the
yearly wage of an unskilled maid, and somewhat less of the salary
of a chambermaid. The effort involved in amassing these sums

[48] Hufton, *The Poor*, p. 29.

TABLE 2.4.
Average Yearly Wages of Female Servants, Aix, 1711–1790
(in livres tournois)

	Unskilled Maids	Chambermaids
1711–20	24	—
1721–30	35	—
1731–40	24	—
1741–50	41	75
1751–60	50	75
1761–70	49	74
1771–80	52	75
1781–90	61	84

Source: See appendix 2

represented much more than six to ten years of hard work. It also meant that every penny earned over this period had to be saved. Any sum that was squandered, lost, or sent home to impoverished parents would prolong one's time in service by months or even years.

Even with bed and board provided, saving money was more of a challenge than might at first appear. Of course gifts and bequeaths from parents and masters came the way of the lucky ones, but they increased dowries by no more than a tenth on average (see table 2.3). Bonuses could also come in the form of Christmas gifts, or *étrennes*, but these amounted to 5 percent of the total salary at most, and are rarely mentioned in account books.[49] On the other hand, most masters expected their servants to take care of their every expenditure outside of food and lodging

[49] A.D.M. IIIE 84, "Livre de Raison de Joseph de Maliverny." The entry for January 1, 1760 reads: "Etraine à Thérèse, 3 livres." Thérèse was getting 60 livres a year at this time. See also M.A., M.Q. 65, Livre de Raison du Baron de Sannes. In 1781 the baron gave a total of 72 livres as *étrennes* to all of his retainers together. Considering that he was employing ten people at the time, including a tutor at 500 livres a year, one suspects that none of them did very well by this gift. See also Jean-Claude Perrot, *Genèse d'une ville moderne: Caen au XVIIIe siècle*, II:1,030.

out of their own pockets, and as a result servants were forever drawing advances on their wages, especially during their first years of work. In the wealthiest households servants benefited from hand-me-downs, liveries, or a fund of clothing available to the staff. But in the middling households where most women worked, every penny (including taxes) spent on a servant or given to her was carefully reckoned and deducted from the final payment.

In February of 1715, Jean Joseph de Bruges, an Aixois doctor, hired Angélique Simon from the nearby village of Rognes at twenty-one livres a year. In April she got an advance of one livre and eighteen sous to buy shoes. She spent six sous in July and one livre in January to have them repaired; in August she borrowed another six sous for her grandmother; and throughout the year she drew advances for ribbon, thread, dressmaking, and clothes, including a heavy serge coat on which she splurged almost half of her salary. In March of 1716 she was paid what remained of her wages, two livres and seventeen sous. The following year Angélique hardly did any better, since she ended up with three livres and three sous in her pocket.[50] Of course most of these clothes would be reckoned into a dowry as *hardes* if they survived ten years of service. But the money spent on an ailing grandmother, a worn-out pair of shoes, or an occasional ribbon would never be retrieved.

This money, we have seen, was crucial to a servant's future. But what sort of future did they want, or could they hope to secure for a few hundred livres? In Marseille at mid-century, female servants brought to their marriage partners fortunes worth, on the average, five to six hundred livres. According to a study of marriage contracts in Marseille at mid-century, this was the sort of dowry that would be expected by young men from the skilled or semiskilled working classes—journeymen and appren-

[50] A.D.A. XXIVHB 41, Livre de Raison de Jean-Joseph de Bruges, docteur en médecine, 1647–1736.

TABLE 2.5.
Occupational Distribution of Servants' Husbands,
Aix and Marseille, 1715–1787

	Aix	Marseille
Unskilled and rural workers	46%	24%
Sailors	—	5%
Servants	21%	9%
Skilled and semiskilled workers	21%	42%
Master artisans	7%	13%
Commerce and urban services	5%	7%
Total number in sample	*115*	*101*

Source: Notarial Records, A.D.A. 301E to 309E; A.D.M. 351E, 363E, 364E

tices, fishermen, sailors, servants, and lower-level employees. Rural and unskilled workers married women who brought them 180 to 320 livres, but master artisans would expect a dowry of 1,000 livres or more.[51] In sum, servants in Marseille could marry into what might be termed the petite bourgeoisie of that town—and judging from their marriage contracts, they did (see table 2.5).

In Marseille the largest proportion of servants in this sample of contracts (42 percent) married skilled workers, another quarter were wed to unskilled workers, and only 13 percent became the wives of master artisans. In Aix the pattern is different: twice as many married unskilled workers or peasants, but the proportion of those who wed other servants is also over double that in Marseille. This reflects no more than differences between the overall occupational structure of the two towns. Aix was a wealthier, more aristocratic town than Marseille, but the pool of skilled working-class men from which husbands could be drawn was smaller. Even servants with respectable dowries had to be content

[51] Mireille Bellenger, "Recherches sur la population marseillaise au milieu de XVIIIe siècle" (Mémoire de Maîtrise, Univ. de Provence, 1963), pp. 76–78.

with one of the *travailleurs* who provided menial work in the gardens and fields belonging to *Parlementaires* and members of the upper clergy. But they could also find more husbands among the servants who staffed the houses of these people. Ironically, it was in the richer town that servants contracted the less glamorous marriages. But all in all, husbands in both towns were evenly distributed between the skilled and unskilled working classes.

Gathering a dowry and finding a husband meant at best definite social promotion since most of these servants came from very modest, even very poor backgrounds. At the very least, it afforded the security that a single female income could not ensure. Even marriage to a day laborer or a peasant represented a measure of success for women whose only chance of a decent life depended on the securing of a marriage partner.

What sort of rewards men got or expected for their labor is much harder to determine. To be sure, they always earned much better wages than women, whatever their skills. In the Mazenod household in Aix, the lackeys hired between 1743 and 1781 made 90 livres a year. In the 1780s and '90s their wages climbed to 160 livres. Over the same period, maids were paid between 35 and 50 livres, and were making 65 livres by century's end. Valets in the same household earned 200 livres a year, at a time when chambermaids were making well under half that amount.[52] In Normandy, wages were lower overall than in Provence, but the same iron rule prevailed. In the Manneville household, upper male servants could expect 80 to 120 livres in the 1770s, when chambermaids were still earning 60 or 70 livres a year. Lackeys in this household made 50 livres at mid-century, and 100 livres a couple of decades later, or systematically double the amount that maids in the same household were paid.[53] At levels of equal

[52] B.M. Mss. 1651 and 1652.
[53] A.D.C. 2E 2810, Fonds Gosselin de Manneville.

qualification, male servants nearly always earned twice as much money as their female counterparts.

Whether they saved their money, and how much they managed to put aside, is difficult to ascertain because of the fragmentary quality of the evidence. Exemplary servants who neither drank, gambled, amassed debts, nor otherwise squandered their earnings could certainly save pretty packets of cash. Antoine Viziot, a servant to the Baron de Sannes in Aix, was paid 480 livres in March 1787 for five years of his wages.[54] But judging from the account books of masters, this was the exception rather than the rule. Menservants drew advances on their wages just as liberally as did maids, and often borrowed much larger sums from their masters since they usually worked for wealthier employers.

In Aix, the Baron d'Audiffren advanced 700 livres to his valet in 1734 so that the latter could repay a debt. Audiffren carefully noted—not without some satisfaction, one imagines—that the servant was thus bound to him for the next seven years, nine months, and nine days. The possibility of repayment or of a rise in wages apparently failed to cross his mind at this time.[55] The lackey of Louis de Thomassin had slipped into the same sort of financial quagmire. He had borrowed 776 livres from his master on different occasions, most recently to contribute to the expenses of his sister's marriage. In 1757, after nine years of service, he still owed his employer 128 livres. Thomassin did record that he reduced this last debt by half, but his tone was self-congratulatory and slightly ominous: "I liberally acquitted him of half, in consideration of his past services, and of those which he will render me in the future."[56]

Between these two extremes were the numerous men who departed or were dismissed before they even collected a full year's salary. Charles-Alexandre de Mazenod must have been no easy

[54] Musée Arbaud, M.Q. 65, Livre de Raison du Baron de Sannes.

[55] A.D.A. XXIVH B 19, Livre de Raison des Audiffren.

[56] B.M. Ms. 1647, Livre de Raison de Louis de Thomassin, entry for July 3, 1752.

employer to live with, to wit the litany that runs through his account book month after month: "Gave him 23 livres and dismissed him . . . 24 livres and dismissed him . . . he was payed 15 livres and gave in his notice."[57] One cannot measure relative likelihoods on such grounds, but the divide seems to fall, here again, between skilled menservants who could, if they were lucky, amass substantial sums, and the lower staff who simply eked out as much money as they could and departed.

Judging from their marriage contracts, menservants were not doing poorly by the time they took a wife. The contracts are a more problematic source in this case, because in many towns only the woman's dowry is mentioned in the document. In Lyon and Paris, however, the contract carries the combined fortune of both parties—though the man's contribution is usually much smaller—and in Toulouse the fortune of the future husband was recorded separately.[58] Even when only the wives' dowries are recorded, social historians have used these sources on the assumption that the men's socioeconomic standing is implicit in these sums: the more wealth and/or status a man enjoyed, the higher was the sum expected of his future wife.[59] At any rate, a comparison between the marriage contracts of men in all of these towns shows them to have held an advantageous position vis-à-vis unskilled

[57] B.M. Ms. 1652.

[58] Garden, *Lyon*, p. 298; Jean Sentou, *Fortunes et groupes sociaux à Toulouse sous la Révolution* (Toulouse, 1969), p. 438; Daumard and Furet, *Structures et relations sociales*, p. 11.

[59] In the wake of Daumard and Furet's pioneering study of Parisian marriage contracts (see note 47), historians have used these documents to study socio-economic structures in Ancien-Régime France on the assumption that, in a rigidly hierarchical society, marriage serves as a means for social reproduction. In other words, they assume that there was, in broad terms, a systematic correlation between the level of the women's dowries and the socioeconomic status of their prospective husbands. Though I have never encountered any evidence that strongly contradicts this notion, the method certainly has its limitations. The only other source for measuring the wealth of different social groups, the *Inventaires après décès*, was unavailable in the towns I studied.

TABLE 2.6.

Fortunes of Male Servants and Other Workers at Marriage,
Aix, 1769–1779

Amount in Livres	Unskilled Workers	Skilled Workers	Servants	Master Artisans
0–150	5%	2%	—	3%
150–300	30%	13%	3%	10%
300–600	45%	32%	27%	9%
600–1200	15%	38%	48%	29%
1200–2400	4%	11%	14%	32%
2400 +	1%	4%	8%	17%
Total number in sample	269	53	37	108

Source: A.D.M. IIC 236, Enregistrement des Actes[60]

and even skilled workers. In Aix in the 1770s, male servants did
better than unskilled workers, journeymen, and apprentices in
the skilled trades. Most of the latter married women who brought
dowries of less than 600 livres but half of the servants had wives
worth 600 to 1,200 livres. The fattest dowries, those over 1,200
livres, were most likely to go to master artisans (see table 2.6).

To be sure, this comparison is based on a very small number
of cases where servants are concerned, and these figures would be
open to question were this pattern not duplicated in other towns.
In Lyon the *affaneurs* were poorer than servants at marriage, since
nearly all of them, in the second half of the century, settled
contracts involving less than a thousand livres, but one-quarter
to one-third of the servants married with more than this amount.
Skilled artisans in that town did not fare as well as servants, but

[60] The source used here is the *Enregistrement des Actes*, A.D.M. IIC 236. The
Enregistrement was a synthetic list, drawn up by the regional *Intendance*, of notarial
acts such as marriage contracts and wills. For marriages, it lists the names of
husbands, their occupations, and the dowry. This is a far more synthetic and
less time-consuming source than notarial records, but far less detailed (it does
not, for instance, record the wife's occupation), and only the lists for 1768–
1791 have survived in the records of the *Intendance* of Provence.

master artisans still cornered the marriage market with deeds involving an average two to three thousand livres.[61] Servants also had an edge over all but master artisans in Paris at mid-century, as they did in Toulouse during the Revolution.[62] Evidently menservants were not poor at marriage, in comparison to other elements of the laboring classes in these towns. At the very least they could perhaps obtain sufficient advances on their salaries to make a good show of wealth and attract the attention of women who brought them substantial dowries. But two caveats are in order here. In the first place, the men who described themselves as servants in their marriage contracts were those most committed to the occupation, those who intended to remain in service. Most likely they were also the wealthier elements of the world of service. In the second place, there was something fragile and insubstantial to their wealth. In Toulouse, when servants married they were twice as rich as other workers; when they died, they were twice as poor.[63]

It was easier for servants to get rich than to stay rich. Their financial survival depended on ceaseless caution and large amounts of ingenuity, for unlike artisans they had no skills, tools, shops, or strong occupational support groups to fall back on should hard times come their way. Outside of service, the alternatives were bleak. Servants, both male and female, were highly vulnerable creatures. The peculiar nature of their occupation exposed female servants, more than any other working women, to the risk of seduction or sexual abuse. Male servants faced no such dangers, but for them there was no escaping their occupation through marriage, and the task of gathering enough money to set themselves up on their own often proved extremely arduous. Finally, servants of both sexes were almost entirely at the mercy of their employers where finances were concerned, for the law offered them

[61] Garden, *Lyon*, pp. 245, 263, 339.

[62] Furet and Daumard, *Structures et relations sociales*, pp. 18–19, 29–33; Sentou, *Toulouse*, pp. 407–438.

[63] Sentou, *Toulouse*, pp. 437–438.

very little protection with regard to their wages. Male and female servants alike spent much of their working lives trying to circumnavigate financial or sexual disasters that might wreck their chances of a decent settlement.

The most abiding threat that a female servant faced was sexual. Illegitimate pregnancy records in every town tell the same dismal tale: the women most likely to be sexually abused and exploited were domestic workers. In Nantes at least 40 percent (but probably more) of the women who reported illegitimate pregnancies were domestic workers, in Aix 50 to 67 percent, and in Marseille 90 percent.[64] It was no coincidence that writers like Richardson, Sade, and Beaumarchais all chose servants as protagonists in their stories of sexual victimization. Sexual abuse is always a tragedy in itself, but for these servants it had far-reaching consequences. Once a woman was known to have lost her virtue, whether willingly or not, her chances of finding a husband were destroyed or at least seriously curtailed.

Many servants, as we saw, were disaster-bound precisely because they aspired to marriage, because perfectly respectable courtships happened to go awry. But a number of cases in the police blotters and illegitimate pregnancy records are tales of outright brutality. One such story is that of Françoise Villevielle, who came before the Sénéchaussée of Aix in 1681 to accuse

[64] In Nantes 40 percent of the women declared that they were in service, but Depaw estimates that there were probably many more since the woman's occupation was not recorded very often. Lottin does not give an exact estimate of the proportion of servants in Lille, but mentions that they were numerous. My own forays into the records of Aix's Hôpital Saint-Jacques yielded proportions of 30 percent of servants between 1695 and 1705, and 47 percent between 1725 and 1735; Fairchilds gives figures of 60.9 percent in the 1720s and 55.4 percent at the end of the century. The proportions are consistently highest in Marseille, where they range between 80 and 90 percent; Depaw, "Nantes," p. 159; Lottin, "Lille," pp. 309–313; for Aix, see records of the Hôpital Saint-Jacques, XXH G 26–33, and Fairchilds, "Female Sexual Attitudes," p. 660; for Marseille, see Marie-Claire Ollivier, "Grossesses Illégitimes à Marseille" (Mémoire de Maîtrise, Univ. de Provence, 1975), p. 73.

Antoine Suchet, a master tailor, of raping her. She claimed that as she was washing dishes, Suchet had entered her master's house to fetch water. Instead of taking leave immediately, as he usually did, he had seized her from behind, thrown her on the ground, stuffed her hair in her mouth to stifle her screams, and had his way with her. The tailor denied that there was any truth to the allegation, and added with ferocious magnanimity: "Let the woman Villevieille be examined, and if I have hurt her I will pay for the damage." When confronted with Françoise, he declared that he knew her, but as a *servante de mauvaise vie*, and that Doctor Brouchard's son had already "thrown her on a bed." Suchet was discharged.[65] A whole century later, at the other end of France, things happened no differently. Marie Anne Hurlin, who worked for a baker in Normandy, pressed charges in 1775 against a blacksmith who entered the shop one evening, harassed her, called her a whore, and tried to rape her after pushing her into the kneading trough.[66] Why were servants especially fated to be the victims of this sort of treatment? Why did these men act as though they could take advantage of them with impunity?

One category of men found it extremely easy to coerce servants. Masters enjoyed both economic power and psychological ascendancy over their employees, and could easily get their way by means of extravagant promises, small gifts, threats of dismissal, or brute force. This prerogative extended to related members of the master class—to sons, brothers, relatives, and friends.[67] But despite the importance of master-servant relationships in the literature of the age, in real life they accounted for few of the occurrences that made the records, especially by the end of the century. In Nantes, master-servant relationships declined from a large proportion of 36 to 9 percent by century's end, and in Aix they fell from 7 to 3.6 percent.[68] Undoubtedly many such liaisons

[65] A.D.A. XXB 2317, May 15, 1681.

[66] A.D.C. 2B 560, July 4, 1775.

[67] Depaw, "Nantes," p. 166.

[68] Depaw, "Nantes," p. 167. According to my calculations for the years

were never recorded, for seducers of high social standing could conceal a pregnant woman, buy her silence, or terrorize her into lying to the officials. Such measures were not always necessary because masters could often get away with indignant denials. A bourgeois named Amphoux who had lived openly in Aix with his mother's servant declared before the police that the girl was not pregnant by him. Was it credible, he asked, that he should have proposed marriage to his own servant, as she claimed?[69]

In most of the instances that made the records, servants were seduced or assaulted by men of their own social class. The reasons for their vulnerability are not hard to guess. Many of these women had entered service upon the death of their father, and a vast majority had left their community of origin. They were, in short, separated from the men who would normally look out for their honor, and those who seduced them were perfectly well aware of this. In addition, there is little evidence of their being either protected or controlled while they were on the job.[70]

Indeed, many of the rapes perpetrated on servants took place in the very houses where they worked, for even modest households were open to a constant stream of friends, visitors, tradesmen, and boarders, not to mention the menservants who worked in

---

1695–1705 and 1725–1735, master-servant relationships in Aix rose from 5 to 7.7 percent; according to Fairchilds, they declined thereafter, from 4.5 percent in 1727–1749 to 3.6 percent in 1750–1789; A.D.A. XXH G 26–33; Fairchilds, "Female Sexual Attitudes," pp. 648–649.

[69] A.D.A. IVB 1228, July 4, 1762. Originally a servant who accused her master was always believed, but by the eighteenth century this presumption in favor of the servant had been abandoned because, as legislators claimed, "A master too often pays for the pleasures of a stableboy or a kitchen helper." Phan, "Essai institutionnel," p. 82.

[70] I found only one instance in the police records in which mention was made of any sort of control: Marguerite Poncet said that her father had explicitly asked her master "not to let her frequent any fellow workers." In the Mirabeau household, a senior servant was in charge of supervising the sexual mores of the lower staff. But this seems to have been the exception rather than the rule. A.D.A. IVB 1274; A.D.A. IVB 1269, January 28, 1786.

them. There was no place a servant could hide if a "regular" had designs on her. The unfortunate Marguerite Laugier suffered from the attentions of a character named Gourel who lived in as a boarder in her master's household. The master did attempt to intervene, but this did not stop Gourel from harassing her, especially while she was making beds. One day she decided that the best answer was a punch in the nose, which she delivered with such force that Gourel had to keep to his room for a few days. But the inevitable had to happen, and a predictably ugly scene took place one evening after supper. It was only when the worst was over that the master threw Gourel out of his house.[71]

Servants often had to work at odd hours in isolated places where nobody could come to their rescue. The kneading of dough and baking of bread kept maids alone with eager helpers into the small hours of the morning. It was in these circumstances that Pierre Gallueil took Marie Castenet by force, "twice, on a chair."[72] Another secluded spot was the wine cellar, the scene of many a brutal encounter such as that of Catherine Martel and the lackey Monier who left her unconscious on the stone steps.[73] During the summer months, servants were moved out to the chateaux that their masters owned in the countryside. In these isolated settings, insincere promises were spoken and acts of violence perpetrated, mostly by fellow workers. Thus the lackey Louis Niel knew Marguerite Burle, but refused to speak to her once they got back to Aix. The cook Antoine Tapoul forced himself upon Marie Crespin one afternoon, then professed honorable intentions, but disappeared to Marseille in the fall.[74]

There is a twist to many of these stories that is likely to shock the twentieth-century reader. A majority of these women, after describing what was manifestly a brutal rape, confessed that after

[71] A.D.A. IVB 1241, October 18, 1769.

[72] A.D.A. IVB 1173, May 6, 1718; also A.D.A. IVB 1239, April 19, 1768; A.D.A. IVB 1250, January 30, 1711.

[73] A.D.A. IVB 1180, March 18, 1726.

[74] A.D.A. IVB 1258, June 11, 1779; A.D.A. IVB 1169, January 25, 1714.

the fact they willingly allowed the seducer to take advantage of them again and again.[75] It may be that they were lying about the rape in the first place, or that they enjoyed sex far more than they would ever admit explicitly to the officials who cross-questioned them. Either of these may have been true in different instances; but it is hard to believe that dozens of women came up with the same story and told the same awkward lies. On the contrary, their very candor suggests that they and the officials who questioned them shared the same assumption: once a woman had succumbed, there was no point in her further resistance; she had, in fact, every interest in allowing the relationship to continue in the hopes that it would lead to marriage.[76]

This strategy must have proven successful in many instances, but the stories with happy endings never made the records. What the documents reveal are the many ways in which an unfortunate romance or a sexual mishap could wreck a woman's prospects for the future. Illegitimate sex often led to petty crime, for a servant known to be sexually involved with a man usually lost her job, and would have trouble finding another one. Eighteen-year-old Rosalie Hommage had barely been serving for a year in Marseille when she struck up a romance with an Italian named Nicolas Fiango. She moved in with him, only to be picked up by the police for robbery a few months later.[77] Marie-Anne Lafarge had served in three households in Aix over a short period of time, but when Charles Vigne started courting her, her current mistress

[75] For instance, the same Catherine Martel who was raped in the wine cellar "suffered that Monier should come and find her in her room, where he knew her again." Jeanne James was abused in the kitchen by the cook Giraud despite her efforts, and "since then she could no longer resist him anymore, and even thought it in her interest to live with him in the most intimate sort of familiarity." A.D.A. IVB 1180, March 18, 1726; A.D.A. IVB 1250, March 1774.

[76] Cissie Fairchilds has also argued, on the basis of similar documents, that the sexual attitudes of most women at this time were strongly oriented toward marriage: "Female Sexual Attitudes," pp. 654–659.

[77] A.D.A. 208U 29/74.

got angry and threw her out one night. She repaired to the tavern where Vigne was eating. There she slept with him, and she went on living with him until the police arrested him for theft.[78] Jeanne Lemaire was arrested for domestic larceny in Bayeux. She confessed that she was pregnant by another servant who had disappeared, and that she stole the money in a moment of panic because she feared for her future and for that of her child.[79]

Even when no other sort of crime was involved, such relationships could bring unhappiness and destitution to women whose prospects had been bright. One of the saddest stories is that of Véronique Argan, the daughter of a dancing master, who was doing well as a chambermaid in Aix when she was seduced by a shady character named Car. After dismissal, pregnancy, and the death of her child, she tried to break off with Car, who had established some sort of ascendancy over her. He managed to wreck her engagement when she found a decent man willing to wed her. She then realized that Car was seeing prostitutes who had given him what she euphemistically referred to as *une galanterie*. When she expressed her fear of being contaminated, Car declared with brutal cynicism that "he acted that way to prevent her from leaving him; that if both of them were sick, they could help each other out." When she came before the police, Argan was physically and psychologically bruised, pregnant again, and desperate.[80]

Where female servants were concerned, affectivity and economics could not be separated. A legitimate relationship, one that was sanctioned by matrimonial vows, held the promise of economic security. Conversely, the temptation or the threat of premarital sex could very easily lead to full-scale disaster. Women who worked as servants had to guard not only their dowries, their trousseaus, and every penny of their savings, but their virtue as well.

[78] A.D.A. IVB 1269, July 1, 1786.
[79] A.D.C. 2L 286/5, June 28, 1806.
[80] A.D.A. IVB 1255, October 7, 1777.

The problems that faced men were of a different nature and ostensibly revolved around purely monetary matters. After all, if a man got married he would still have to provide for himself and for a family as well. Marriage could in fact create more problems than it solved because, according to a sixteenth-century law, a servant who married without his master's express consent could lose not only his job, but all the wages owed to him as well.[81] The haunting problems for male servants were illness and old age. Masters were morally bound to provide for their servants in such cases, but there were no legal underpinnings to this obligation.[82] The archetypical servant's lament, an item from the repertoire of popular poems of the Ancien Régime entitled *L'Etat de servitude ou la misère des domestiques*, suggests that few masters lived up to their duties:

> Lorsqu'on est attaqué de quelque maladie
> Aller à l'hôpital comme un gueux qui mendie.[83]

In 1750 a lackey names Jacques Viollet de Wagnon produced the century's only major piece of writing—other than memoirs—by a servant who identified himself as such. His long pamphlet, entitled *L'Auteur laquais* was a response to a ponderous tract by an ecclesiastic, Toussaint de Saint-Luc, which upheld the life of the virtuous lackey Jasmin as an example to other servants. Viollet's concerns went beyond just debunking the seraphic Jasmin, which he did with a vengeance. His was the only voice of the century to make known the anxieties that haunted servants. In Paris especially, supply exceeded demand, and a host of servants roamed the streets of the city, vying for each others' jobs:

[81] Merlin, *Répertoire*, IV:3.

[82] I have found no legal texts requiring that masters take care of ill or aged servants, but this is a standard injunction in contemporary handbooks; see Introduction.

[83] *L'Etat de servitude ou la misère des domestiques* (Paris, 1711), p. 21. "When illness strikes/ You go off to the hospital like a begging tramp."

When I see the number of those who are jobless [*sur le pavé*], their ranks swollen by misery, a number too great for the places our estate can offer, I tremble within myself, and fear that I may fall back into this awful precipice.

Onto the end of his work Viollet tacked a strange utopia: a plan for an old people's home for aged and faithful retainers.[84] His preoccupations, and those of his brothers in service, were well illustrated by an anecdote reported by the peripatetic Jean-Joseph Esmieu. Traveling south through the Alps, Esmieu met an old man who had been afflicted by paralysis after forty-two years in the service of the Marquis de Joucques, and was turned out with a mediocre pension of fifty livres a year:

As for me, my brother took me in out of charity. It is hard to have to eat his children's bread; yet without my brother, I should have to go die in a hospital. These are the rewards of a great lord's servant.[85]

Male servants stood in ambiguous relation to the underworld of poverty. While in service, they were protected from the threats that faced the day laborer, or even the artisan. They had bed and board provided, and clothes in many cases; they were literate, earned good wages, and could flatter themselves with a sense of superiority. Yet when illness, unemployment, or old age came upon them, nothing would stand between them and destitution. Who but their masters needed the skills of men who knew only how to powder wigs and shine shoes? As a result, male servants, just like their female counterparts but for somewhat different reasons, had to wage an unending battle to lay hands on every

---

[84] Jacques Viollet de Wagnon, *L'Auteur laquais, ou réponses aux objections qui ont été faites au corps de ce nom sur la vie de Jacques Cochois, dit Jasmin*, pp. xxviii, 111–149; also Toussaint de Saint-Luc, *Le Bon laquais, ou vie de Jacques Cochois, dit Jasmin.*

[85] Pierre Dubois, ed., *La Vie pénible et laborieuse de Jean-Joseph Esmieu, marchand-colporteur en Provence sous la Révolution Française*, p. 13.

penny that could come their way. Servants of both sexes invested vast amounts of energy into securing what was due to them and devising expedients to increase their earnings.

As a group, servants enjoyed very little legal protection in financial matters. The contract between master and servant was regulated by custom alone, and the agreement was purely verbal. There are no traces in notarial documents of any sort of written contract comparable to the *contrats d'apprentissage* that bound apprentices to their employers. Customarily the terms of the agreement would be settled, usually over a glass of wine, after which the servant received a small advance known as an *aleu* or a *denier à Dieu*.[86] While no contract could, theoretically, bind a servant for life, neither could he or she leave "without dismissal or a cause legitimating departure," the interpretation of which was of course subject to great variation. If any disagreement occurred between the parties, the master's word was considered final. A master could therefore dismiss an employee whenever he chose to, but a servant risked a substantial financial loss if he or she broke the agreement.[87] What is more, a servant could not demand wages due more than a year after leaving a master's employ, and there had to be some written proof of the claim, to boot.[88]

In 1714 Vitalis, a silk merchant in Aix, hired Jean Cauvet to serve him for the coming year. The deal was settled, and Cauvet received an *écu* as a deposit, but before he had even begun to work he changed his mind. The merchant refused to listen to him, so Cauvet burst in one day and flung the coin on the floor, "believing that thus he would be disengaged." "It is inadmissible for a valet to take back his word," snapped the silk merchant,

---

[86] Léon Hom, *De la Situation juridique des gens de service*, p. 5; Henri Richard, *Du Louage des services domestiques en droit français*, p. 12. In 1779, François de Verigny, a minor nobleman in Normandy hired a maidservant. She came with her mother and "il y eut aleu fait et vin payé." A.D.C. 2B 1060, 1779.

[87] Hom, *Situation juridique*, pp. 8–12.

[88] Richard, *Louage des domestiques*, p. 18.

and the police supported his claim, condemning Cauvet to find a replacement, to pay eighteen sous as compensation for resigning, and to double the deposit.[89]

Despite the vagueness and harshness of contemporary legislation, many servants did bring their claims for unpaid wages before the judicial authorities. The police records of Aix are peppered with cases of servants who assigned their masters to pay wages—and of masters who retaliated with accusations of theft or untimely departure. And for one servant who spoke up, how many never dared to protest, how many settled the matter privately? Sometimes they found the strength to assert their claims in the bitterness provoked by flagrant injustice. To Honorade Granette's demands for her unpaid wages and the clothes which her mistress had confiscated, the latter responded with a clumsy accumulation of justifications. Honorade, she said, had received part of the sum; the clothes had no value, anyway, and one of her husband's shirts was missing. Honorade could only fling her mistress's paltriness back into her face, and point out that "as long as there was no question of paying wages, [her mistress] had not been missing any of her linen, and only came to accuse her four months later, apparently to pay her back with this pretty money."[90]

Putting in such a claim could be a risky business, for the master had the upper hand, legally, if the servant had left before his or her term in service was up. Not only could the employer flatly refuse to pay, but the simplest course for the authorities to take in such a case was to coerce the servant into returning to work no matter how harsh the conditions might be. This happened to Anne Martine, who had complained "that master Rippert mistreated and beat her all the time"; to Nanon, who pleaded "let him pay for the time she spent working for him, and return her *hardes*, for she was too ill-treated, and fed like a dog"; and to Isabeau, who claimed that her master had tried to trick her

[89] A.M.A. FF 68, fol. 256.
[90] A.M.A. FF 68, July 12, 1714.

3. A bourgeois mistress and her maid, late seventeenth century.
(Phot. Bibl. nat. Paris)

into stealing, "having tested her very often and put money in different places to see if she would say nothing if she found it." All three women were sent back to their masters' houses by the police.[91]

Even when masters did not have the law on their side, they could exert pressure by withholding not only a servant's wages, but her *hardes* as well, and many a servant counterattacked by stealing and selling household objects. The financial tug-of-war between master and servant could easily take on the appearance of a game of chess, with objects belonging to either party serving as pawns. In Aix in 1720, Madame de Cameron's chambermaid sold a mirror in order to recover her wages. The Bureau de Police had her turn over the money to her mistress, but also ordered Madame de Cameron to return her maid's housecoat.[92]

The masters' fears of grasping servants were not necessarily paranoid delusions, for whether or not as retribution for unpaid wages, domestic larceny was a widespread business.[93] Even the numerous cases of domestic theft that made the records represent only the tip of the iceberg. Until the Revolution, death was theoretically the only form of punishment meted out for domestic theft, and this brutal archaism put a check on denunciations. Masters often preferred to deal privately with the matter rather than expose their employees to capital punishment for a trifling offense.[94] Atrocities did not cease, even late in the century. In Bayeux, Bernardin Marie was indicted in 1772 for the theft of a jar of jam, a few shirts, and a hat buckle. It was his second offense, and he was duly hanged.[95] But even this barbaric legal holdover did not stop many servants from absconding with everything they could lay their hands on, from butter or nails to linen

[91] A.M.A. FF 73, August 13, 1722; A.M.A. FF 73, April 4, 1723; A.M.A. FF 73, September 17, 1722.
[92] A.M.A. FF 72, February 15, 1720.
[93] Hufton, *The Poor*, p. 258.
[94] Richard, *Louage des domestiques*, p. 45.
[95] A.D.C. 2B 1037, 1772.

or hard cash. The typical *vol domestique* in Marseille at the turn of the century was the act of a dowry-hungry female servant, egged on and helped by friends and relatives outside of the house, who aided her by hoarding objects that a maid could not possibly conceal in her small room.[96]

Naturally, servants knew that they were doing wrong. But they and the friends who helped them often justified the act with a crude sort of egalitarianism. They were surrounded by wealth but lived in misery; why on earth should they not take their share? Elizabeth Bayle-Mouillard, wrote indignantly in an early nineteenth-century handbook: "The remarkable thing about these sad affairs is that these people do not think of themselves as thieves."[97] When Rose Isque's cousin pushed her into committing larceny, she advised her: "You should take everything you can because you are with rich people . . . it will help you when you get out." The woman Bidot, who urged Marie Jeanne Auvray to take her share of the riches, presented it as a precautionary measure: "They are going to throw you out, so you had better take a few things to reward yourself."[98] Servants themselves doubtless felt few qualms, notwithstanding the tall tales they served to the police. In Bayeux two servants, Françoise de la Haye and Saint-Pierre, made off with possessions belonging to their master. La Haye had been overheard complaining that she was underpaid, but her mate was considerably more earthy about the whole business: "*Foutre*, here is a shirt, but he won't see it again, I need it *foutre sacredié* more than he does."[99]

Given the risks involved, most servants probably stopped short of outright theft, but they cheated and chiseled for all they were worth. Therese Aulanière, who worked for an innkeeper, poured

---

[96] A.D.A. 208U 29/14, 23 Thermidor, Year XI; A.D.A. 208 U 29/305, May 23, 1814; A.D.C. 2L 289/1, October–November 1806; A.D.C. 2L 275/1, Year XII; A.D.C. 2L 281/5, Year XIII.

[97] Elizabeth Bayle-Mouillard, *Manuel complet des domestiques*, p. 3.

[98] A.D.A. 208/U 29/129; A.D.C. 2L 281/5, Year XIII.

[99] A.D.C. 2B 559, 1779.

two jugs of water down a wine barrel for fear that the wine she had spilled should be deducted from her wages. It turned out to be a poor calculation, since her master and the police caught up with her and fined her twelve livres.[100] Servants lucky enough to be entrusted with shopping duties pocketed the change, not to mention commissions from tradespeople. The two picturesque expressions that meant chiseling off the shopping money, *ferrer la mule* and *faire danser l'anse du panier*, were as widespread as the practice itself, and probably as old.[101] Cooks could make substantial profits by setting aside animal fats and skins, and masters were forever trying to put a check on this custom. Louis de Thomassin firmly noted that his cook was hired at 150 livres a year, "with no profit except hare and rabbit skins"; and Charles de Mazenod wrote elliptically: "180 livres, and the meat will be trimmed by the butcher."[102] But cooks felt entitled to these kickbacks, and one of them put in a claim for his profits in 1722, which he estimated at ten livres a month over and above his wages.[103]

Extra money could be milked out of everyday duties, but as often as not even well-paid servants such as valets and chambermaids tried their hardest to find auxiliary sources of income. If a manservant were allowed to marry, his wife might engage in a little retail business on the side. In Aix the spouse of Monsieur de Saint-Tropez's manservant rented a room in town where she sold wine. Apolonie Serique, whose husband served Monsieur de Cabanes, was allowed to keep *her* wine in the cellar of the latter's house; trouble broke out among the staff when it was discovered that the Cabanes's maidservant was engaging in a little commerce

[100] A.M.A. FF 68, July 12, 1714.

[101] *Recueil de pièces rares*, passim. As late as the mid-nineteenth century, Flaubert had one of his characters, Rosanette, use the expression *faire danser l'anse du panier: L'Education sentimentale* (Paris, 1965), p. 348.

[102] B.M. Ms. 1647; B.M. ms. 1652, see entries for May 3, 1762, April 27, 1768, and June 20, 1783.

[103] A.M.A. FF 73, November 5, 1722.

of her own, selling Serique's wine on the sly.[104] Male and female servants throughout the century dealt in wine, wheat, and clothes, with the consent or even the blessing of their masters, who may have seen in this a justification for keeping their employees' wages at a minimal level. In the police records of Aix we see the chambermaid of Monsieur de Broglia in 1709 engaging in a profitable commerce in grains, right in the marketplace. Fifty years later another chambermaid, Marie Bonnet, negotiated with a baker for the payment of eight *charges* of wheat.[105] In neither of these two cases is the name of the employer mentioned. But even if they were carrying out their employers' business, it is hard to believe that they did not pocket some of the profits for themselves.

With or without the help of a spouse or the approval of their masters, servants trafficked in commodities of every kind and exploited every possible source of income. Nicolas Girard dealt in large quantities of fruit near the gates of Aix; the cook Jacques Ipert sold cotton stockings; Gabrielle, the chambermaid of Monsieur de Clapiers, set up a lucrative commerce with the leaves from her master's country home.[106] César Vallantin, the valet of Monsieur de Forbentin, even devised a booby trap for pigeons of the neighboring farmhouses, "for which purposes he has made a particular study," the investigating agent gravely reported, "with the result that pigeons once landing in this place never again see the light of day."[107]

If all else failed, a servant's major recourse was to change households. The wages of unskilled servants especially tended to remain fixed by custom at the same level in any given household over years or even decades. Charles-Alexandre de Mazenod steadfastly doled out ninety livres a year to every lackey who entered his service between 1743 and 1782. Reyne, a young maid who

[104] A.D.A. IVB 1258, March 5, 1779; A.D.A. IVB 1172, May 26, 1717.

[105] A.M.A. FF 66, August 22, 1709; A.D.A. 306E 974, April 20, 1763.

[106] A.D.A. IVB 1186, July 1, 1731; A.M.A. FF 72, fol. 20; A.M.A. FF 93, fol. 135.

[107] A.D.A. XXB 717, 1726.

was hired in 1776, started out at thirty-six livres, exactly the same salary that Catherine Borelli was making thirty years before.[108] The only recourse was to change jobs once one had acquired the necessary skills and connections, and this may largely account for the much decried instability of lower servants. Among twenty-one of the women whose employment records were kept by the Hôtel-Dieu of Marseille, only four stayed a year or more, on the average, with each employer they served. Most of them stayed six to ten months in each job, and nearly every move entailed a corresponding raise in pay. Anne Roze got her first job in 1739, and was paid eighteen livres a year; seven years later she had changed employers nine times, and was making over three times that amount. Marie Claire started work in 1754 at thirty livres; five years and seven households later she was making ninety livres a year.[109]

Olwen Hufton has described the mode of life of the poor of eighteenth-century France as an "economy of makeshifts."[110] This expression could well apply also to the ways in which servants of both sexes went about securing their nest egg. It may be strange to think of these domestic workers, some of them well-dressed, well-fed, and literate valets and chambermaids, scrounging for every sou they could collect. They were not poor, but they were virtual citizens of the world of poverty, and they knew it. Those reflexes which members of the master class often took for ingratitude or greed were usually careful strategies aimed at self-preservation.

[108] B.M. Ms. 1652. This problem was apparently not specific to eighteenth-century France. Rosina Harrison, who entered service just after the First World War in London, had exactly the same complaint: "I don't know whether there was a conspiracy among the upper classes to keep servants' wages down, but everyone I knew in service at that time met with the same brick-wall attitude. The only way to get more was to change employers, and this couldn't be done too often; otherwise you earned the reputation for being unreliable and having itchy feet." Rosina Harrison, *Rose: My Life in Service* (New York, 1975), p. 35.

[109] A.D.M. IV G 103, 104, 106.

[110] Hufton, *The Poor*, chaps. 3–4.

To the lucky, the hardworking, and the thrifty, domestic service did open up genuine possibilities of social promotion or at least of decent settlement. A woman who accumulated a few hundred livres in savings could, after a decade or so in service, hope to marry an apprentice, a journeyman, or even a shopkeeper; a male servant, whose earnings would be considerably greater, could save enough money to open a tavern, a shop, or a small business. Yet there were many obstacles to be surmounted and dangers to be avoided on the road to independence and security. Low wages, dishonest or grasping employers, fickle suitors and brutal seducers, unemployment, illness, pregnancy—any of these could set one back by several years or even destroy one's chances for good. Domestic service offered substantial rewards to some workers; but it exposed many of them to great dangers as well.

The servants' continual preoccupation with monetary matters suggests that many masters failed to live up to the ideals of material responsibility toward their servants that were laid out in their handbooks. Yet they still expected servants to uphold their end of the covenant. We may begin to understand what lay behind these expectations of obedience and loyalty if we take into account both the dangers and the promise that shaped a servant's working life. On the one hand, employers were well aware of the economic, legal, and sexual vulnerability of their servants. This made it easy to demand absolute subservience of their household employees. On the other hand, most servants looked upon their occupation as a temporary plight, as a prelude to a better life. Women hoped for a good marriage, men for the means to acquire independence and financial security. Paradoxically, the servants' view of their occupation as transitional did not encourage resistance, but compliance: what point was there in resisting the will of a master if one's goal was to relinquish the occupation as soon as possible? No doubt, masters were well aware that their servants' ultimate goals contradicted their own expectations. And it was probably this very conflict between two different views of the purpose of service that generated the satirical portrayal of servants in literature as venal and grasping creatures. No matter how well he played his role while in service, Sganarelle would always scream for his wages when his master disappeared.

In light of the evidence presented in this chapter, it is easy enough to understand why masters could expect their servants to be obedient and tractable. But there is a great difference between simple obedience on the one hand, and identification with or loyalty to one's employer on the other. The hard-nosed pursuit of gain and marriage was only one aspect of the servants' experience. One cannot understand the nature of the psychological bonds that tied them to their masters without knowing of the rewards they found and the dangers they faced in their relations with other workers or with each other. What sort of life did servants lead, what place did they occupy, in the towns of pre-revolutionary France?

CHAPTER 3

Life on the Threshold

Un laquais en tout lieu passe pour un vaurien
Est raillé des méchans, haï des gens de bien.
Fût-il de bonnes moeurs et d'honnête famille,
Il porte, c'est assez, la honteuse mandille. . . .[1]

These lines from *L'Etat de servitude ou la misère des domestiques* announce one of the central themes in this anonymous poem lamenting the fate of domestic workers. The gist of it is that nobody likes a servant.

The poem belongs to a specific genre of popular literature, the *misères*. *Misères* were popular laments, circulated in chap-book form, which detailed the complaints of workers in different trades or occupations. There were *misères* of clerks, of bakers, of printer's boys, of apprentice surgeons.[2] The servant's *misère* runs through the catalog of trials and tribulations intrinsic to *l'état de servitude*: freezing garrets, poor food, insufficient sleep, and the indignity

---

[1] *L'Etat de servitude, ou la misère des domestiques*, p. 4.
   A lackey is everywhere taken for a scoundrel
   The laughing-stock of villains and the scourge of decent folk
   Though his manners be good and his family respectable
   He nevertheless wears that shameful garb.

[2] Geneviève Bollème, *La Bibliothèque bleue: La Littérature populaire en France du XVIe au XIXe siècle* (Paris, 1971), p. 104; see also Peter Burke, *Popular Culture in Early Modern Europe* (New York, 1978), pp. 120–121.

of living at the beck and call of a capricious master or mistress. But it also dwells insistently on an aura of infamy which allegedly surrounded the occupation. Honorable women shrink away from the livery; your "friends" ignore you in the street, shower you with compliments if they want access to your master, but turn their backs on you when you are in trouble.[3]

Whether or not a servant wrote this pamphlet, its author was not voicing an idle complaint. Just about every contemporary moralist, chronicler, social critic, or novelist who cared to comment on the subject described the servant as *persona non grata*. In fact, the denunciation of servants was one exercise that brought together writers of widely divergent ideological slants. The Carmelite Father Toussaint de Saint-Luc wrote that "the vices that [lackeys] contract in their youth make them wicked and vicious for the rest of their lives";[4] on that score he would encounter no opposition from that scion of the Enlightenment, Sébastien Mercier, who never missed an occasion to pass censure on servants:

> Today, servants who go from house to house, indifferent to the masters whom they serve, can meet an employer they just left without feeling any sort of emotion. They assemble only to exchange the secrets they have unearthed: they are spies, and being well paid, well dressed, and well fed, but despised, they resent us, and have become our greatest enemies.[5]

At first sight there is nothing very novel or surprising about these sorts of complaints. For centuries, servants had been accused of every vice under the sun. Luther himself apparently loved them no more than he did rebellious peasants, for he labeled them "disobedient, unfaithful, ill-mannered and rapacious . . . a scourge

[3] *L'Etat de servitude*, pp. 4–5.

[4] Toussaint de Saint Luc, *Le Bon laquais, ou vie de Jacques Cochois, dit Jasmin*, p. 110.

[5] Louis-Sébastien Mercier, *Le Tableau de Paris*, II:122.

sent by God."[6] It is not hard to imagine why exasperated masters were, and always had been, ready to accuse their servants of greed, impudence, or disobedience. But the criticisms expressed by eighteenth-century writers often crystallized around themes that had nothing to do with the complaints of angry employers.

One of the recurring motifs was that of ambiguity. The uneasiness that servants provoked was often triggered by their tendency to imitate their masters. Mercier, again, was quick to point this out:

> A fashionable lackey will usually take his master's name when he is with other lackeys; he also borrows his habits, gestures, and manners. . . . With young men, he is Monsieur's confidante when the latter has no money, his procurer when a lady strikes his fancy, the most brazen liar when it comes to dealing with creditors and getting his master out of trouble.[7]

In the eyes of contemporaries, servants were threatening creatures because they imitated their masters too well, while retaining the baser instincts of the class they came from. The Abbé Leblanc, writing in the 1750s, expressed this with pithy brutality: "By education, servants have all the vices of the populace; by imitation, all those of their masters."[8] Another observer, writing of Montpellier in 1768, thundered: "They are not supposed to be free, or integrated into the body of citizens," and went on to suggest that servants be obliged to wear a mark on their clothing to distinguish them from the rest of the population.[9] But ambiguity was not so easily disposed of.

The stigma that derived from servility, imitation, and social

[6] Quoted in Paul Katz, *Situation économique et sociale des domestiques en France, en Allemagne, et en Suisse depuis le moyen-âge jusqu'à nos jours*, p. 27.

[7] Mercier, *Tableau de Paris*, II:124

[8] Abbé Jean Leblanc, *Lettres de Monsieur l'Abbé Leblanc*, I:151.

[9] Joseph Berthélé, ed., *Montpellier en 1768 et 1836 d'après deux manuscrits inédits*, p. 69.

109

THE WORLD OF THE SERVANTS

ambiguity was usually attached to male servants, especially lackeys and valets. Criticisms of female service more usually revolved around themes of sexual corruption. Even Marivaux, a writer who depicted servants with great sympathy in his plays, was not free from this sort of prejudice. In *Le Paysan parvenu*, the hero Jacob, himself a servant and a man of questionable morals, bluntly refuses to take a servant as his bride:

> In our village, it is the custom to take only maidens as brides, and if one of them had been the chambermaid of a gentleman, she would have to make do with a lover; as for a husband, *néant*; if it rained husbands, not one would fall for her.[10]

As for Marianne, the protagonist of his other great novel, she bursts into tears and goes into something akin to a fit of hysteria at the mere suggestion that she should serve:

> The suggestion made me blush. "Alas, sir, though I have nothing and know not who I am, I feel that I would rather die than go to work as a servant," I replied sadly, shedding tears. "Since I have to work in order to support myself," I sobbed, "I would prefer the meanest and hardest work there is, if I can keep my freedom, to the occupation you proposed, were it even to bring me fortune."[11]

Ostensibly, Marianne's attitude comes from her fear of jeopardizing her independence. Elsewhere in the novel, however, she does not hesitate to place herself under the protection of powerful patrons. Her shame and panic at the very mention of the occupation suggest that domestic service would endanger her virtue much more than her independence.

The feelings of these writers about service, ranging from distaste to downright repulsion, could very well be interpreted as

---

[10] Pierre Carlet de Marivaux, *Le Paysan parvenu*, p. 44.
[11] Pierre Carlet de Marivaux, *La Vie de Marianne*, pp. 38–39.

just the pieties of middle-class men who feared and despised their social inferiors, especially those who took on mannerisms inappropriate to their station in life. But these feelings were apparently shared by a majority of native urban dwellers, even those of very modest social standing.

As we have seen, native town dwellers accounted for a very small proportion—often less than 5 percent—of the domestic workforce in most eighteenth-century towns.[12] No doubt this was partly due to the availability, in most towns, of a large pool of immigrant workers from which masters could hire their servants at very cheap rates. But it is also clear that native urban workers tended to avoid an occupation which they considered dangerous and degrading. The town girl, writes Hufton, "did not seek to become a servant; the degree to which she shunned such employ is remarkable."[13] In Lyon, the children of *affaneurs, journaliers,* and above all the offspring of artisans would never dream of becoming servants if they could avoid it, no matter how poor their families.[14] The same was true in Marseille. To the Marseillais worker, service was a disgrace because it robbed him of his independence; to native women it was the last and worst resource. In artisan families in Marseille only the boys contributed their earnings to the family budget. Girls were allowed to save their wages for their dowry and thus avoid the perils and dishonor of service.[15]

This revulsion may not have been shared by every native town dweller, but evidently large segments of the laboring poor despised the idea of service and shunned the occupation. Contempt for an occupation is rarely a notion that is entertained in the abstract, and the conspicuousness of servants made them into natural targets for the animosity of those who rejected the "ul-

[12] See chapter 1.

[13] Olwen Hufton, *The Poor of Eighteenth-Century France*, p. 33.

[14] Maurice Garden, *Lyon et les lyonnais au XVIIIe siècle*, pp. 250–251.

[15] François Mazuy, *Essai historique sur les moeurs et coutumes des marseillais au XIXe siècle*, pp. 141, 178.

timate resource." Aversion to service and antipathy toward servants undoubtedly fed upon one another. In the concert of denunciations, the educated middle and upper classes called the tune. But the laboring poor, who might have recognized servants as wretched, hard-worked souls like themselves, also turned their backs on them, and their attitude demands some sort of explanation.

Perhaps the very origins and identity of servants as migrant paupers, as strangers to the town, exposed them to the suspicions of their peers and their superiors. This factor must surely be reckoned with, but the explanation does not suffice in itself. Servants were foreigners, and must have suffered on that account, but so were large numbers of other workers, day laborers, craftsmen, or textile workers, who provoked no such systematic resentment.[16] The foreignness of servants must be taken into account, but only as part of the explanation.

Were servants perceived as threatening because they were actually dangerous? Contemporaries were certainly inclined to believe this. The journal that the lawyer Barbier kept under the Regency and the reign of Louis XV is peppered with dark tales of murder, theft, and blackmail carried out by servants. Barbier's complacent comment on the execution of a cook in 1726 speaks for itself: "They did well in hanging him to set an example, especially since he was a servant, for no price is too high for public safety."[17] Were one to look only at contemporary legislation, one might also be led to suspect that within every servant lurked a dangerous homicidal maniac. Between 1609 and 1685, no less than twenty-six different ordinances were issued in Paris prohibiting lackeys, pages, and valets from carrying swords, daggers, knives, or clubs under penalty of death. The text of the *Déclaration* of 1655 explained that the violence of servants had reached such a degree that they had been responsible for the

---

[16] Hufton, *The Poor*, chaps. 1–3.
[17] Edmond Barbier, *Chronique de la régence et du règne de Louis XV*, I:420.

murder of "several persons of quality." These laws and regulations were reiterated throughout the eighteenth century, albeit less frequently.[18]

The fears of masters and legislators had little grounding in facts. Young pages and lackeys may well have had violent habits in the sixteenth and seventeenth centuries, but most statistical studies of criminality under the Old Regime indicate that as a group eighteenth-century servants could have qualified as one of the most tranquil and law-abiding segments of the urban popular classes. Of course they were still more prone to criminality in the larger towns where bands of lackeys roamed the streets looking for a fight. In the second half of the century, 7 percent of the criminals brought before the Châtelet court in Paris were domestic servants.[19] Early in the Revolution they accounted for 6 percent of those indicted by the provisional criminal courts.[20] But in Aix domestic workers were involved in only 2 to 3 percent of the cases that came before the local *Sénéchaussée*, and not one servant made the criminal records of the small town of Digne over the entire second half of the century.[21]

It is possible that many crimes committed by servants never made the records, if some masters succeeded in concealing misdeeds or in protecting their servants from the law. Nonetheless,

---

[18] B. N. Ms. 21800, fols. 39–41, 134, 169, 171, 183–184, 207–208, 210–211. F.-A. Isambert el al., *Recueil général des anciennes lois françaises depuis 420 jusqu'à la Révolution*, XXVI:94, XXVII:117.

[19] Yves Castan, ed., *Crimes et criminalité en France sous l'Ancien Régime* (Paris, 1971), pp. 64–66, 245.

[20] Antoinette Wills, "Criminal Life and Criminal Justice during the French Revolution: The Six Provisional Criminal Courts of Paris, 1791–1792" (Ph.D. diss., Univ. of Washington, 1975), p. 178.

[21] Out of 2,041 cases that came before the Sénéchaussée of Aix between 1711 and 1735, and 2,264 between 1766 and 1790, servants were implicated in 44 and 60, respectively, or 2.1 and 2.6 percent. A.D.A. IVB 1166 to 1189, and IVB 1232 to 1275; Annie Eyglunent, "Délinquance, criminalité, et troubles sociaux dans la Sénéchaussée de Digne, 1750–1790" (Mémoire de Maîtrise, Univ. de Provence, 1969), p. 114.

even the highest of these figures suggest remarkably low rates of criminality, given the fact that servants of both sexes made up one-tenth or more of the population of these towns, and a larger proportion still of the urban poor. Police records do suggest that male and even female servants in groups could be obnoxious, rowdy, even bellicose. This cannot have endeared them to the public. But by no means were they particularly dangerous, or any more offensive than the bands of journeymen and apprentices who raped, brawled, and charivaried to their hearts' content in these very same towns and villages.[22]

Both Marivaux's heroine and the Marseillais artisans described by Mazuy invoked servility and the loss of independence as the main reason for their abhorrence of servants and service. Historians such as Yves Castan and Jeffry Kaplow have suggested that native workers despised servants as men and women who lived in bondage to others and eked out a living as unproductive parasites.[23] But both Marivaux and Mazuy were middle-class men whose perceptions were refracted through their own social prejudices. As Kaplow himself admits, freedom and productivity were notions mostly hauled out by middle-class writers when they wished to cast aspersion on *l'état de servitude*. In some instances such ideas may have filtered down to the prouder elements of the artisanal world, who were not unaware, for instance, of the servile connotations inherent in the wearing of liveries. But on the whole these notions were as yet unfamiliar to the laboring poor in a society imbued with hierarchy and patronage, in which bourgeois notions of productivity had not yet taken hold.[24]

[22] See Natalie Davis, "The Reasons of Misrule," in *Society and Culture in Early Modern France*, pp. 97–123; Jacques Rossiaud, "Prostitution, jeunesse, et société dans les villes du sud-ouest au XVe siècle," *Annales E.S.C.* 31:289–325.

[23] Jeffry Kaplow, *The Names of Kings: The Parisian Laboring Poor in the Eighteenth Century*, pp. 51–52; Yves Castan, *Honnêteté et relations sociales en Languedoc, 1715–1780*, p. 181.

[24] Kaplow, *Names of Kings*, p. 52.

Neither the characteristics of servants themselves, their foreignness, or their allegedly violent behavior, nor any abstract prejudices harbored by other workers against servility or parasitism really suffice to make sense of the contempt in which domestic workers were held. Rather, the bias against servants was rooted in the mundane trappings of everyday life. Servants were anomalous workers, ill-integrated into the world of the laboring poor. Nearly every aspect of their life and work placed them in a world apart from that of their peers.

The gap between servants and other workers was first of all a spatial one. Within the urban milieu, the confines of servants' lives were separate from those of other workers. Nostalgic myths notwithstanding, the geographic segregation of social classes in French towns long antedated the Paris of Haussmann and Napoleon III. While such divisions were anything but hermetic, rich and poor *quartiers* were clearly marked off from one another in the towns of the Old Regime.[25] And in every case that we know of, servants were more likely to reside in the *beaux quartiers* inhabited by the middle and upper classes. In Paris, the concentration of servants was highest in the areas surrounding the Palais Royal, in the Faubourg Saint-Germain, and around the Place Royale, and lowest in popular districts like the faubourg Saint-Antoine. In Lyon domestic servants were numerous in wealthy sections of town such as the quartier d'Ainay to the east of the Saône, but few of them lived in the crowded districts to the west of the city like la Croix Rousse, the traditional abode of silk-workers.[26]

In Aix and Marseille the same sort of sociogeographic separation existed between the old popular sections of these towns, teeming with artisans and day laborers, and the newer residential districts where servants and their masters lived. In Marseille at the end of the century, the oldest parts of the city to the north and south

[25] Pierre Goubert, *L'Ancien Régime*, pp. 196–197.
[26] Kaplow, *Names of Kings*, pp. 50–51; Garden, *Lyon*, p. 249.

of the port were inhabited mostly by fishermen and unskilled workers, many of whom crowded the boardinghouses of the old Butte des Carmes adjacent to the northern quay. The newer *quartiers* sprawled to the east, northeast, and southeast of the port. These were elegant commercial districts where merchants and bourgeois lived and worked, and which also housed a great majority of the town's domestic servants.[27] In Aix, finally, the contrast between popular and aristocratic sections was equally clear. Aix was divided, for administrative purposes, into six *quartiers* of uneven size. To the north lay the three most ancient districts: the medieval Bourg Saint-Sauveur, the bourgeois and popular district of Bellegarde, and the predominantly artisanal Quartier des Cordeliers, spreading west into the rural suburb, le Faubourg. To the south were Saint-Jean and Les Augustins, where, on either side of the stately Cours à Carosses, luxurious townhouses in the Italian style, sculpted fountains, and formal gardens had been erected since the seventeenth century.[28]

In Aix the residential distribution of servants and unskilled workers (*travailleurs*) was almost exactly complementary (see table 3.1.)

In the 1750s, three quarters of the town's servants inhabited the two elegant southern districts, whereas eight out of ten laborers lived in the northern *quartiers*. The only significant overlap occurred in Saint-Jean, the town's biggest and most populated district, which extended north into the more plebeian sections of town. The social segregation of the urban milieu had increased

[27] Françoise Rouget, Muriel Sauty, and Dominique Patouillard, "La Population de Marseille en 1793: Approche sociologique," (Mémoire de Maîtrise, Univ. de Provence, 1971), appendixes; Michel Vovelle, "Le Prolétariat flottant à Marseille sous la Révolution Française," *Annales de démographie historique* (1968), pp. 111–138.

[28] On the evolution of Aix during the Old Regime, see Michel Vovelle et al., *Histoire d'Aix-en-Provence*, chaps. 5–7; Cissie Fairchilds, *Poverty and Charity in Aix-en-Provence, 1640–1789*, chap. 1; A. Roux-Alpheran, *Les Rues d'Aix, ou recherches historiques sur l'ancienne capitale de la Provence*.

TABLE 3.1.

Residential Distribution of Servants and Day Laborers, Aix, 1695 and 1755–1756*

| | 1695 | | 1755–56 | |
	Servants	Day Laborers	Servants	Day Laborers
Poorer Districts				
Les Cordeliers	9.5%	28.0%	6.0%	27.0%
Bellegarde	10.4	13.0	7.0	16.5
Bourg St. Sauveur	10.0	12.0	8.5	13.7
Faubourg	0.3	11.0	4.0	22.0
	30.2%	64.0%	25.5%	79.2%
Wealthy Districts				
Saint Jean	43.8%	24.0%	38.0%	15.0%
Les Augustins	26.0	12.0	36.5	5.8
	69.8%	36.0%	74.5%	20.8%
Total number in sample	1,906	1,087	1,527	655

* Figures in this table are percentages of total group

Sources: Jean-Paul Coste, *La Ville d'Aix en 1695*, vol. II, maps SP 610 × 710; A.M.A. CC 68 and 69

over the first half of the century. Just as in Marseille and Paris, it lasted out the century, and persisted even at the height of the Revolution.[29] In all of these towns servants lived and worked in the world of the rich, separated from the laborers who crowded the shops and *garnis* of the more popular urban districts.

[29] Bérénice Grissolange, "Aix-en-Provence sous la Révolution: Structures sociales et familiales" (Mémoire de Maîtrise, Univ. de Provence, 1974), appendixes. According to the *contribution mobiliaire* of 1795–96, the highest concentration of artisans (over one-fifth of the group) was still to be found at this date in the northwestern *section* corresponding to the old quartier des Cordeliers. Most servants still resided in the areas corresponding to the old districts of Saint-Jean and Les Augustins, and were very scarce in the northern and western sections of the town.

The barriers separating servants from other workers were not only geographical, they were sartorial as well. In these towns, every article of clothing took on great symbolic weight. Even very late in the century, in the town of Angers described by François Besnard, fine sartorial distinctions left no doubt as to the status of the wearer:

> Custom had determined the clothes and general attire of every person to such an extent that not only could one recognize the dress of the upper classes from that of the lower orders, but that even within the latter certain nuances were significant enough to reveal the estate or the profession of the wearer at a glance. Thus, the serving girl's clothes were different from those of the chambermaid, and even more so from those of her mistress.[30]

But to other observers, the vestimentary signs that distinguished servant from master or mistress were, on the contrary, not clear enough. The chronicler of Montpellier acidly remarked:

> Nothing is more distasteful than to see a cook or a valet, wearing trimmed and embroidered clothes and a sword at his side, hobnobbing with high society in the town's public walks; a chambermaid as artfully decked out as her mistress; simple maids as well attired as young ladies. All of this is revolting.[31]

The quality of servants' clothing varied enormously, of course, depending on their masters' wealth and their own status within the household. The information we have, however, clearly indicates that a servant was likely to be better dressed than the average worker. Iconographic evidence suggests that the wearing of cast-offs was more the exception than the rule, but also that

[30] François-Yves Besnard, *Mémoires d'un nonagénaire*, I:142.
[31] Berthélé, *Montpellier*, p. 69.

no servant went around barefoot or in rags.[32] Rousseau himself recalled that as a young lackey to the Comtesse de Vercellis he wore a simple costume in the colors of the household, and that since it was adorned with neither shoulder knots nor braids, "it looked more or less like a bourgeois suit."[33]

The most characteristic apparel sported by servants was the livery, a uniform costume worn by the male servants of wealthier households. The garments making up the livery could be roughly in the fashion of the day, or else slightly outmoded, and resembled the clothes of the wealthly though they were often made of coarser materials. Liveries were in any case highly visible because masters tended to choose them in bright colors, ideally those of the family coat of arms. In addition, the outfit was supposed to include a visible sign of the servant's condition, originally badges worn on the back or the arm, which in the eighteenth century were replaced by shoulder knots or wide ornamental braids running down the front of the coat and around the sleeves.[34] (See illustrations 1, 4, 7, 9.) This costume was only worn by lackeys, coachmen, doormen, and some upper servants—in other words, by a substantial minority of servants. But so powerful was the symbolism implicit in the ribbons, gold braid, or shoulder knots that decorated the uniforms of these retainers that throughout the Old

---

[32] Jean Emelina, *Les Valets et les servantes dans le théâtre comique en France de 1610 à 1700*, pp. 396–397.

[33] Jean-Jacques Rousseau, *Les Confessions*, I:122.

[34] Phillis Cunnington, *The Costume of Household Servants from the Middle Ages to 1900*, pp. 15–28. Cunnington's study is the only work on the subject, and concerns only Britain. But iconographic and descriptive evidence suggest that French servants sported much the same sort of costume, with some variants. French menservants rarely wore hats, as did their British counterparts, and the ornamental braid (*galon de livrée*) was more common in France than was the shoulder knot. See *L'Etat de servitude*, p. 4:

> De galonds bleus et verts son habit est chargé
> Sans nul autre examen par un faux préjugé
> On le croit entâché de l'humeur libertine
> Naturelle et commune à la gens laquesine.

4. Liveried servants waiting at table: *Le Midy*, late seventeenth century. (Phot. Bibl. nat. Paris)

Regime the entire category of domestic servants was known simply as *la livrée*. From the seventeenth century on, royal legislation attempted to contain the elaborateness of servants' attire by prohibiting the wearing of gold or silk, or by prosecuting masters who dressed their servants up in the royal colors of scarlet, white, and blue.[35] But the authorities never really succeeded in putting a check on the expensive habits of status-hungry employers.

For the servants themselves, the livery created a painful dilemma. In theory, the costume served as a safeguard, since these sartorial advertisements of the master's power were supposed to protect the wearer from attacks and insults. The Abbé Collet, for instance, wrote of the livery as a blessing bestowed on servants: "Your master's livery shelters you from insults; and the respect which he commands redounds on those who belong to him."[36] Servants did, occasionally, invoke the respect due to the livery in the hopes of deflecting insults and blows, but nothing in the police records suggests that this ploy was especially effective. In Aix early in the century, Monsieur de Pigenat's livery certainly did not protect two of his footmen from the wrath of a husky fishmonger. In fact, their indignant complaints suggest that the tradesman was delighted to lambast these two puny, overdressed fellows: "This is a case of premeditated murder," they complained, "committed in cold blood by this fishmonger who should have respected the livery of the Lieutenant de Pigenat, but who on the contrary showed contempt for it, and let out a quantity of filthy, insulting and threatening utterances."[37] Life on the street was not easy for workers clad in garments so visibly at odds with their true social standing.

The servants themselves were ill at ease with the livery, and

[35] Emelina, *Les Valets et les servantes*, pp. 397–399; Pierre-Jacques Brillon, *Dictionnaire des arrêts, ou jurisprudence universelle*, II:722–723; B.N. Ms. 21800, Fos. 144–146, 148–149.

[36] Abbé Pierre Collet, *Instructions et prières à l'usage des domestiques et des personnes travaillant en ville*, p. 24.

[37] A.D.A. IVB 1175, May 29, 1720.

looked upon it at best as an inconvenience, and at worst as a badge of infamy. The author of *L'Etat de servitude* equated the indignities of bondage with this servile garb, *la honteuse mandille*, and lamented:

> Et lorsqu'avec l'habit j'endossai tant d'affront
> D'une honnête pudeur on vit rougir mon front.[38]

Viollet de Wagnon, the lackey-author, was no less adamant: "All of these disgraces befall [our estate]", he wrote, "only through the scandal of [our] clothing." Servants, he added, did their best to avoid wearing *les couleurs* because of the contempt in which the livery was held.[39] There is evidence in legal texts as well that liveried servants tried to doff any sign of their condition as soon as they were out of the sight of their masters. Between 1679 and 1725, six different police regulations and royal ordinances were issued in Paris against servants who removed their shoulder knots, braids, and other characteristic pieces of clothing. As soon as they leave their masters, explained the ordinance of 1725, servants don *l'habit bourgeois* and the sword, and go mingle with the public in the promenades and theaters. Those who engaged in this sort of sartorial hocus-pocus could incur the severest of punishments, such as whipping, branding, and banishment.[40] These laws demanded that servants wear a distinctive mark on their clothing because, as the ordinance of 1717 explained, when servants were "confused with persons of every condition," they became a threat to "order, decency, and public safety."[41]

Servants were considered a class apart, and as such they had

---

[38] *L'Etat de servitude*, p. 4.
> And when, with these clothes, I donned such disgrace
> An honest blush of shame spread over my face.

[39] Jacques Viollet de Wagnon, *L'Auteur laquais, ou réponses aux objections qui ont été faites au corps de ce nom sur la vie de Jacques Cochois, dit Jasmin*, pp. lii, 35–36.

[40] B.N. Ms. 21800, fols. 41, 134, 136–137, 207–208.

[41] B.N. Ms. 21800, fols. 136–137.

to remain visibly distinct. One can only sympathize with these poor souls caught between two fires, despised by the public if they wore their liveries, and prosecuted by the police if they did not. A source of pride and a focus for resentment, an ostentatiously wealthy costume, yet too rich for the wearer and laden with degrading implications, the livery perfectly captures the wrenching ambiguity of the servant's condition. Though it was only the dubious privilege of some menservants to sport it, the shameful opulence of *la livrée* rubbed off onto the whole class of domestic servants.

As the authors of handbooks and prayer guides for servants pointed out, often at tedious length, domestic workers enjoyed an unquestionable privilege over other workers in that their occupation sheltered them from immediate economic disaster. The Abbé Collet exhorted his servant readers:

> Compare yourself to the multitude of wretched beings with whom you meet every day. Cast your eyes upon the poor man with crippled limbs who begs you for charity. He goes almost naked, and you are well dressed. He suffers from the hardships of winter, while on that count you have steady resources both at home and abroad.[42]

With bed and board provided, servants were indeed protected from economic cycles, from the subsistence crises which, with grim regularity, wrought havoc in the budgets and very lives of peasants and workers alike throughout the Old Regime. This no doubt goes a long way toward explaining the surprisingly low rates of criminality of servants: the job might be rough and the hours long, but at least one was not tempted to snatch a loaf of bread or a handful of fruit in the street. As a group, servants were much less vulnerable to sudden hardship than any other category of workers, as the records of charitable institutions demonstrate. Only 11 percent of the inmates of the Hôpital de la

---

[42] Collet, *Instructions et prières*, p. 24.

Charité in Aix in the late 1740s were servants, as were a mere 3 percent of those of Paris's Bicêtre in 1750.[43]

The material security that servants enjoyed while employed must have conditioned their perceptions of themselves and influenced the attitudes of other, poorer workers toward them. But this one positive aspect of their occupation provoked little comment since it was less blatantly visible than others. Much of the hostility vented at domestics was triggered by a more conspicuous but also more illusory advantage: to other workers, servants never seemed to perform an honest day's work.

Throughout the century, the same indignation swelled up in Christian tracts and Physiocratic treatises alike. "It is a great injustice to want to be paid to do nothing," complained the author of a religious pamphlet in 1713. Fifty years later, the enlightened Turmeau de la Morandière echoed the same anger in a different mode: "All of these superfluous people have no merit but the insolence and wickedness that proceeds from idleness, and no talent but that of consuming considerable goods to the detriment of the whole body of civil society."[44] Servants must have been outraged at these allegations, for by all accounts most of them worked extremely hard. The misunderstanding arose from the erratic patterns of work and leisure characteristic of their occupation.

The d'Entrecasteaux servants in Aix were cross-examined by the police in 1784 after their mistress was discovered murdered in her bedchamber. From the accounts they gave of their whereabouts and occupations on the night before and the morning after the murder, it seems that they could count themselves lucky if

[43] Fairchilds, *Poverty and Charity*, p. 78; Jeffry Kaplow, "Sur la Population flottante de Paris à la fin de l'Ancien Régime," *Annales Historiques de la Révolution Française* 39 (January–March 1967):10.

[44] *Devoirs généraux des domestiques de l'un et l'autre sexe envers Dieu, leurs maîtres et maîtresses*, p. 50; Turmeau de La Morandière, *Police sur les mendians, les vagabonds, . . . , les filles prostituées, les domestiques hors de maison depuis long-temps, et les gens sans aveu*, p. 134.

they were able to get in six hours of sleep on a weekday night. Most of them, regardless of rank, had waited until after midnight for the return of their masters from various dinner parties, and all of them rose the next morning as early as any peasant or artisan in time to go to mass and to be on duty by six or seven.[45] The author of *L'Etat de servitude* complained bitterly of this exhausting schedule, which he judged to be one of the worst plights of the servant's existence. The loss of dignity, lack of security, and miserable wages were nothing, he grumbled, in comparison to those four-hour nights.[46]

But if servants put in extremely long hours, they were also blessed—or cursed—with what Jean-Claude Perrot has called *des plages de tranquillité*. The daily routine of servants, especially men, included long hours spent waiting at doorsteps and in antechambers and loitering in the street during their leisure hours.[47] Since their pace of work slackened during the middle of the day, those few moments of leisure to which they were entitled were all the more conspicuous. This apparent idleness exposed them to the gibes and resentment not only of their social superiors but also of artisans and laborers who would be hard at work during those hours.

In sum, it was the very ambiguity of their status and the privileges which they seemed to enjoy that set servants at odds with the rest of urban society. A bourgeois or a merchant might himself employ a maid, but waxed nervous at the sight of the valets and footmen of the rich who dressed too well and worked too little. As for the laboring poor, they could not fail to resent these men and women of lowly origins whose apparently comfortable style of living differed so markedly from their own. The cruel irony of the servants' fate was that nearly every advantage they enjoyed, every boon that earned them such antipathy, was more illusory than real. They lived in elegant neighborhoods,

[45] A.D.A. B 6270.

[46] *L'Etat de servitude*, p. 19.

[47] Jean-Claude Perrot, *Genèse d'une ville moderne: Caen au XVIIIe siècle*, II:1029.

but slept in garrets or on the floors of antechambers; they were decked out in silk and gold ornaments, but made every effort to divest themselves of costumes that kept them out of public promenades and theaters; they were sheltered from economic crises, but defenseless in the face of illness, unemployment, or old age; finally, they loafed away long stretches of the day in symbiosis with their masters' own idleness, but could rarely hope for a decent night's sleep.

Servants came to grief on account of the privileges, be they real or apparent, that differentiated their occupation from others. But even the most obvious drawbacks of domestic service earned them no sympathy because they too marked servants off as anomalous workers. Wealthy surroundings, flashy clothes, and ostentatious sloth were the prerogatives of the servants of the rich, and especially of male retainers hired for display, such as pages, lackeys, and coachmen. But female servants and the smaller fry of male domestics were not immune from criticism either. For one thing, the opprobrium heaped indiscriminately on *la livrée* for the reasons described above was no doubt extended to them as well. But beyond this most servants, regardless of sex or status, shared two characteristics which marked them off from the respectable mainstream of the artisanal world: servants were transients, and they were unmarried.

The turnover rate of servants, especially on the lower echelons, was extremely rapid. As we saw in the last chapter, many unskilled servants stayed in a job from six months to a year before moving on out of whim or necessity. Besides the faithful retainers who stayed on year after year, the staff of a large house usually comprised at any given moment a number of transient figures in the kitchens and the stables. In 1771 the Conseiller de Charleval in Aix employed eight servants, three of whom had been with the household for less than a year, and another who had been there for less than two. In the same town the Marquis d'Entrecasteaux had a staff of ten in 1784, which included two valets and a maid hired in the last four months, and two lackeys employed there for less than two years.[48] Some masters were clearly responsible for this high turnover rate, but others professed indignation at what they perceived as selfishness and unreliability. The Abbé Grégoire, a prominent revolutionary who was otherwise quite sympathetic to the plight of servants, vented the frustration of those of his class when he wrote: "There are numbers of servants who go from house to house, and whose lives are no better than those of tramps . . . they enter households on a sort of probation, so as to find one where they can steal and waste time with impunity."[49]

Domestic workers were well aware that this sort of instability gave them a reputation for fickleness. Rosalie Chabert, charged with domestic larceny, was asked why she had deliberately shortened the list of her previous employers. She answered that she had lied "so as not to seem to change masters too often."[50] And Jacques Viollet, writing in defense of the maligned Parisian *corps des laquais*, assured his readers that only steady employment could redeem the reputation of his brothers in service: "Since the instability of service is the principal reason for the contempt in which we are held, we will never manage to redeem our occupation unless it is made as solid as other professions to which it bears resemblance."[51] There is a measure of ambiguity to Viollet's pleas for sympathy and respect. Strictly speaking, servants themselves were largely to blame for their reputation as volatile workers, since it was often they who took the initiative of quitting their jobs in search of better-paid employment in or out of service. But who can tell how many such departures were made necessary by harsh treatment or low wages?

It is also true that other workers, even skilled ones, were just as restless as servants. The well-paid and highly skilled printers

[48] A.D.A. IVB 1245, March 1771; A.D.A. B 6270.

[49] Abbé Henri Grégoire, *De la Domesticité chez les peuples anciens et modernes*, p. 144.

[50] A.D.A. 208U 29/200, December 11, 1811.

[51] Viollet de Wagnon, *L'Auteur laquais*, pp. 104–105.

hired by the Société Typographique de Neuchâtel, for instance, remained on average less than a year on the job before moving on—and this wanderlust did little to endear them to their employers.[52] On the whole, however it was accepted that a skilled worker should move from job to job, and his reputation suffered no damage providing he possess a *billet de congé* or a *livret* attesting to his character.[53] As for day laborers, the very nature of their occupation commanded that they pick up work here and there according to what opportunities might be available. The mobility of servants, by contrast, was not built into the theoretical definition of their jobs. In theory a servant "belonged" to a master who expected the covenant to rest upon notions of reciprocal *fidélité*. No matter that mobility was in fact widespread, and that masters frequently dismissed their employees. If a servant left of his or her own volition, such a move was frowned upon as somewhat immoral.

Finally, when Viollet yearned that service become as "solid" as other occupations, he was plotting his old people's home for faithful retainers. To his mind, servants enjoyed no safety or stability because unlike other workers they lacked a strong occupational network that could protect them from destitution. Servants had to move from house to house and from job to job. The injustice of it was that they were transient because they were vulnerable, and distrusted because they were transient.

The servants' reputation for volatility and rootlessness also derived from the fact that most of them were unmarried. With the increase in the size of eighteenth-century cities and the influx into towns of rootless, unmarried migrant workers, the urban elites became all the more adamant in their advocacy of marriage as the foundation of social stability. In 1789 Louis Vastel, a lawyer in Caen, concluded a fiery tract in defense of traditional

[52] Robert Darnton, *The Business of Enlightenment: A Publishing History of the Encyclopédie*, pp. 203–212.

[53] Emile Levasseur, *Histoire des classes ouvrières et de l'industrie en France avant 1789*, I:668–669, 742–746, 798–799.

virtues by exhorting the reader: "Take a wife, and become a loyal member of society."[54]

Most male servants and nearly all females were unmarried, and at the very least their bachelor- or spinsterhood made for lifestyles somewhat different from those of the more established segments of the urban laboring poor.[55] At least it exposed them to the same accusations of debauchery regularly levied at those elements of urban society whose occupations kept them de jure or de facto in a state of celibacy, such as monks, soldiers, apprentices, and migrant workers.[56] Many a middle-class writer or ecclesiastical moralist expatiated with insistence—and occasionally some relish—on the alleged depravity of servants. To be fair to these writers, they sometimes laid the blame where it actually belonged: on the masters who insisted that their valets and footmen remain unmarried, corrupted them by their own example, or took advantage of their maidservants.[57] In the eyes of the upper classes, the corruption of both sexes was equally reprehensible.

But among the laboring poor, suspicion and anger were directed primarily at maidservants rather than men. If pages and lackeys sowed their wild oats, what self-respecting worker, in a society where the double standard flourished, would think of casting the first stone? Female servants, on the other hand, were isolated and unprotected, and it was the ambiguous, implausible celibacy of these women that gave rise to torrents of ugly accu-

[54] Perrot, *Caen*, II:832–834, quote p. 833.

[55] Kaplow, *Names of Kings*, pp. 50–51. In Marseille in 1793, 96 percent of all female servants were unmarried: Thérèse Reynaud-Lefaucheur, "Les Femmes dans la population marseillaise en 1793" (Mémoire de Maîtrise, Univ. de Provence, 1975), p. 110 and table E10.

[56] Perrot, *Caen*, II:839–842.

[57] Jean-Louis Flandrin, *Familles: Parenté, maison, sexualité dans l'ancienne société*, p. 140; Claude Fleury, *Devoirs des maîtres et des domestiques*, reprinted in Alfred Franklin, *La Vie privée d'autrefois: La vie de Paris sous Louis XIV*, p. 241. Other handbooks took the opposite stance and advised masters against hiring or retaining married servants. See Duchesse de Liancourt, *Règlement donné par une dame de qualité à M*** sa petite-fille pour sa conduite et celle de sa maison*, p. 114.

sations. The repertoire of abuse against female servants, a series of variations on motifs of prostitution, pimping, and pregnancy, was high in color, if limited in thematic scope. If a worker screamed at a maidservant that she was "a bitch, a whore, a madam, a brothel keeper,"[58] she could consider herself lucky on account of the banality of such insults. Not infrequently, abuse took the form of the most wildly elaborated sorts of calumny. The woman Aguillon in Marseille, pursuing a ruthless vendetta against the servant Anne Arnaud, informed her audience in the street that Arnaud "would hitch up her skirt for two *liards*, that she had had six bastards, that she was pregnant right now and about to destroy the fruit of her womb."[59] This sort of lavish vituperation had nothing to do with any specifically Mediterranean talent for debunking one's neighbor in public. The widow Guenon in Normandy was just as ferociously inventive when she accused Marie-Anne Beaulieu of repeated pregnancies and infanticides. Beaulieu, said the widow, had been involved with most of the male population of Bayeux including her master, and, she added, "if the basket is full right now, it's no wonder why."[60]

Sexual calumny was a common form of abuse in the towns of early modern France. The accusation of prostitution was the most drastic sort of insult that could be preferred in public against a woman, while men were more commonly accused of dishonesty. The streets of any town or village frequently rang with violent verbal exchanges, with the cries of *voleur* and *putain*.[61] Police records suggest that the risk of verbal aggression was greater for defenseless female servants, who were assumed as a matter of course to engage in prostitution or to carry on affairs with their masters.

[58] A.D.M. IIB 1237, July 31, 1764.
[59] A.D.M. IIB 1208, December 12, 1787.
[60] A.D.C. 2B 1057, June 1778.
[61] Castan, *Honnêteté et relations sociales*, pp. 79, 170–171; Arlette Farge, *Vivre dans la rue à Paris au XVIIIe siècle*, p. 118; Kaplow, *Names of Kings*, pp. 105–107.

Few of these women had a chance to fight back, and they were unlikely to have the last word when they did so. Anne Chave, who worked for the police lieutenant in Aix, was out walking with some friends when they ran into a peasant who stared at her rudely and exclaimed: "I know her; I want my share!" Her friends' half-hearted attempt at defending her ("What are you saying, she's not what you think.") proved unsuccessful. Chave stepped forward and threw a stone at her aggressor, screaming: "Yes, it is I, *visage de banny*; you want your share, go get it on the galleys, or from the hangman"; if she was a whore, she added, he was a thief. The peasant picked up a rock and dashed it at her, breaking her arm.[62]

That female servants were choice targets for accusations of prostitution and loose living is, on the face of it, easy enough to explain. They were known to be economically and sexually vulnerable, and many of them did succumb to threats or promises. Even the most chaste and respectable maidservant was exposed to suspicions: if a defenseless woman sold her work in someone's household, might she not sell her body as well? But these scabrous attacks also revealed deeper and more complex forms of hostility. Servants were usually assumed to be promiscuous creatures, but accusations usually crystallized around the notion that maidservants slept with their masters. Even a married woman like Cécile Bernard, the wife of an Aixois carter, was harassed in this fashion by a group of women, one of whom declared that "she was a whore, and was kept by her master, and last year she had a child by him."[63]

Both men and women were incensed by these real, or more often imaginary, relationships between masters and their servants. Such involvements were invoked to underline and explain the ambiguous status and allegiances of domestic workers. The daughters of a musician taunted the chambermaid of a Conseiller

[62] A.D.A. IVB 1174, March 23, 1719.
[63] A.D.A. IVB 1235, June 30, 1760.

au Parlement in Aix, "telling her that she wanted to pass for a lady, because her master had her anytime he wanted."[64] The intricate mixture of contempt and jealousy provoked by high-ranking servants thus poured out in the form of the coarsest of sexual slurs.

The men who insulted maidservants in this way often harbored other grievances against them. Servants were the most usual victims of gang rapes in late medieval southern towns. The frequency of this type of collective crime subsided, only to be replaced by individual aggressions and prolific verbal abuse.[65] Louis Houlu, the blacksmith who tried to take advantage of Marie Anne Hurlin, was foiled in his attempt but he angrily called her "a bitch, and the whore of Monsieur de Graffy."[66] As Jacques Rossiaud has suggested, humiliating a woman by calling her a prostitute, and thus objectifying her before raping her, was probably a means for the aggressor to allay his guilt by presenting the victim as already guilty.[67]

Young unmarried men especially resented and attacked servants because these women were unmarried but unavailable, except by means of force or patience. The hundreds of young women who worked as domestics in these eighteenth-century towns represented a social and sexual capital hoarded by masters who had social power over society at large, sexual power over their employees, and were already married to boot. The rage and frustration that men felt at the sight of these women could just as easily be turned against their masters. When the notary Pierre Chabaud tried to defend his maidservant from the obscenities of a laborer named Belair, the latter made a quick about-face and screamed at the master: "Come down you rascal, you miserable wretch, I'm going to break your arms and legs, you are a shameless man, you have four bastards by the slut, the whore who serves

---

[64] A.D.A. IVB 1271, July 9, 1788.
[65] Rossiaud, "Prostitution et société," p. 301.
[66] A.D.C. 2B 560, July 4, 1775.
[67] Rossiaud, "Prostitution et société," p. 297.

you, you are infamous, and your servant is a whore."[68] The real
or alleged sexual exploitation of maidservants thus became an
explosive symbolic issue when tensions between the poor and the
not-so-rich happened to surface. In 1772 a fight broke out in a
tavern in Bayeux between Le Midou, a merchant, and the farmer
Le Tourneur who owed him money. Le Tourneur roared at the
merchant: "Hold your peace, you wretched scoundrel, you upstart
. . . no servant ever left your house without her guts being full;
you wanted to make one of them into your whore."[69] On this
count, as on many others, servants paid for the sins of their
masters.

Male and female servants encountered distrust, hostility, or
just aloofness from other townsfolk for different but fundamentally related reasons. The nature of their work and the demands
of their masters placed them in either a social or a sexual limbo,
if not both. Men were more likely to wear good clothes, to live
in fine houses, and to enjoy long stretches of apparent leisure:
they belonged, yet not entirely and not legitimately, in the world
of the rich. Female servants who worked for poorer masters more
often encountered hostility on account of their unmarried status.
Their sexuality provoked uneasiness and suspicion, for they were
unmarried, unprotected, yet "possessed" by their masters.

What of the servants themselves? How could they respond to the
suspicions, diffidence, or anger which they encountered daily in
the towns where they worked? In many instances they fought
back, and repaid their aggressors in kind with jibes, insults, or
blows. In other cases, they draped themselves in defensive arrogance, and tried to crush those who insulted them with disdain.
Elizabeth Bayle-Mouillard wrote in her handbook that servants
resented their dependence on their masters and vented their frus-

---

[68] A.D.A. IVB 1245, July 2, 1770.
[69] A.D.C. 2B 1037, 1772.

tration by lording it over those whom they considered inferiors.[70] This may have been more typical of the nineteenth century than the eighteenth, but the earlier sources do occasionaly suggest that the servants' reputation for superciliousness may not have been undeserved. In Aix a servant named Pierre Ricard had attempted to seduce the sister of a mason. When the man vented his rage, Ricard snapped back

> that he had nothing to do or to say to a villain of that sort; that he wanted to fight, but not with his fists; that he was going to fetch his sword and that he, referring to the plaintiff, should go fetch his pickaxe and start digging his grave.[71]

But most servants were too vulnerable to make a habit of this sort of obnoxious behavior. More often they protected themselves by retreating to the territory that was really their own: the doorsteps of their masters' houses.

The scenes of love or violence that punctuated the lives of servants were usually acted out in the vicinity of this strategic spot. Women were courted on the threshold: Louise Telenne was on her master's doorstep when her future lover Antoine Imbert first caught sight of her; Magdeleine Cotton received the attentions of the valet Blondin who "sometimes would come to talk to her when he found her at the door of her mistress's house."[72] Skirmishes and fights, always preceded by the obligatory exchange of insults, frequently exploded at the doorstep. Anne Chave explained before the police in Aix that she was standing at her master's door when her archenemy and neighbor, a tailor's wife named Ginouvesse, brought matters to a breaking point by means of an obscene gesture.[73] Marianne Audric, the chambermaid of

---

[70] Madame Celnart (Elizabeth Bayle-Mouillard), *Manuel complet des domestiques*, p. 11.

[71] A.D.A. IVB 1248, May 1773.

[72] A.D.A. IVB 1178, February 12, 1724; A.D.A. IVB 1239, April 19, 1768.

[73] A.D.A. IVB 1181, August 29, 1727.

Madame Lange de Saint Suffren, was sitting on the bench in front
of Monsieur de la Brillane's house one Sunday evening in the
company of two servants from that household when a woman
named Dondon showered insults on the three of them, touching
off a general brawl.[74] From the haven of the threshold, servants
not only responded to attacks, but initiated them as well. Jean
Gaue in Bayeux complained to the police that his uncle's servants
had provoked a family feud by calling him a *bougre de fripon* and
a *plat-pied* every time he strolled by his relative's door.[75]

Entrenched on the doorstep, servants could better protect
themselves from a potentially hostile environment. The thresholds
of wealthy houses offered them asylum, but in some instances
the doorstep gave them power as well. From this vantage point,
lackeys, valets, and especially the burly doormen known as *suisses*
could farm out menial work to the errand goers, shoeshiners,
chimney sweeps, and others who stationed themselves outside
the houses of the rich.[76]

The authority that servants wielded in such situations, and the
petty rivalries rampant among their dependents, are vividly illustrated in an episode from a contemporary novel, Mouhy's *Avantures galantes de Bigand*. The hero, Bigand, surviving temporarily
as a shoe cleaner, one day ambles up to the doorstep of a wealthy
house. The threshold is ruled by a colossal *suisse* with a thick
mustache, whose vassals of the moment include a couple of nasty-
looking Savoyard chimney sweeps. This new arrival is not to the
liking of the Savoyards, and within minutes the three are locked
in a deadly struggle from which Bigand emerges victorious. The
doorman and lackeys of the household, having enjoyed the fight,
applaud his courage, and as a reward grant him permission to
clean all of their shoes and to set up his trade at their door.[77]

[74] A.D.A. IVB 1222, September 1758.

[75] A.D.C. 2B 857, July 1716.

[76] Hufton, *The Poor*, p. 101.

[77] Charles de Fieux, Chevalier de Mouhy, *Le Mouche ou les espiègleries et avantures
galantes de Bigand*, 2 vols. (Paris, 1777), I:272–273.

The episode is fictional, of course, but in its details it does correspond to what we know of the reality of life on the threshold. The doorstep gave some servants authority over the jobless, and control over creditors and parasites who tried to gain access to the masters within. The power they wielded from this strategic point can only have further contributed to their unpopularity.

Like the livery, the threshold symbolically captures the essence of the servants' condition. They stood poised in this spatial limbo for they belonged neither in the master's house, nor in the street among the laboring poor. The resentment that servants provoked, and their own defensiveness and isolation, thus derived from the special conditions under which they worked, from the privileges as well as the strictures of their occupation. Their living conditions, clothes, rhythms of work and leisure, their immunity from economic hazards and their ambiguous celibacy all contributed to setting them apart in a sort of social limbo. Little wonder that servants took refuge behind their employers' liveries and on their masters' doorsteps.

It would be an exaggeration, however, to conclude from all this that servants led totally isolated, pariah-like existences. Evidence cited in the previous chapter shows that many of them were successfully integrated into urban society through marriage or the accumulation of a small capital, that townsfolk traded with servants, and that artisans, tradesmen, and laborers courted maidservants in the hopes of marrying them. The hostility that servants encountered was not systematic, and above all it did not outlast their time in service. Once they relinquished the occupation, the opprobrium disappeared. One is inevitably led to conclude that it was the occupation itself that provoked uneasiness, rather than the persons involved in it.

Servants were despised and feared because they were different, but above all because their social status was ill-defined, because they were marginal creatures. Anthropologists such as Mary Douglas and Victor Turner have devoted much attention to the stigma which, in most societies, attaches itself to those persons and groups that reside at the margins or in the interstices of society. Witches, novices, and unborn children are threatening, Douglas argues, because they have no official place in the patterning of society: "They may be doing nothing wrong, but their status is undefinable."[78] Marginal creatures, groups where status is ambiguous or weakly defined, are profoundly menacing, she explains, because margins are the most vulnerable point in any socioideological structure: "If they are pulled this way or that, the shape of fundamental experience is altered. Any structure of ideas is vulnerable at its margins."[79] Servants, in preindustrial societies, were socially and sexually marginal creatures par excellence. They were liminal beings, and quite literally so, since the Latin word *limen* signifies threshold. And they shared some of the attributes which, in archaic and modern societies over the ages, have marked off liminal groups from the mainstream of the social order. Groups placed in a state of transition or marginality, Victor Turner tells us, are usually stripped of their names and clothing, clad in uniforms, forced into humility, silence, and sexual continence, and regarded as fools and simpletons.[80] Yet such persons are feared because their very marginality invests them with powers that challenge the ordering of society.[81]

Viewed within this sort of explanatory framework, some of the issues around which the fear of servants crystallized are easier to explain. Marginal persons and groups, Douglas argues, are usually seen as carriers of pollution and disorder—hence the often unjustified accusations of debauchery or violence regularly levied at servants. Liminal creatures must be visibly marked off from the mainstream of society to prevent their corrupting the social order—hence the strident insistence that domestics wear sartorial symbols of their condition. Finally, though some servants did

[78] Mary Douglas, *Purity and Danger*, p. 115 and passim.
[79] Ibid., p. 145.
[80] Victor Turner, *The Ritual Process: Structure and Anti-Structure*, pp. 95, 102–107.
[81] Turner, *Ritual Process*, p. 108; Douglas, *Purity and Danger*, passim.

wield power over the little world of the threshold, it is hard to explain the absurd contentions of writers such as Mercier or Montesquieu that servants were taking over the families of the aristocracy and the very court itself, unless one pays heed to anthropologists who explain that "the danger which is risked by boundary transgression is power."[82]

Domestic service was a "threshold" in two important respects—a state of passage between celibacy and marriage, and a boundary zone between the upper and the lower classes. Be they unmarried maidservants or livery-clad lackeys, in the eyes of other workers they were neither fish nor fowl. Service did not mark these men and women for life; but the peculiarities of this state of passage not only estranged them materially from large segments of the urban population, but also provoked in others the fears and dislikes to which social ambiguities and contradictions frequently give rise.

Within the urban setting, servants were isolated from others not only by virtue of their poverty and foreignness, but by the very nature of their occupation. They might make friends and contacts among the laboring poor, but were ill-accepted while they were in service. Since this was the case, where did servants find support and conviviality? Did they compensate for their estrangement from other workers by setting up their own network of relations? Is it possible, in short, to document the existence of a servant subculture?

---

[82] Douglas, *Purity and Danger*, p. 190. In many societies, the thresholds of houses and temples have been charged with a great deal of religious significance. The doorstep was often the site of the sealing of covenants, of animal and human sacrifices, of the acting out of rites of hospitality and rites of passage—the latter having survived to our own day in the custom of carrying the bride over the threshold. See H. Clay-Trumbull, *The Threshold Covenant: The Beginning of Religious Rites* (New York, 1896). The fear of the alleged power of servants is demonstrated by the popularity of satirical literature in which servants ruled the houses of the rich through their intrigues. See for instance the English *High Life Below Stairs* (London, 1788), and its earlier French equivalent, *Les Amours, intrigues et caballes des domestiques des grandes maisons de ce temps.*

There can be no doubt that servants in eighteenth-century towns knew each other, helped each other, and sought out each other's company. Contacts among servants even preceded their trek into the foreign world of the city. Since most of them were immigrants, many secured their first job with the help of a friend or relative already established in town, and like most immigrants they spontaneously sought out the company of men and women from their own native villages or regions. Marie Lami, a young serving girl in Bayeux, told the police that she obtained her first job through a maid whom she met in the fish market, "because we were from the same area."[83] Of course the servants' first concerns were for their siblings and relatives. In 1787 Elizabeth Gallier wrote from Grenoble to a homesick sister in Lyon: "If you can no longer endure the town you are in, you can come here, masters are easy to find, but I warn you that you will not earn such good wages."[84] And in Caen, Madame Simon de Franval wrote to her husband about the hiring of a young lackey: "He is a close relative of [our maid] Madelon."[85] Such "family ties" could be remote or even completely phoney, as Legrain revealed in his account of his arrival in Paris:

> Upon arriving in Paris, I stayed with a coachman cousin of mine. We went to see his friends. Within two days we met one of them, who worked as a postilion for the Comte de Rougé, the brother of the Marquise de Tourzel. He said: "What can we do to present you?" We decided that I would also be a relative of his.[86]

Even after servants had secured their first jobs, they continued to operate within this nexus for reception and placement. Most

[83] A.D.C. 2L 275/1, Year XII.

[84] Bernard Fradin, "Domestiques d'établissement et domestiques de maison à Lyon au XVIIIe siècle" (Mémoire de maîtrise, Univ. de Lyon 1976), p. 60.

[85] A.D.C. 2E 6645, Fonds Simon de Franval, letter of November 8, 1742.

[86] Legrain, "Souvenirs de Legrain, valet de chambre de Mirabeau," *Nouvelle Revue rétrospective* 1 p. 2.

jobs, whether in service or not, were secured through contacts, and many servants were in touch with those who could offer them. When Jean-Joseph Esmieu arrived in Marseille from the Alps, he sought out at least five people from his native region. Typically, the very first person he approached was an upper servant of the wealthy Foresta-Collongue family.[87] But the system operated on a more modest level as well: in Bayeux, Anne Le François was offered employment as a maid to Mademoiselle Saint-Gilles by Anne Banioche, the lady's current (and disenchanted) employee.[88] Shreds of information of this sort surface frequently enough in police records to suggest that some very active trafficking in jobs was constantly going on. Servants established and maintained contacts with one another in order to procure employment for themselves, and for friends, relatives, and even total strangers; but just how strong or lasting these ties were is impossible to determine.

Servants who worked in the same household were of necessity forced into each other's constant company. The relationships that flourished under these circumstances crisscrossed the lines of the servant hierarchy, and could naturally take a myriad different forms depending on the sex, status, and personalities of the individuals involved. The hothouse atmosphere of the "world below stairs" could nurture the sort of solidarity and compassion of which police records offer an occasional glimpse. In 1775 Pierre Perrée, a young lackey in Bayeux, was accused of stealing his master's silverware, a charge that he denied vehemently though he could only offer the flimsiest of alibis for the night of the theft. In the days before his arrest, the male servants of the household rallied around him. Eighteen-year-old Jacques Le Boiteux, who shared a room with Perrée, found the lad lying disconsolately on his bed. Le Boiteux entreated him, using the formal

---

[87] Pierre Dubois, ed., *La Vie pénible et laborieuse de Jean-Joseph Esmieu, marchand-colporteur en Provence sous la Révolution Française*, p. 17. See also Hufton, *The Poor*, pp. 100–101.

[88] A.D.C. 2B 875, 1722.

vouvoiement: "But Perrée, why are you acting like this? I'm not saying that you are the culprit, I know nothing of this; but if you are to blame, they are giving you every chance of justifying your behavior. Why do you not justify yourself?" The coachman Thomas Guillot, a forty-one-year-old longtime retainer in the household, promptly stepped into a fatherly role. He spoke to Perrée on the morning after the theft, using the familiar *tu* form: "My boy, this is a nasty business for you." After some palavering, Guillot and Perrée, in the company of the master's valet, took off to consult a magician in the hopes of discovering the name of the real culprit.[89]

As we saw in the last chapter, relations between male and female servants in the same household could easily turn into sentimental or sexual involvements. Such relationships ran the gamut from friendship or flirtation to hostility or brutal rape. Any such closed environment can produce extreme manifestations of devotion or hatred. In Marseille, Anne Vachier hanged herself in May of 1772 after her only friend, a chambermaid in the same household, had left service to get married.[90] Conversely, petty rivalries and hatreds often came close to a breaking point in smaller households, while clannishness and cabals flourished in larger ones. Many a servant, like Thérèse Reynaud in Aix, complained to the police of having lost a job because of the aggravations and calumnies of other members of the staff, and Rousseau himself suffered greatly as a young lackey from the persecutions of a trio of scheming domestics who had established control over the Vercellis household.[91]

From the diverse welter of evidence on these relationships between coworkers, it is impossible to determine the dominant tenor of these bonds born of circumstance. But few servants can have found much solace or stability among their fellow workers. For one thing, only a minority of domestic workers resided in

[89] A.D.C. 2B 1049, May 1775.

[90] A.D.M. IIB 2089, May 21, 1722.

[91] A.D.A. IVB 1250, January 1774; Rousseau, *Confessions*, I:111–112.

multiservant households, and still fewer in houses with a staff of more than two or three. What is more, many such relationships, except among a few stable retainers, had a necessarily transient quality built into them. The turnover rate among servants in any given household was likely to be very high. Pauline Casagne, the chambermaid to Madame de Charleval, told the police in 1771 that in the four years she had been with the household,

> she had always seen the same coachman and the same cook, but that the younger Madame de Charleval changed chambermaids very often; as for the lackeys of [the latter lady], she saw them change very often too, but she does not know any of these people and cannot say where they are serving now.[92]

Even when passions did not run high, it seems that servants could expect little more of their fellow workers than an ad hoc sort of camaraderie.

If so, did stronger, more lasting ties develop between servants of different households? Outside of their masters' houses, did servants of comparable status seek each other out during their leisure hours? The answer to this question is definitely yes. In the streets, on the doorsteps, in kitchens and taverns, servants enjoyed an informal but flourishing social life. It was not until the nineteenth century that some masters, imbued with new notions of morality and productivity, began to restrict severely the mobility of their staff, keep tabs on their servants' acquaintances, and impose draconian "no followers" rules.[93] Eighteenth-century employers concerned themselves little with such matters

---

[92] A.D.A. IVB 1245, March 5, 1771.

[93] Guy Thuillier and Pierre Guiral, *La Vie quotidienne des domestiques en France au XIXe siècle* (Paris, 1978), p. 28; Charles Ozanam, *Manuel des pieuses domestiques*, pp. 193–204; Madame Pariset, *Manuel de la maîtresse de maison, ou lettres sur l'économie domestique* (Paris, 1821), p. 177. For England see John Gillis, "Servants, Sexual Relations, and the Risks of Illegitimacy in London, 1801–1900," *Feminist Studies* 5:150–151.

and even seem to have encouraged the commingling of their servants with those of their friends and relatives. Legrain, in his memoirs, told of several instances in which his master actually suggested that he go drinking with the servants of Mirabeau's father or those of other hosts.[94] Since many a master or mistress went traveling or visiting with a servant or two, friendships naturally developed between the servants of allied or friendly households.[95]

In town the servants of different households visited each other quite freely. Many a young girl met a lover this way. Rose Chanut, the chambermaid of Monsieur Siméon in Aix "often saw the man named Claude Segond, the servant of Monsieur le Marquis de Vauvenargues, who came to visit Dauphiné and other servants in the household."[96] Another maid was courted by a cook named Arnaud who spent long hours in the kitchens of the Marquis de Marignane "pretending to visit the household cook who was a mate of his, but in truth it was in order to see her more easily."[97] Evidence in the police records suggests that the kitchens of larger households were noisy, convivial places, open to a stream of visitors; and while the occasional laborer or artisan came to court a female member of the staff, the regular crowd was almost exclusively composed of servants.

Habits of conviviality among servants were not confined to the staffs of larger, wealthier houses. Maidservants who worked alone in bourgeois or artisan households also tended to rely on their

[94] Legrain, "Souvenirs," pp. 18–19, 92–93.
[95] See, for instance, A.D.A. IVB 1270, December 24, 1787. The case concerns one Claudine Charézieux, whose close friendship (?) with a married man, Blache, got her into trouble with the latter's wife. Charézieux said that Blache, with his master the Chevalier de Toussaint, came to visit the household in which she was serving: "There, he had occasion to get to know all of the staff of the household one by one, and had many chances to see the plaintiff either in the house of Monsieur le Camus, or else in that of Madame la Présidente de Cabre, where she also served."
[96] A.D.A. IVB 1269, January 28, 1786.
[97] A.D.A. IVB 1263, May 12, 1782.

sisters in service for help and company. A makeshift system of mutual aid operated among serving women in Bayeux, though it did not always remain within the bounds of legality. Marie Lami absconded wood and butter from her master's house for her friend Anne Guerin, and the latter cleaned Lami's clothes in return; Marie Anne Le Gageu stole butter from her employer to make a cake which she wanted to share with three other maid-servants.[98]

In documents spanning the entire century, one finds hints of the alliances that jelled spontaneously among servants from different households, and brought them together for fights, drinks, or games. In their clashes with other townsfolk, servants demonstrated a solidarity with one another that frequently ran along specific occupational and status lines within the domestic underworld. When François Pochon, the cook of the Marquis de Sabran in Aix, was attacked by a group of young men—a cobbler, a tanner, and a soldier—two other cooks from aristocratic households rushed to his defense; among the six people who testified on his behalf were three other cooks and a maître d'hôtel.[99] When Madame de Mazaugue's sedan-chair carriers were ambushed late one night, they were rescued by their colleagues in the service of Madame d'André.[100]

But servants turned just as easily against one another when tempers ran high. The staffs of large aristocratic households, bonded together by the prestige of their masters' names, collided in violent encounters. In Aix in 1712, some of the Archbishop's servants complained that they had been attacked by one of the Prieur de Saint Jean's men, who had advanced upon them brandishing stones,

> swearing, profaning and blaspheming the holy name of the Lord . . . saying that he would stone to death the first man

[98] A.D.C. 2L 275/1, Year XII; A.D.C. 2L 257/1, Year X.
[99] A.D.A. IVB 1229, December 1763.
[100] A.D.A. IVB 1230, March 1763.

to step forward . . . that he knew them to be the Archbishop's men and that he was the chair carrier of the Prieur de Saint Jean.[101]

But such clashes also opposed the servants of those lesser masters who employed only one or two domestics. Networks would form, solidified by weeks or months of harassment. In Aix in 1787, a campaign of mutual aggravation had been going on between two rival groups. On one side was Elizabeth Valin, the servant of Maître Tamisier, whose main ally was a cousin who worked for Maître Eymond. On the other was Marguerite Bonnet, the maidservant of Maître Arbaud, whose troops included her master's clerk and an assortment of other servants named Brémond, Babet, Julien, and Grégoire. The final showdown took place near the Fontaine des Trois Ormeaux. After both sides had exhausted their particularly rich repertoire of libels, a general brawl ensued in the course of which Elizabeth Valin took a severe beating at the hands of the clerk.[102]

These instances of collective violence reveal the patterns of alliance into which servants tended to fall. But the day-to-day social life of servants did not always take on such explosive qualities. Some servants promenaded with their suitors, others congregated on benches near their masters' houses or stood chatting in groups on the main street.[103] Wine and *eau-de-vie* brought them together in tight-knit groups in the town's taverns and inns. After the servant François Pochon exchanged harsh words with a group of young ruffians, they knew exactly where to find him that evening; they made straight for Jean Baptiste Alexis's tavern, where Pochon was drinking in the company of six other servants.[104]

[101] A.D.A. IVB 1172, June 14, 1717.
[102] A.D.A. IVB 1174, June 21, 1719.
[103] For instance, A.D.A. XXB 3975, August 4, 1738; A.D.A. IVB 1222, September 1758.
[104] A.D.A. IVB 1229, December 1763.

In certain instances, gregariousness was reinforced by the needs and habits of the masters themselves. Male servants were likely to meet in the vicinity of the theaters, for they escorted their masters there but were not allowed inside if they wore liveries.[105] The coachman Pouillard told the police that "when he was at the comedy yesterday, he was invited to play cards by François, the lackey of Madame de la Roque and the chair carrier of Monsieur de Blanc Popinot."[106] He most certainly did not mean that the three of them were inside enjoying the performance, but that they were biding their time around the coaches outside. In other cases, it is clear that servants took some initiative in shaping their own social life: Marie Roustan told of her courtship by a cook who invited her out to a ball given in a big house in town by all of the town's cooks.[107]

It is evident that domestic servants tended to seek each other out, and to spend much of their free time together. The picture should not be overdrawn, however, for though their world was homogeneous, it was by no means watertight. Friendships frequently crossed occupational lines and extended to other workers. The same Pierre Perrée who was suspected of stealing his master's silver described the group of people with whom he had been drinking on the night of the theft: his own sister, a man called Taillenfant and his sister, one Perrette and his wife and child, another woman, and a worker. None of these people, apparently, were in service.[108] And such examples could be multiplied. Many a servant kept company with relatives, friends, or compatriots. What is more, servants were sought out in certain situations because they had more contacts, more sophistication, or simply

[105] Henri Lagrave, *Le Théâtre et le public à Paris de 1715 à 1750*, pp. 237–238. This prohibition was in fact hard to enforce, for lackeys and pages were always slipping into the theaters. See John Lough, *Paris Theater Audiences in the Seventeenth and Eighteenth Centuries*, pp. 56–57, 75–79, 95, 115.

[106] A.D.A. IVB 1174, June 21, 1719.

[107] A.D.A. IVB 1269, January 28, 1786.

[108] A.D.C. 2B 1049, 1775.

more spare cash than others. A case in point is the heavy involvement of domestic servants in the major form of illicit amusement in eighteenth-century French towns—gambling.

Legal or illegal games provided an important framework for servant sociability, especially but not exclusively where male servants were concerned. In Paris, long hours of leisure were spent around the billiard tables during the winter months, and some servants acquired such an intimate knowledge of the poolroom that they could set one up upon retiring. The chronicler of Montpellier dryly observed of the town's *billiardiers*: "This is a lazy man's occupation, usually practiced by former servants."[109] Billiards and other games of skill which in theory did not involve financial risks were legal, if subjected to strong disapproval because they supposedly encouraged idleness. But male servants were also heavily involved in illicit gambling, as organizers of forbidden games and as principal offenders.

Jeux prohibés became more and more popular as the eighteenth century progressed. One of the numerous ordinances issued by the Bureau de Police of Aix at increasingly shorter intervals described the phenomenon as something of a minor earthquake, "a scourge that can make families tremble and alarm society itself," whose adepts could only sink further and further into moral turpitude.[110] Despite the official hue and cry, forbidden games of cards and dice with strange and beautiful names like le Pharaon, le Lansquenet, le Torpetinque and le Quinquenove were regularly organized at dead of night in secluded backyards, country houses, and the back rooms of inns. In Aix servants played a major role in such gatherings. Nearly every time that the police broke up one of these parties, they noted the presence of one or more lackeys or valets whose conspicuous clothing gave him away. One police

---

[109] Nicolas-Edmé Restif de la Bretonne, *Les Nuits de Paris* (Paris, 1967), p. 89; Berthélé, *Montpellier*, p. 104.

[110] Ordinances against gambling were issued in Aix in 1738, 1754, 1758, 1771, 1775, and 1784. A.M.A. FF 98, fols. 118, 210 and FF 99, fols. 159–164.

147

officer reported in 1775 that he had caught eight or nine people gambling, "all of them peasants except for a person wearing a red costume with silver facings, which led us to believe that he was the servant of some gentleman."[111]

There is good reason to suspect that servants played the role of initiators and organizers for such assemblies, for they acquired skills and predispositions toward gambling by acting as intermediaries for their masters. La Reverdit, a butcher's wife in Aix, told the police that she had been pressured into renting out her house for such purposes by a woman named Françoise and the valet of an influential personage who assured her that "the profits of a single evening would be enough to pay her rent . . . and in any case there were people in the party with enough power to get her out of trouble."[112] But even when only the *menu peuple* was involved, servants were natural ringleaders for such affairs. They had time and opportunity to practice, had access to cards, dice, and carpets, and maybe possessed some flourish and sophistication in their manner.

Gambling brought the servants themselves together in exclusive gatherings—in fact, their games were unofficial institutions. On February 10, 1781, an informer came to warn the police in Aix that "the lackey's vandôme game was taking place at the house of Lambert, a servant on the rue du Port." The police rushed onto the scene, snatched a pack of cards from the coachman Perier, and arrested him along with nine other servants including one Dauphiné "known as le Comte d'Estaing, a servant also but unemployed."[113] But lackeys and valets also infiltrated many another such assembly, hence the usual composition of these gambling parties: two aristocratic servants and six artisans in one case;

---

[111] A.M.A. FF 105, January 5, 1775; see also A.M.A. FF 106 April 18, 1776.

[112] A.M.A. FF 105, February 25, 1775.

[113] A.M.A. FF 107, February 10, 1781.

seven servants, eight artisans, and three farmers in another; three peasants, a tailor, and four domestics in yet another.[114]

These tales of forbidden pastimes are emblematic of the lives led by servants in the towns of eighteenth-century France. They tended to associate with one another, for they shared the same patterns of work and leisure, the same problems, the same opprobrium. Yet they did maintain contacts with other workers outside of the world of service. "Others" could be friends, relatives, or simply acquaintances with whom they shared some wine on occasion. But such associations must have been shot through with ambiguity. Even if a servant shared the thrill of a game of dice late at night with half a dozen artisans, he was still clad in the telltale livery. Perhaps he played with greater skill, or could afford higher stakes, or had used his contacts to set the party afoot. Thus friendships and sociability did extend beyond the world of service, but the social lives of men and women in service were nonetheless determined by the bonds they formed with one another within that occupation.

A world of service did exist; yet from the instances of sociability and collective life described above, one cannot piece together a picture of a very strong or coherent servant subculture. In comparison to the cultures of other large preindustrial laboring groups—peasants, artisans, or slaves—the servants' world conspicuously lacked any concrete or lasting manifestations of creativity or solidarity. With some minor exceptions,[115] servants produced no

[114] A.M.A. FF 104, January 5, 1774; A.M.A. FF 106, November 4, 1777; A.M.A. FF 107, August 15, 1783.

[115] One finds mention, for instance, of a religious confraternity, Notre-Dame du Bon Repos, formed by the sedan-chair carriers of Aix. However, sedan-chair carriers did not systematically qualify as domestic servants since many were in fact independent workers who hired out their services on a short-term basis. This confraternity is mentioned in a police blotter, A.D.A. IVB 1230. Very few works of literature or polemical pieces were written in the eighteenth century by servants. *L'Etat de servitude* and Viollet de Wagnon's *L'Auteur laquais* have already been cited, and a pamphlet entitled *Avis à la livrée par un homme qui la*

festivities, tales, or songs. They never gave any institutional bases to their collective existence and of necessity had little or no family life; still less did they engage in strikes or rebellions. In the larger towns where servants were more numerous, the group took on very marked characteristics, and servants displayed a remarkably strong *esprit de corps*. In Paris at midcentury, Viollet de Wagnon wrote in defense of something he dubbed the *corps des laquais*. His writing reveals much about the bonds that united Parisian lackeys in the 1750s:

> We do however still count a few among our number who in all that they do imitate this man [Jasmin], but we call them in lackey's terms *pisse froids*, meaning people who are unsociable and useless to the world . . . that if for instance their colleagues were unfortunately out of work or penniless, they could expect no help from people of that sort.[116]

But even such extreme reflexes of solidarity and group identification never gave birth to anything like confraternities, organized festivities, or institutionalized mutual aid. Street fights, gambling and drinking parties, conversations around the kitchen table or at the doorstep, plus some makeshift mutual assistance were the only forms of collective life that servants were able to engage in during the Old Regime. Their culture—if such a word can be used—was amorphous, and it was fragile.

This is hardly surprising, given the characteristics of their occupation. Servants were allowed to consort with one another, but lived scattered in different households, working at the beck and call of their masters. Their opportunities for creation or

---

porte was published in Paris in 1789—though there is no way of knowing whether the authors of the two anonymous works were in fact servants. Françoise Thérèse Dalibard, who wrote novels under the name of Mademoiselle de Saint-Phalier, was a former chambermaid, but her *Les Caprices du sort ou l'histoire d'Emilie* (n.p., 1750), can hardly be said to bear the imprint of its author's onetime occupation.

[116] Viollet de Wagnon, *L'Auteur laquais*, pp. 62–63.

recreation were therefore seriously curtailed. In addition, most of the servants themselves viewed their occupation as transitional, and would not be tempted to invest large amounts of energy into elaborating a durable collective life. They sought each other out from necessity more than by choice, for they were ill-integrated into the mainstream of society. The subculture that servants generated was defensive and tenuous. They were forced to resort to one another, but neither their masters nor they themselves could allow these friendships to jell into lasting bonds.

Servants found companionship and support in one another, but the strength and stability of their collective life left much to be desired. Certain forms of deviance that are characteristic of servants are symptomatic of the fundamental isolation of domestic workers. Servants in nineteenth-century France accounted for a disproportionate percentage of total suicides.[117] What little quantitative evidence we have on the matter for the eighteenth century is contradictory,[118] but the stories of servant suicides are telling enough. Barbier cites the case of a maidservant who threw herself out of a window after having been accused of domestic theft.[119] François Achard in Marseille also dashed himself onto the street, apparently because he had caught a venereal disease; Anne Mortier took her own life because, her mistress explained, "she was in the depths of misery, and had no other belongings than the clothes she wore, having drawn all her wages in advances."[120]

Equally tragic, and far more numerous, are the stories of alleged

[117] Theresa McBride, *The Domestic Revolution: The Modernisation of Household Service in England and France, 1820–1920*, p. 108.

[118] Astrid Bernicot, "Etude de la délinquance à Marseille au XVIIIe siècle" (Mémoire de Maîtrise, Univ. de Provence, 1974), p. 91; Richard Cobb, *Death in Paris, 1795–1801* (London, 1978), pp. 14, 15, 124–125. Bernicot cites three servant suicide cases out of twenty-three in Marseille, whereas Cobb notes the "surprising absence" of domestic servants who account for half a dozen at most of the 262 suicide victims whose occupation he details.

[119] Barbier, *Chronique de la régence*, I:284.

[120] A.D.M. IIB 1206, September 29, 1783; A.D.M. IIB 2090, June 13, 1775.

infanticides committed by women who became pregnant out of wedlock and had to deliver their children in total solitude. Suzanne Eguillon, who was arrested in Marseille in July of 1759, unsuccessfully attempted to conceal her pregnancy and deplorable physical condition from her masters and neighbors. She was hanged in December. Some forty years later, Nannette Vernoux's sentence was less harsh: two hours on the pillory and four years in prison. But she had gone through the same ordeal. She had been violently sick for several months, had lived in terror of being discovered, had fainted while giving birth in absolute solitude to a stillborn child, and had been obliged to resume work immediately so as not to arouse suspicions.[121] In Normandy, instances of alleged infanticides were hardly less gruesome. There was Elizabeth Barthelotte, for instance, who panicked when she heard footsteps approaching and thrust the dead infant into the pocket of her skirt; or Marie Morel who struggled unsuccessfully to tie the umbilical cord, and finally threw the child into a hole she had hastily dug out with her clog.[122] Most of these women, driven into hysteria by the repeated cross-questionings of the police, swore that they never intended to harm the child they were bearing. "Why did you kill your child?" they asked Félicité Gance in Bayeux. "I did not kill him; if I could buy back his life I would do so," she answered. The examination had to be interrupted for the accused was "in a state of stupor and imbecility."[123] Nanette Michel in Marseille explained three times to the police, in tones of increasing panic, that she had concealed her pregnancy for fear of losing her job. "As God is my witness," she sobbed, "I never for one moment entertained the thought of harming the child I was bearing."[124]

There was not a soul to whom these women could appeal during

[121] A.D.M. XXB 5560, July 1759; A.D.A. 208/U 20/4, 23 Germinal, Year III.

[122] A.D.C. 2L 140/6, Year III; A.D.C. 2B 1050, 1775.

[123] A.D.C. 2L 302/8, 1809.

[124] A.D.A. 208/U 20/5, January 6, 1806.

their ordeal. Not one of them admitted to having received any assistance, psychological or otherwise. The families were far, their lovers had deserted them, and friends were not to be trusted with so grave a secret. Loneliness, misery, insecurity—the same syndromes that drove some servants to suicide—made these women conceal their pregnancy and deliver stillborn infants whom they threw into wells and cisterns or buried under handfuls of dirt.

Suicide and infanticide are but extreme symptoms of the fundamental isolation of domestic servants. Cut off from family and community, isolated by occupation from the mainstream of the urban laboring classes, domestic servants could count on only makeshift and limited support from their brothers and sisters in service. Confronted with an alienating and sometimes hostile environment, in the company of fellow workers as vulnerable and transient as themsleves, servants were naturally led to opt for the one remaining alternative, that of casting in their lot with their masters.

In recent decades some magnificent pieces of historical writing—the works of Edward Thompson and Eugene Genovese, in particular—have demonstrated that apparently vulnerable and downtrodden groups such as artisans and slaves were able to maintain a sense of dignity and autonomy by means of coherent separate cultures.[125] Collective traditions, autonomous forms of culture, religious movements, and family life helped English artisans and slaves in the American South to withstand even the enormous pressures of nascent capitalism on the one hand and the white man's hegemony on the other. The strength of their separate cultures gave these workers the wherewithal to elaborate overt or more subtle forms of resistance to the wills of those who exploited them. As these first chapters have sought to explain, particular features of the servants' experience precluded the possibility of

[125] Edward Thompson, *The Making of the English Working Class* (New York, 1963); Eugene Genovese, *Roll, Jordan, Roll: The World the Slaves Made.*

any major forms of resistance. Not only were servants highly vulnerable in nearly every respect, but they themselves viewed their condition as transitional. Domestic workers withstood the hardships of their situation by means of minor transgressions: they stole, cheated, played truant, or wasted time. But in the end the problem is one of allegiance rather than resistance.

Servants tended to accept the dictates of their masters, and even to identify with those who employed them. They did not do so out of ingrained servility or snobbery, but out of sheer necessity. Most of them had no recourse but to act in public as extensions of their masters, for their social marginality alienated them from other workers. The isolation of servants from their peers resulted just as much from the advantages of their occupation as from its drawbacks. In many ways, servants were privileged workers. They enjoyed a measure of material security that was denied to other workers, and some of them even wielded considerable power over other segments of the laboring poor. But these very privileges only contributed further to their isolation.

Domestic workers defined the shape of their own occupation less than did any other category of workers. Their poverty and foreignness, their instrumental attitudes toward the occupation, and their isolation from other workers all go a long way toward explaining why servants so often agreed to play the roles assigned to them by their employers. But the masters themselves also actively sought, within the confines of their homes, to ensure the dependency and loyalty of their menials. How masters and mistresses established control over their servants within the domestic setting and how they put that authority to use outside of the household are the subjects of the next two chapters.

Part Two

THE WILL OF
THE MASTERS

CHAPTER 4

Life in the Household

Foreign and poor as they were, isolated from one another and from their peers by the nature of their occupation, eighteenth-century servants often had no option but to cast in their lot with their employers. Yet these very circumstances might seem to preclude a servant's investing his or her identity in the job. If for most of them the main concern was with the financial rewards of the occupation, if their ties to their masters were born of circumstance and necessity, how could any deep attachment or spontaneous loyalty be expected to them? How could masters demand anything beyond obedience and hard work of salaried workers whose only apparent incentive was financial?

The deeper bond between master and servant was forged within the household. It is in the hallways, the antechambers, the bedrooms and kitchens of eighteenth-century households that we must go looking for the roots of *fidélité*. Since employers were by far the dominant parties in the relationship, we must enter their world in order to understand why they could expect—and often obtain—the allegiance of their servants. What was the tenor of domestic relations in eighteenth-century France? How could masters hold sway over the hearts and minds of the menials who worked in their houses? How did they use rewards and punishments, affection and authority, in order to coerce or cajole their servants into *fidélité*?

The argument that servants espoused their masters' interests only because they had no other recourse may seem simplistic or unduly cynical. Surely, one could object, some masters must have cared for their servants. In the intimacy of the household, strong emotional ties must have developed between master and valet, between mistress and chambermaid, between the artisan family and their maid-of-all-work. Was it not natural that servants should identify with men and women who at the very least gave them bed, board, and protection?

That some servants were genuinely attached to those whom they served is beyond doubt. Among domestics who drew up wills in Aix and Marseille, about one in twenty named a master or mistress as one of his or her heirs.[1] Some of them bequeathed large sums of money to their employers: Marguerite Olive of Marseille left her master four hundred livres, and Jeanne Gondram left eighteen hundred livres, which she described as her savings and wages in arrears. Others, like Françoise Colombe and Suzanne Parete, named their employers or employers' children as principal legatees. But most touching were the small gifts of women like Françoise Giroud of Aix, who left her master's wife a calico apron and four muslin sheets, "begging her to accept this little present."[2]

Eighteenth-century police blotters never record feelings as such. But the attitudes and gestures described sometimes leave no doubt as to the emotions that underlay them. Auguste Reynaud had been employed by the Marquis d'Entrecasteaux for five months when the latter's wife was discovered savagely murdered in her

---

[1] This estimate is based on an analysis of 133 wills, 81 in Aix and 46 in Marseille. A total of six servants—three in each town—left a legacy to a master or mistress. The wills sampled are those of servants in the notarial archives of Aix and Marseille A.D.A. 301E to 309E, A.D.M. 351E, 363E, and 364E for the years 1715–1718, 1730–1733, 1749–1752, 1764–1767, 1784–1787.

[2] A.D.M. 351E 1153 fol. 225; A.D.M. 364E 419, fol. 419; A.D.M. 351E 1178, fol. 942; A.D.A. 306E 962, fol. 19; A.D.A. 302E 1283, fol. 457.

bed. He was in his bedroom, he told the police, when he heard of the murder:

> He combed his hair, and just as he was about to put on his shoes, Dauphiné came up crying and threw himself on the bed, crying Madame is dead. [Reynaud] ran down immediately, entered Madame's room, and found her bathing in her blood . . . he only remembers that Binet [another servant] was there as well as Monsieur who entered at the same time holding a handkerchief to his eyes; and as he rushed toward the bed, [Reynaud] put his arms around him and dragged him back to his room.[3]

It is unlikely that Reynaud invented either Dauphiné's tears or his own spontaneous gesture of compassion. To these instances of deep affection or spontaneous warmth, one could add examples from the autobiographies of servants such as Gourville, Legrain, or Madame de Staal, or of others, like Rousseau, who began their working lives as servants.[4] All of them professed to have felt affection for at least one of their employers. Late in the century, many servants were arraigned before the revolutionary courts for having followed their masters into emigration. In 1792 Pierre Chevalier, aged thirty-nine, took off with his employer, Madame de La Porte, on a trek that led them to Holland, Germany, and England, and lasted four years. Chevalier had been in the lady's employ for fourteen years. He had left his wife behind in Bayeux to work as a chambermaid for Madame de La Porte's mother.[5]

It is quite possible, then, to find evidence of the deep attachment that some servants felt for their masters. But to every such

---

[3] A.D.A. B6270, June 1784.

[4] Gourville, *Mémoires de Monsieur de Gourville concernant les affaires auxquelles il a été employé par la cour depuis 1642 jusqu'en 1698*; "Souvenirs de Legrain, valet de chambre de Mirabeau," *Nouvelle Revue rétrospective* (Paris, 1901); *Mémoires de Madame de Staal de Launay* (Paris, n.d.), p. 78; Jean-Jacques Rousseau, *Les Confessions*, I:108–112.

[5] A.D.C. 2L 152/4, Fructidor, Year XIV.

example one could pose a counterexample, a story of loathing or deceit. We have already seen the bitterness that was vented when servants put in claims for unpaid wages, and their lack of compunction about stealing or cheating. These were quite mundane occurrences, for resentment or disloyalty could drive them further still. Sometimes swindling was carried out on a grand scale when a vulnerable employer fell into the clutches of particularly unscrupulous servants. In 1772 the heirs of Monsieur de la Houblonnière of Bayeux brought a lawsuit against his former servants, Marie Le Queux and her husband, Jean Gueroult. Le Queux and Gueroult had apparently taken advantage of their master's physical and mental decrepitude to extort large sums of money from him and take over the management of his estate. They had pushed their brazenness so far as to rifle through the old man's pockets as he lay on his deathbed.[6]

Some servants physically aggressed their current or former employers, or insulted them publicly in the coarsest of manners. In Bayeux in 1772, a Monsieur de Betteville summoned his former servant Bidard to a meeting in the back room of an inn, because the servant had been threatening him with a lawsuit. The conversation soon got heated, tempers flared, and Betteville tried to eject his former employee from the room. Bidard grabbed him by the hair and dealt him a blow across the face, which Betteville countered by stabbing at the servant with a hunting knife.[7] In Aix, a master saddler named Joseph Gaillard dismissed his maidservant Anne, who protested loudly that "he would be sorry someday." He was indeed sorry a couple of weeks later when Anne descended upon his dog and crippled the poor beast, and, confronted with her misdeed, screamed at her former master that he was "a scoundrel and a thief."[8]

Perhaps masters were prepared for the animosity of servants whom they had dismissed, but one wonders how many of them

---

[6] A.D.C. 2B 1036, 1772.

[7] A.D.C. 2B 1052, December 1776.

[8] A.D.A. IVB 1250, October 18, 1774.

expected blows or insults from men and women who actually worked for them. Margouton Garcin pummeled her mistress over the head with a bunch of keys because, her hapless employer explained, "she was in a bad mood"; Joseph Nizon called his masters names "that decency prohibits from reporting"; and André Marion, the valet of a miller, responded to an order from his master with "a thousand insults" and some ungracious remarks directed at his employer's wife and sister-in-law.[9] The victims of this sort of behavior were usually masters of lower social standing. The servants of aristocrats and wealthy bourgeois would naturally have to check their violent impulses and resort to more devious tactics in order to get back at their employers. But at every level of society, callousness and resentment surfaced at least as often as attachment and trust.

Any and every sort of relationship could exist between servants and their masters. The attitudes of domestic workers ranged from indifference to devotion to deep loathing, and the attitudes of the masters themselves were just as varied and unpredictable. Yet no matter what the circumstances, masters always seemed to assume that servants owed them not just formal obedience but an allegiance that extended even beyond their time in service. Monsieur de Betteville wound up his peroration: "If these different outrages deserve punishment no matter who commits them, all the more so in the case of this man, a former servant."[10] Joseph Gaillard, the saddlemaker, spoke the same language: "One senses how vexing were these impertinent utterances, coming from a servant and directed at a master whom she had left only a fortnight earlier."[11]

Every challenge to the master's authority was met with the same mixture of outrage and incredulity. Catherine Le Rendu in Bayeux complained to the police that her master had refused to

[9] A.D.A. IVB 1234, September 24, 1766; A.D.A. IVB 1180, March 18, 1726; A.D.A. IVB 1174, October 20, 1719.
[10] A.D.C. 2B 1052, December 1776.
[11] A.D.A. IVB 1250, October 18, 1774.

pay her a half year's wages, and had called her a *bougre de salope*. The master acknowledged this, but retorted that "though this treatment may be hard on a woman, nonetheless it is not a compelling reason to quit one's job."[12] Jean Tropey of the same town complained of the misdeeds of his unruly valet Le Viandier and went on to explain emphatically that "at the time Le Viandier was his servant, and by necessary consequence, Tropey and his wife had every right to give him orders, and all of his glory should consist in obeying them." It might be true, he went on, that his wife had seized Le Viandier by the hair and beaten him, as the servant claimed, but in light of his "ridiculous disobedience" she would only have been doing her duty.[13] Here again the complaints emanate from masters of lower or middling social standing. Not surprisingly, one seldom finds traces in police blotters of cases of this sort involving the servants of very wealthy or powerful masters. But judging from the handbooks that set the standards for domestic relations in aristocratic households, wealthy masters were even more adamant in their demands for absolute obedience and *fidélité*.

Feelings are volatile quantities. One cannot hope to make sense of the ties that bound masters and servants in the eighteenth century by merely lining up specific instances of love or loathing, illuminating as such examples may be. Masters and servants were locked into a system of paternalistic relations that transcended the accidents of individual personality and life history. It was a system implemented by the masters and by and large accepted by the servants, though of course neither party consciously apprehended it as such. It was made up of deeply ingrained habits and patterns of behavior that ensured the dependency and malleability of servants. The unspoken conventions that governed the daily lives of masters and servants will tell us much more about the relationship than will the feelings consciously expressed on

[12] A.D.C. 2L 226/1, Year VII.
[13] A.D.C. 2B 856, February 1715.

such momentous occasions as the drawing up of a will or the aftermath of a fight. As Jacques Le Goff has argued, inarticulate habits and reflexes are the true stuff of the history of mentalities, which he defines as the history of "that which is mundane and automatic . . . that which escapes the individual subjects of history for it reveals the impersonal content of their thought."[14]

Of course, masters had perfectly explicit precepts to guide them in their dealings with their servants, those which were hammered out in religious tracts, sermons, and domestic handbooks. But these lofty ideals of compassion and responsibility had to be adapted to the less exalted realities of day-to-day life. Employers wanted dependent and obedient servants whose behavior they could control. In order to achieve this, they adopted methods that ranged from financial pressure to sheer physical brutality to extremely subtle forms of psychological coercion. At the same time, they allowed their servants a great deal of freedom in some areas of their lives, and struck up familiar and even intimate relations with some of them. The behavior of masters and mistresses was very often anything but Christian. But the particular brand of paternalism they adopted allowed them to maintain within the household the rigid social hierarchy that was the hallmark of their whole society.

At the most fundamental level, masters dictated the terms of the legal and financial bases of the relationship. As we have seen, they could dismiss their employees whenever they chose, while servants who departed without permission risked the loss of their wages and sometimes legal prosecution as well. Masters protected their own interests but in this way also made it clear that the covenant was really in their hands. Employers reacted with hostility to the suggestion that servants could have any control over the situation, as is evident in the story that Auguste Reynaud

[14] Jacques Le Goff, "Les Mentalités, une histoire ambigue," in Jacques Le Goff and Pierre Nora, eds., *Faire de l'histoire*, 3 vols. (Paris, 1974), III:80.

told the police in Aix in 1784. Reynaud had been serving a Monsieur de Guerit in Marseille on a six-month contract, but he left for another job after five and a half months and lost his wages as a result. His next job with Monsieur Barthe was evidently a disaster, for he left without pay after only five days. De Guerit showed unusual flexibility in allowing Reynaud to return for two weeks in order to complete the six months and recover his pay. Unfortunately, Barthe was feeling bitter about the servant and told De Guerit that Reynaud had bragged about forcing his first master to pay him his wages. De Guerit accused the servant of theft and had him beaten and thrown into prison.[15] The master had acted with benevolence as long as he felt that he controlled the situation. He only flew into a fury when it was suggested that his servant had "forced" him to hand over the wages.

Most employers acted in high-handed ways when it came to paying their servants. Legal texts were vague as to the desirable form and frequency of remuneration, and in the standard seventeenth- and eighteenth-century domestic handbooks wages were not considered an important matter. Theoretically, the master's main responsibility lay in providing food, work, and moral guidance for his servants. In the seventeenth century, some masters were reputed not to pay their staff at all. Such was Monsieur d'Angoulême who, according to Tallemant, countered his servants' timid pleas for wages with the arrogant response: "There are four streets leading to the Hôtel d'Angoulême; you may take advantage of this convenient location if you wish."[16] By the eighteenth century, however, masters universally acknowledged the financial factor in their dealings with their servants. A salary was decided upon in advance, and was paid unless the servant broke the contract or committed a serious misdemeanor, such as domestic theft. The account books of eighteenth-century masters also show that when employers dismissed their servants they

---

[15] A.D.A. B 6270, June 1784.
[16] Tallemant des Réaux, *Historiettes*, I:96.

always paid them a sum proportional to the amount of time spent in the household, no matter how small.[17]

Though these basic principles were respected, employers tended nonetheless to manipulate the financial agreement to their own advantage. Since the contract was usually established on a yearly basis, servants could theoretically collect their wages once a year. In fact, this principle of yearly payment was not at all systematically respected, since some servants drew sizable advances on their wages while others were paid by quarter or semester, and others still over several years or even decades. What with servants coming and going, drawing advances or letting wages accumulate, eighteenth-century account books are a maze of names and figures. But some method may be discernible in the overall madness.

In modest households, financial arrangements between masters and servants—usually maids-of-all-work—were at once straightforward and quite flexible. In Aix the doctor Jean-Joseph de Bruges, the farmer De Curbans, and the Eyssautier family all followed roughly the same practice: they hired maids on a yearly basis, lent them small sums of money throughout the year, and settled the balance at the end of twelve months, whether the servant was to stay on or not.[18] In wealthier households, some servants were paid at regular intervals while others—usually the

[17] These and subsequent general remarks are based on my reading of the account books in the Archives of Aix, Marseille, and Caen, and the Bibliothèque Méjanes and Musée arbaud in Aix, listed in the bibliography. Those that have proved the most useful are Bibliothèque Méjanes, Mss. 1645–1648, Livres de Raison de Louis de Thomassin, Président de Peynier; Mss. 1651–1652, Livres de Raison de Charles-Alexandre de Mazenod; Musée Arbaud MQ 65, Livre de Raison du Baron de Sannes; A.D.A. XXIV H B 41–43, Livre de Raison de Jean-Joseph de Bruges; A.D.A. XXIV H B 19–21, Livre de Raison, Famille Audiffren; A.D.C. 2E 2810, Fonds Gosselin de Manneville, Registre des Gages des Domestiques (hereafter Manneville).

[18] A.D.A. XXVI H B41–43, Livre de Raison de Jean Joseph de Bruges; A.D.M. IIIE 83, Livre de Raison Famille de Curbans; A.D.A. XXIV H B 73, Livre de Raison de Melchior et Joseph Eyssautier.

higher-ranking ones—were bound to their masters by more complex financial ties. In households where servants remained for only short periods of time, monetary dealings were quite perfunctory. A case in point is the household of Charles-Alexandre de Mazenod, a middling nobleman in Aix who employed about six servants at a time. Mazenod was forever firing servants, and as a result 135 of them entered his household over the half century between 1743 and 1792, most of whom remained less than two years on the job. The Mazenod account books are cryptic and record only lump sums of money handed over to servants every year or half year, or upon dismissal.[19] This high turnover rate certainly worked to Mazenod's financial advantage, for it allowed him to keep wages at very low levels by not having to grant his servants raises. But it is hard to imagine that many of his servants felt deeply attached to their master, with the exception of a few stable characters like the valet Bonnet whose wages doubled in the eleven years he spent in Mazenod's employ.

But this case was extreme. Few masters were that quirky or predatory, and few staffs quite that volatile. The Gosselin de Manneville family in Caen was probably closer to eighteenth-century aristocratic norms when it came to hiring and paying servants.[20] The Mannevilles were habitually served by a staff of eight or nine: a steward, a cook, a valet, a gardener, a groom, two lackeys, a chambermaid and a maid-of-all-work. The account books that they kept between 1743 and 1775 record the names of fifty-five servants. Some of them were extremely stable retainers. The steward Vergeon stayed on for nineteen years, the lackey Mutel and the maidservant Catin Le Marchand for twenty-four, and the record was held by a groom named La Rose who remained with the family for close to three decades. Other servants departed quickly, like the seven cooks hired and fired between 1769 and

19 Bibliothèque Méjanes, Mss. 1651–1652, Livres de Raison de Charles-Alexandre de Mazenod.

20 A.D.C. 2E 2810, Manneville. The analysis that follows is based on this document.

1773. Differences in commitment to the household commanded differences in modes of payment—or vice versa. Vergeon waited fourteen years to collect 2,090 livres, the lackey Lantrin was paid at the end of eleven. La Rose, who was making 40 livres a year in the 1740s and 80 livres a year two decades later, had accumulated 2,000 livres by 1771. "La Rose has left me this money until he needs it," noted Manneville. But the servants who stayed for shorter periods of time—from a few months to a decade—were usually paid once or twice a year; clearly, their relationship to their employers was different. All of this suggests that the paying of servants was by no means a standardized affair. The form and frequency of payment varied from household to household and from servant to servant within the same household. Monetary dealings only took on a routine appearance where transient servants in large households were concerned. In many, perhaps most, cases the cash nexus was complicated and obscured by endless financial transactions between masters and servants.

In many households, masters allowed their employees to draw advances on their wages. This widespread practice involved sums of money that ranged from the few sous advanced to a maidservant for the purchase of a pair of shoes to the hundreds of livres that wealthy masters lent to their valets to help them repay debts or support their relatives.[21] But in all cases the result was the same in that many servants were materially and psychologically bound to masters who in effect acted as bankers for them. This was the most common sort of transaction between master and servant; but because domestics worked for men and women who had connections, material resources, and capital, and were better educated than they, the possibilities were endless. In the Manneville household, a cook bought an annuity from the master by paying him a lump sum in cash and promising several years of free work; a very young boy named Adeline worked for three years without wages as a *petit laquais* in exchange for food and clothing and a

[21] See chapter 2.

few lessons from a schoolmaster.[22] Other domestics worked for lower wages and received a compensation in kind: the Manne-villes' cook was paid 250 livres, and was allowed to keep animal skins and trimmings of lard; the gardener's salary of 100 livres was supplemented by whatever produce from the garden the masters did not need; the doorman got 50 livres a year and fifty bundles of wood, Madame's lackey received 50 livres and an unspecified amount of wine.[23] These payments in kind may in fact have worked to the servants' financial advantage, but in any case they involved domestic workers in the household economy and reinforced their dependency on their master's largesse. Be-cause their exact value was usually left unclear, material bonuses accentuated the paternalistic character of domestic relations.

The financial embroilment of master and servant reached a paradoxical extreme in those occasional instances where masters borrowed money from their own employees. In 1720 an Aixois lawyer, Monsieur d'Albert, borrowed thirty livres from his valet André to send to an ailing sister; Louis de Thomassin, a nobleman in the same town, noted in 1755 that he had reimbursed his servant Valois of the sum of thirty-five louis which he had owed him for two years; and in 1775, a valet named Jean-Baptiste Perret sued the heirs of his master: Monsieur d'Albinot had been pumping small sums of money out of his servant for several years before his death, an arrangement he found so embarrassing that he systematically burned his account books.[24] No doubt, most servants who lent money to their employers did so of their own volition, and were promised rewards for their pains. Thomassin did record that his man Valois received a bonus of four livres when the debt was repaid. But what servant could think of leaving the employ of a master who owed him money?

In short, masters tended to deal with their more transient

[22] A.D.C. 2E 2810, Manneville.
[23] Ibid.
[24] A.D.A. MQ 186, March 1720; Bibliothèque Méjanes Ms. 1647, fol. 49; A.D.A. IVB 1252, March 27, 1775.

employees in straightforward and perfunctory ways, but where more stable servants were concerned the relationship between employer and employee was consolidated by complex financial transactions. By lending their servants money, saving their wages, providing them with payments in kind that were presented as benefits, or borrowing from them, masters made it clear that they were in a position to control their servants' finances, and thus attempted to secure their loyalty. Many servants went along with their masters and played the game willingly, especially when long-term commitment to the household held the promise of further financial rewards in the form of raises or bequeaths.

Eighteenth-century employers were singularly reluctant to raise the wages of their servants, especially of those who remained with the household for only short amounts of time. They preferred to dole out bonuses (*gratifications*) as a reward for outstanding services. But they also made it clear that their employees had no right actually to expect compensation for extra work. Louis de Thomassin recorded in his account book that he gave one of his lackeys an extra twelve livres "for the extraordinary services he performs in the household in addition to serving my son, it being understood that this cannot be a rule for the future."[25] One poor woman complained before the police in Aix that her masters wanted to pay her as a simple maidservant after she had cared for them during a lengthy illness. Her master snapped back that "the illness he suffered did not in any way change her status."[26]

When masters did raise wages, they usually bestowed this favor on those employees who remained with the household for very long periods of time. The Mannevilles very rarely increased the salaries of servants who stayed in their employ for less than ten years. They apparently preferred to raise wages when new servants entered the household. But the salaries of their most faithful retainers, Mutel, La Rose, and Catin Le Marchand, doubled over

[25] Bibliothèque Méjanes Ms. 1647, Livre de Raison de Louis de Thomassin, fol. 12, July 3, 1752.
[26] A.M.A. FF 72, January 8, 1722.

the course of twenty or thirty years.[27] In some cases, raises were roughly proportional to the amount of time spent in the household. This was the pattern in the Audiffren family in Aix. The valet, Hyacinthe Desissart, remained in their service for ten years, over which period of time his wages went up by a fifth. The wages of the lackey Beaudieu Menffre inched up by a third, from 150 to 200 livres, over the course of twenty years. The maidservant Armande was earning 100 livres in 1773, two-thirds more than the salary that she received upon entering the household thirty-four years before.[28] The paternalistic ethos that masters adopted commanded that domestic workers be rewarded not for extra hard work or efficiency, but for *fidélité*, for commitment to the household. Servants were well aware that unless they could find better-paid work in another household, they had every interest in remaining with the same masters for as long as possible. They must also have been aware that substantial bequeaths only came the way of those whose loyalty was proven by their presence at their master's deathbed.

Out of 227 wealthy Aixois who drew up wills between 1681 and 1789, 111 or 40 percent named one or several servants as legatees.[29] The legacies bestowed on servants varied with the wealth and generosity of the testator, ranging from a few sticks of furniture or assorted castoffs to very large sums of money. The constable Bessonet left six shirts to his maid Delphine, the Comtesse de Forbin bequeathed thirty livres to each of her servants, while the Marquis d'Agoult gave his head valet an entire wardrobe, the bedroom silver, ten thousand livres, and a pension for

---

[27] A.D.C. 2E 2810, Manneville.

[28] A.D.A. XXIV H B 21, Livre de Compte des Audiffren.

[29] A.D.A. IVB 112 to IVB 118. This sample of wills is drawn from the *Insinuation Laïque*. The *Insinuation* was a series of copies kept by the local *Intendance* of all of those notarial acts of which a public record had to be kept in order to prevent frauds. In practice, this means that the wills of persons of moderate or substantial wealth are usually found in the *Insinuation*, making it a conveniently synthetic source for examining the wills of the elites.

his servant's son.[30] As a rule, the servants of well-to-do masters could expect to inherit a few hundred livres, a small annuity, or a year's worth of their wages. Some masters made it clear in their wills that they were genuinely grateful to individual servants, and wanted them rewarded under any circumstances. Honorade Gazel, the widow of a bourgeois, left most of her possessions to Anne Andourine, "her servant for thirty-eight years to whom she has infinite obligations, and who cannot be rewarded enough." Andourine was to receive a bed, vast quantities of household linen, the contents of the cellar—wine, barrels, and all—and on top of this one thousand livres. Anticipating the jealousy of her family, the widow Gazel repeatedly insisted that these provisions be executed in full.[31] Without waxing quite this eloquent or insistent, many masters named servants whom they wished to reward, and attached no conditions to the bequeath.

But in most of the wills the wording was different. About two out of three of the testators specified that the servants whom they named would be entitled to the legacy only if they were still in the master or mistress's employ at the time of his or her decease. Even the warmest eulogy of a servant's virtue and devotion was likely to be capped by the brutal codicil: "If he (or she) is in my service, and not otherwise." Among the legatees of Pierre Gaillard de Longjumeau, a judge in the *Cour des Comptes* of Aix, was Magdeleine Paris,

> who has served in my house with zeal and loyalty, particularly the late lady, my mother, in the last years of her decline and during her lengthy illness, and was particularly recommended to me—a life annuity of two hundred livres and the sum of two thousand livres and my wardrobe, provided that she still be in my service.[32]

[30] A.D.A. IVB 116, fol. 219; A.D.A. IVB 112, fol. 204; A.D.A. IVB 113, fol. 308.
[31] A.D.A. IVB 112, fol. 351.
[32] A.D.A. IVB 116, fol. 439.

Many of those who drew up wills did not even deem it necessary to mention servants by name. They simply left a gift of money or an extra year's worth of wages to whichever valet, chambermaid, or lackey would be serving them at the time of their death. Others worded their wills in such a way as to ensure the continuing attachment of their favorite servants to the household even after their own decease. The Président de Bourbon left his servant Joseph Dou an annuity of one hundred livres a year "on condition that he be well-behaved and satisfy my heiress hereafter named."[33] Mademoiselle de Chenevilles bequeathed to her valet Lionnois a sum of thirty livres if he were still serving her, with an extra thirty over and above his wages for every year that he remained in the service of her great-nephew.[34]

Whether or not servants were singled out for special bequeaths or mentioned by name, it was made clear to them in this way that no matter how hard they worked or how faithfully they served they would jeopardize their chances of inheriting if they left the household before the master's death. Employers pursued the same goal when they drew up wills as when they paid wages, lent money, or granted raises. Their generosity may have been genuine, but at bottom it was aimed at securing the continuing attachment and dependency of some, if not all, of their servants. These various forms of financial pressure were, for the most part, aimed at the more promising or stable servants in the household. But masters and mistresses also needed to establish their authority over roving menials who could not be cajoled by promises of raises or bequeaths. To this end, they adopted methods that were a great deal cruder and more direct than these relatively sophisticated forms of financial pressure.

In domestic handbooks, physical punishment was recommended as a means of moral education while erratic or gratuitous violence was frowned upon as unchristian. One of the questions

---

[33] A.D.A. IVB 112, fol. 210.
[34] A.D.A. IVB 116, fol. 608.

asked of masters in a confessional guide published in 1736 was: "Did you mistreat your servants out of ill humor or anger?"[35] Needless to say, few masters, if any, drew such fine distinctions when it came to chastising their servants. Marivaux's character Arlequin spoke for many a servant when he grumbled at his master: "The marks of your friendship are always impressed upon my shoulders."[36] In a world where husbands routinely thrashed their wives, parents their children, and artisans their apprentices, employers felt few qualms about beating the men and women who worked for them. Aristocrats usually had upper servants flog their pages and lackeys, but were not loath to handle the whip themselves upon occasion. Even high-ranking masters and mistresses sometimes indulged in downright sadistic behavior. Madame d'Amet thrashed her chambermaid a first time and then locked her in the cellar, "intending to come back and beat her when she returned from town."[37]

Instances of scandalous abuse spanned the century. In Marseille in 1752 a maid named Louison was accused of stealing a coin worth six livres. Her mistress forced her to undress, and beat her unconscious. Like many another maidservant, Magdeleine Agnelle was kicked by her master when she refused to give in to his advances. As late as 1787 Marie Rolland, in Toulouse, was sequestered and brutalized for nineteen days. Two decades later Rose Isque in Marseille, suspected of stealing from her masters, was also locked in a room, harassed, and beaten.[38] Only these sorts of cases of extreme brutality ever made the records. Servants who left their masters prematurely sometimes explained that sys-

[35] Antoine Blanchard, *Essai d'exhortation pour les états différens des malades*, II:219.

[36] Marivaux, *l'Île des esclaves*, scene 1.

[37] Tallemant, *Historiettes*, II:291.

[38] A.D.M. IIB 1206, January 21, 1752; A.D.M. IIB 1209, December 31, 1760; Yves Castan, *Honnêteté et relations sociales en Languedoc 1715–1784* (Paris, 1974), pp. 586–587; A.D.A. 208U 29/129, Pluviôse, Year XIII.

tematic brutality had driven them out of their jobs,[39] but normally no servant would think of complaining to the police of the slaps, kicks, and beatings that punctuated his or her daily life. Masters were legally and morally entitled to exercise the fatherly prerogative of corporal punishment, and be they noblemen or artisans they exacted obedience from their servants by using and abusing this right.

Violence and threats of violence were the crudest means—and also the most widespread—whereby masters asserted their authority. Employers also established control over servants in symbolic fashion by stripping them of the signs of their previous identities. In many households, domestics were outfitted with clothes that were not their own and rechristened with names that their masters chose for them. Clothing could be used for purposes of coercion in several different ways. We have seen that masters could and did exert pressure on servants by withholding their personal belongings if they lost or damaged household goods, threatened to leave, or actually took off.[40] This tactic was most usually adopted by masters of lower social standing. Ostensibly it was a purely economic sanction, but it must have had some symbolic meaning as well since a servant's *hardes* represented his or her future independence from the household. If these clothes and trinkets were confiscated, the road out of service became all the more arduous.

In the eighteenth century, articles of clothing were economically important because of the high prices that they fetched. But they were also fraught with meaning in situations that involved patterns of protection and dependency. The bonds created by gifts of clothing are evident, for instance, in a series of episodes in the opening sections of Marivaux's *La Vie de Marianne*. Marianne, while not strictly speaking a servant, is in a similar position of destitute dependency, and the wicked Monsieur de Climal's

[39] See A.M.A. FF 73, August 13, 1722; A.M.A. FF 68, January 11, 1714.
[40] For instance, A.M.A. FF 66, October 6, 1707; A.M.A. FF 66, December 16, 1706; A.M.A. FF 68, July 5, 1714.

first attempt at seducing her involves mainly the purchase of clothes. Marianne soon learns of Climal's designs on her virtue, and her very first reaction is to return the garments, ripping off the cap he gave her as she showers him with abuse. Immediately after this disagreeable scene, Marianne places herself under the protection of Madame de Miran, and the covenant is sealed, once again, with clothes:

> My benefactress had me dressed as if I had been her daughter, and provided me, in this fashion, with all of the clothing I needed. You may well imagine my feelings toward her: I never could see her without being overwhelmed by transports of joy and tenderness.[41]

Masters operated under these same assumptions when they gave their servants castoffs or dressed them in liveries. As a rule, only upper servants—essentially valets and chambermaids—wore the masters' used clothing, while lower male servants were dressed in uniform liveries.[42] But giving servants expensive clothes or forcing them into uniforms were both expressions of the same impulse on the part of masters: gifts of clothing would reinforce the servants' sense of identification with, and dependency on, their masters' households.

Once a servant had been clad, he had obligations and his master had rights. In 1725 in Aix, an ex-servant named Jean Decanys begged his former employer, the Chevalier de Meynier-Francfort, to keep the police from seizing his goods. Meynier agreed, but demanded in return that Decanys's son enter his service. The boy complied and was given a whole new set of clothes, but eventually his parents removed him from the job, and the master brought the case before the police. Young Decanys had no right to leave, he argued, because there had been a moral agreement, but above all because the boy had been clad. Decanys's wife appeared as a

---

[41] Marivaux, *La Vie de Marianne*, pp. 48–49, 122–123, 156.

[42] Paul Kreiss, "The Valet in French Comedy, 1670–1730" (Ph.D. diss., Northwestern Univ., 1968), I:279–281.

witness and retorted that the position was meant to be temporary, and that the clothes "were old rags belonging to Monsieur de Meynier, and are worth almost nothing."[43] The boy's mother and his master were talking at cross-purposes: she evaluated the clothes for their monetary value, whereas he spoke of them as a symbol of his rights.

Besides being given new clothes when they entered a household, some servants were often given new names as well. Jacques Viollet de Wagnon, defending the dignity of his fellow lackeys, became indignant at the thought of servants changing their names. Jacques Cochois, he surmised, must have called himself Jasmin out of shame of his state of bondage: "For I cannot see what forced him to change his name from that of Cochois, which was his father's."[44] In fact, servants rarely gave up their names of their own volition. Masters chose names suggested to them by whim, custom, or fashion, and foisted them upon their employees.[45] The onomastic habits of masters tended to reinforce the domestic hierarchy: lower menservants were renamed, while upper servants of either sex were usually known by their last name and maidservants by a shortened version of their given name. In renaming their menservants, masters followed a number or practices that varied according to time and place. Jasmin was a botanical name, as were other popular nicknames for lackeys such as La Rose, Lépine, Lolive, or Bocage. Some employers tried to give an aristocratic ring to the names of young peasants who entered their service: in the Manneville household Jean Groscol

---

[43] A.M.A. FF 75, January 11, 1725.

[44] Jacques Viollet de Wagnon, *L'Auteur laquais, ou réponses aux objections qui ont été faites au corps de ce nom sur la vie de Jacques Cochois, dit Jasmin*, p. 36.

[45] The following discussion is based on Kreiss, "The Valet in French Comedy," II, chap. 1, and Jean Emelina, *Les Valets et les servantes dans le théâtre comique en France de 1610 à 1700*, part 4, chap. 2. Both are works of literary criticism, but in the passages cited the authors are dealing with social realities, not the names of servants in plays. The fictional names of servants—Arlequin, Crispin, and so on—were determined by literary tradition.

and Gilles Brehy became respectively Saint-Jean and Saint-Gilles.[46] Nicknames that referred to personal attributes or physical characteristics were becoming outmoded by the eighteenth century, though names like Gros-René, Petit-Jean, or La Jeunesse were still used in the provinces. By far the most common practice was that of giving domestics the names of provinces that traditionally supplied servants, whether or not these were really their birthplaces. Dauphiné was the most popular manservant's name throughout southeastern France, and in other parts of the realm servants by the hundreds were named Picard, Champagne, Flamand, Provençal, or Le Breton. Masters were less inclined to tamper with the names of maidservants, but given names like Louise, Elizabeth, and Catherine were routinely transformed into Louison, Lisette, and Catin.

The motivations of masters in their choice of names can be variously interpreted. They probably considered these nicknames more elegant than their servants' original names, though this concern with style was not always devoid of sarcasm: in Bayeux Thomas Le Boucher became Jolycoeur, and in Caen one Le Boeuf was rechristened La Rose.[47] The use of nicknames no doubt encouraged masters to look upon their servants as children or even mere commodities. Geographical surnames most likely served to underscore the poverty and foreignness of domestics from rural areas whose real or presumed origins were flung in their face with every order that the master gave. Whatever the specific implications of different names, there can be little doubt as to the overall meaning of this custom of renaming servants. The use of nicknames or aliases has usually been a characteristic feature of institutions that are cut off from the mainstream of society, and whose inmates or inhabitants are subject to highly authoritarian forms of control, such as armies, plantations, or prisons.[48] Eight-

[46] A.D.C. 2E 2810, Manneville.

[47] Ibid; and A.D.C. 2B 875, 1722.

[48] Kreiss cites a text by François Eudes de Mezeray which explains that in the eighteenth century soldiers took the names of their native provinces, of

eenth-century households were by no means as tightly organized and controlled as were, or still are, veritable "total institutions" such as monasteries, boarding schools, or asylums. But inasmuch as masters sought to establish control over the domestic sphere, albeit with varying degrees of success, they spontaneously adopted some of the methods characteristic of these sorts of institutions, humiliation, physical punishment, the stripping of names and clothes, and the parsimonious doling out of rewards and minor privileges.[49]

Brutality and coercion were not systematic, nor were they universal. Indeed, in many cases the line between manipulation and genuine closeness and concern is very hard to draw. A case in point is that of religion. The bonds that developed between masters and servants were sometimes cemented by the sharing of a common religious experience. In theory the master's fundamental responsibility toward his servants was to provide for their religious education and to make sure that they acquitted themselves of their duties toward the Church. In standard handbooks, like that of Claude Fleury, masters were enjoined to provide catechism lessons for their employees, to conduct daily services within the household, and to make sure that they took communion at least four times a year.[50] It is doubtful that many masters ever lived up to these lofty ideals. No evidence, for instance, suggests that servants were given the day off on Sunday,

---

flowers or plants, or of "some adventurous action" (see "The Valet in French Comedy," II:376); on names in American plantations, see Eugene Genovese, *Roll, Jordan, Roll: The World the Slaves Made*, pp. 443–450; for a general discussion of these institutions and the modes of control adopted in them, see Erving Goffman, *Asylums: Essays on the Social Situation of Patients and Other Inmates*, pp. 1–124.

[49] Goffman, *Asylums*, pp. 12–60.

[50] Audiger, *La Maison réglée* and Claude Fleury, *Devoirs des maîtres et des domestiques*, both in Alfred Franklin, *La Vie de Paris sous Louis XIV: Tenue de maison et domesticité*, pp. 21–22, 222.

notwithstanding the admonitions of the likes of Fleury.[51] But in other ways faith did often play an important role in the master-servant relationship. Some masters were unabashedly cynical about their use of religion as a tool for exacting obedience. Madame de Genlis in 1818, evoking the bygone mores of the Ancien Régime, lamented: "In those days religion came between you and your servant, to soften your authority and purify his obedience. What can you place between the two of you now? Surely not his confessor."[52] But this sort of amoral self-consciousness was probably not widespread.

It was assumed that masters could easily hold sway over their servants' religious beliefs. Hence, Jews were not allowed to employ Christian servants, and after the Revocation of the Edict of Nantes, Huguenot masters were prohibited from hiring Catholics—though the latter law was quickly reversed when it was discovered that it encouraged clannishness among Protestants.[53] No doubt, most masters simply hired domestics of their own persuasion, and if they themselves were devout they hired those with a reputation for piety. But isolated and lonely servants, especially women, were malleable matter for employers with strong doctrinal commitments. Barbier noted in 1728 that chambermaids provided the Parisian Jansenist party with some of its most fiercely devoted recruits: "The Jansenist party is ever stronger, and as stubborn as the devil . . . even chambermaids would get chopped to bits for its sake."[54] By the eighteenth century, Jansenism had become popularized, and as Barbier also remarked, the heresy was particularly attractive to women.[55] It is possible

---

[51] Fleury, *Devoirs des maîtres*, p. 223; Abbé Pierre Collet, *Instructions et prières à l'usage des domestiques et des pesonnes travaillant en ville* p. 121.

[52] Comtesse de Genlis, *Dictionnaire critique et raisonné des étiquettes de la cour*, 2 vols. (Paris, 1818), I:140.

[53] Henri Richard, *Du Louage des services domestiques en droit français*, p. 8; Paul-Ernest Vêtu, *De la Domesticité en France et dans l'ancienne Rome*, p. 49.

[54] Edmond Barbier, *Chronique de la régence et du règne de Louis XV*, II:29–30.

[55] Ibid; on the popularization of Jansenism, see B. Robert Kreiser, *Miracles,*

that servants played a significant role in the dissemination of a faith that may have been passed on from mistress to chambermaid, and from there spread through the popular classes. At any rate, the heresy could prove a strong ingredient in the bonds that tied mistress to maid, and sometimes split households along the lines of gender and religion rather than class.

The disorders that these patterns of allegiance could create within a household, when Jansenist women were pitted against orthodox men, are well illustrated in the diary of a Provençal nobleman, Pierre César de Cadenet Charleval. Charleval's mother, Catherine de Gueidan, passed away in June of 1754, apparently to nobody's great regret:

> She would not recognize the Pope's authority, still less the Unigenitus constitution; in sum, she was a most determined Jansenist, and took pride in it, and all the [women] zealots in the party courted her to maintain her in her erroneous opinions. . . . She had by her side a rascally chambermaid as enraged as herself, named Honnorade Louchon.

During Madame de Gueidan's agony, members of the family rallied around her deathbed, vying with one another to secure her soul—and her money. The priest who was to administer the last rites insisted that she return to the fold of the Church, but the sly old lady was not to be moved. Would she submit to the doctrine of the Church? "She said yes; but namely to the Unigenitus constitution, added the priest, to which my mother replied, 'I know nothing of that, I am no theologian.' " Also present were Madame de Gueidan's brother, "a two-faced man with no religion," who sided with the priest, and her sister, a fellow traveler, who kept muttering under her breath, "O Lord, save her from seduction, give her the strength to resist this sophistry." As if, wrote Charleval in disgust, this had been a minister from

---

Convulsions, and Ecclesiastical Politics in Eighteenth-Century Paris (Princeton, 1978), chaps. 4–7.

Geneva asking her to give up the Catholic faith! The chambermaid was silent throughout the scene, but once the men had pretended to leave the room,

> We heard Honnorade the chambermaid, who was standing behind the bed curtain, now holding my mother on her cushions and saying to my mother and to her sister, "What temptations; they are worse than the Devil, but I was sprinkling a lot of holy water over you, to keep you from giving in."[56]

In this case, heretical beliefs cemented the alliance between women in the household. But even independently of religious commitment, strong attachments were allowed to flourish between upper servants, especially, and their employers.

A spontaneous solidarity often jelled between maidservant and mistress, especially if the latter was married to a brutal, unfaithful, or peripatetic man. Court cases often reveal the depths of such attachments, and the pandemonium that they could create in the household if husband and wife were on bad terms. In 1752 in Marseille a nobleman named De Gâtines went to the length of staging the theft of his own silver spoons in order to dismiss a servant named Thérèse Rabier because he felt threatened by her attachment to his wife. He managed to get rid of the girl; but when Madame de Gâtines placed her with a friend of hers, he threatened and brutalized his wife, and forced her to have Rabier dismissed from her new job.[57]

The strongest bonds usually developed between master and manservant or between mistress and maid, but servants could also demonstrate fierce loyalty to an employer of the opposite sex. In wealthy households, servants were explicitly hired to serve one employer: they "belonged" to Monsieur *or* to Madame. Madame

---

[56] Musée Arbaud, MF 79, Livre de Raison de Pierre César de Cadenet-Charleval, entries for 1754.

[57] A.D.A. XXB 5639, March 1752.

de Liancourt, in her handbook, warned her readers against drawing such distinctions:

> One must never distinguish between one's servants and those of one's husband, nor suffer that servants make such distinctions themselves in order to avoid serving both masters equally or in order to make alliances among themselves.[58]

Nonetheless, servants did tend to form alliances and to fall into rival clans when clashes occurred between husband and wife. The d'Ollivary family in Aix, for instance, was torn asunder by rivalries that were aggravated by the geographical separation of the spouses. Monsieur d'Ollivary lived in the country with his housekeeper, Thérèse Reynaud, and Madame in town with a fiercely devoted chambermaid, Marie Pichegrude. Monsieur's servants circulated rumors that his wife was leading a dissolute life in town, and that her servants were plotting to murder the housekeeper; Madame's chambermaid told the police that Thérèse Reynaud had become "the absolute mistress of her master's house and mind," and that Madame d'Ollivary was being denied the basic necessities of life. When the marquis moved his wife to the country, the situation rapidly deteriorated, and masters and servants exchanged the most vile accusations. The village priest, brought in to testify, cautiously declared that "there was dissension in that household, and the servants were mixed up in it."[59]

Loyalty was not always thrashed into servants, nor was it entirely secured by the manipulation of such potent weapons as money or religion. In many cases attachment flourished spontaneously because of the intimate quality of master-servant relationships in seventeenth- and eighteenth-century households. Masters displayed their power in a hundred different ways, by beating, threatening, or coercing domestics, or by enmeshing

---

[58] Duchesse de Liancourt, *Règlement donné par une dame de qualité à M*** sa petite-fille pour sa conduite et celle de sa maison*, p. 27.

[59] A.D.A. IVB 1250, January 1774.

them in a web of obligations. But they also shored up the relationship by granting their servants access to their intimacy and by tolerating surprisingly large measures of familiarity and freedom.

The social and cultural gap between masters and servants may have been wide and deep, but the physical one certainly was not. Modern notions of privacy were totally alien to preindustrial society, and in the big houses of the seventeenth and eighteenth centuries daily routines were acted out under conditions of extreme physical proximity. In seventeenth-century aristocratic houses, suites of large rooms of imprecise function opened on to each other, and eating, sleeping, and conversing took place amidst a bustle of visitors, children, servants, and animals.[60] Within such houses, the spatial boundaries between masters' and servants' domains were, to say the least, ill-defined.

Masters paid little attention to the quality of their servants' living quarters, and parked them wherever space was available. The author of *L'Etat de misère* complained bitterly of the freezing garret that he used as a bedroom:

> Dans un grenier qui n'a ni porte ni serrure
> Où pendant tout l'hiver pénètre la froidure
> En un mot dans un sale et vil galetas
> Est étendu par terre un mauvais matelas.[61]

Lackeys and grooms sometimes bedded down in the stables, and inside the house even high-ranking servants were crowded into

[60] Philippe Ariès, *Centuries of Childhood*, trans. Robert Baldick (New York, 1962), pp. 391–398; Jean-Louis Flandrin, *Familles: Parenté, maison, sexualité dans l'ancienne société*, pp. 91–94; for example of floor plans, see Anthony Blunt, *Art and Architecture in France, 1500–1700*, pp. 224, 234, 238.

[61] *L'Etat de servitude, ou la misère des domestiques*, p. 19. "In an attic with no door and no lock/ Open to cold air all winter long/ In a filthy and vile sort of garret/ A rotten mattress is laid out on the ground."

small and poorly lit and heated rooms. Madame de Staal de Launay, who worked as a chambermaid for the Duchesse du Maine in the early eighteenth century, complained of being forced to crowd into a small cupboard-like room with the rest of the female staff during the day in order to keep warm. At night she shared a miniscule bedroom with another maid whose husband sometimes spent the night there, too. At Versailles it was worse, with two maids vying for space in a room with no windows, where the only alternative to freezing was risking suffocation from the fumes of the coal stove.[62] The stoves that were commonly used to heat servants' rooms could prove extremely dangerous. Barbier reported that the fumes from one of them killed two of the Abbé Dromesnil's servants, and left four others who were sleeping in the room in a sorry state: "They were ill for a long time, and the doorman is still in a state of stupor."[63] The living quarters assigned to servants were so exiguous that sometimes they were forced to share their very beds. Despite the efforts of the Counter-Reformation church at encouraging sexual purity, masters thought nothing of having servants of the same sex sleep two or three to a bed. Fleury, Madame de Liancourt, and the Prince de Conty all gave masters the same advice in their handbooks: no servants, especially pages and lackeys, should be allowed to share the same bed.[64] But at the end of the century in Angers, communal bedding was still a widespread custom.[65]

Servants did not enjoy much privacy, but then neither did their masters. In modest households, especially in the countryside, masters and servants often bedded down together. In Nor-

---

[62] *Mémoires de Madame de Staal*, p. 64.

[63] Barbier, *Chronique*, I:251.

[64] Fleury, *Devoirs des maîtres*, p. 235; Liancourt, *Règlement*, p. 116; Prince de Conty, *Mémoire de Mgr. le Prince de Conty touchant les obligations d'un gouverneur de province et la conduite de sa maison*, p. 82.

[65] François-Yves Besnard, *Mémoires d'un nonagénaire*, I:84: "It was the custom in those days [the 1790s] for not only servants, but even friends and relatives who were on good terms to sleep in twos or threes in the same bed."

mandy, Marie Alexandre told the police in 1725 that she had regularly shared a bed with her mistress and the latter's son, and was pregnant by the boy as a result.[66] In wealthy houses the lower staff usually slept in separate quarters, in dormitory-like arrangements, but upper servants settled down for the night on benches and mattresses within calling distance of their masters, sometimes in their very bedrooms.[67] The practice was widespread, and is recorded in many contemporary works of fiction. Gil Blas, in Lesage's novel, just takes a candle and huddles up in the antechamber, "in a little bed without curtains"; in Caylus's *Histoire de Guillaume*, Guillaume's wife is a chambermaid whose mistress has her sleep in the next room with the door open, much to the frustration of her newlywed husband; and in one of Mouhy's novels the heroine Agnès shares her bed with her chambermaid Babet.[68] It was considered proper for mistresses at least to share a room, if not a bed, with one of their maidservants. Madame de Liancourt advised her granddaughter:

> You should never sleep alone in a room, and should even have two women rather than one share your room if it is convenient, but not your bed; that is contrary to the respect they owe you, and goes against cleanliness and decency.[69]

The reasons for this injunction are left unclear, but presumably the nightly presence of one or more maidservants was to serve as a guarantee of the lady's virtue. If so, such precautionary measures could backfire against the master of the household: in one of her letters, Madame de Sévigné advised her daughter to move a ser-

[66] A.D.C. 2B 883, March 1725.

[67] Kreiss, "The Valet in French Comedy," I:294-297; floor plans in Blunt, *Art and Architecture*, pp. 224, 234, 238.

[68] Alain-René Lesage, *Gil Blas de Santillane*, 2 vols. (Paris, 1973), I:208; Charles de Fieux, Chevalier de Mouhy, *Mémoires d'une fille de qualité qui ne s'est point retirée du monde*, 4 vols. (Amsterdam, 1747), I:49; Anne Claude de Caylus, *Histoire de Guillaume, cocher* (Paris, n.d.), p. 75.

[69] Liancourt, *Règlement*, p. 45.

vant into her bedroom for fear that another pregnancy should endanger her health.[70]

Only a few servants actually slept in the masters' living quarters; a few chambermaids and valets slept in or near the masters' rooms; some lackeys slept in the antechambers; and some governesses and maids bedded down in the children's rooms. But during the daytime a crowd of servants was usually present in the antechambers and *garde-robes* that flanked bedrooms and drawing rooms in every house of distinction.[71] Even in the new *hôtels* of the eighteenth century, where a sharper demarcation began to appear between reception rooms and living quarters, the new smaller, more intimate bedrooms were still coupled with antechambers of equal size where domestics were permanently stationed.[72] Masters and mistresses not only tolerated, but in fact required, the constant physical proximity of servants, day and night. (See illustrations 5 and 6.)

Physical intimacy and even bodily contact with servants came easily to most employers. One aspect of this lack of self-consciousness is the ease with which they undressed in front of servants, even those of the opposite sex. Madame de Liancourt

[70] Marquise de Sévigné, *Lettres*, 3 vols. (Paris, 1953–1957), letter of December 23, 1671.

[71] Blunt, *Art and Architecture*, pp. 224, 234, 238. In these houses, the servants' quarters—kitchens and common rooms—were on a separate floor (Hôtel de Beauvais), or separated from the main reception rooms by a monumental staircase and hall (maison de Monsieur Rolland). But on the upper stories the rooms are arranged in galleries, with masters' bedrooms alternating with antechambers of equal size. In the Hôtel Lambert, the *garde-robes* and servants' sickroom were contiguous to the masters' apartments. The same overall arrangement existed in contemporary country houses in England, though in the latter the masters' bedrooms and antechambers were never as public as in wealthy French houses; see Mark Girouard, *Life in the English Country House*, pp. 128–130. There is unfortunately no equivalent for France to Girouard's fine socioarchitectural study of preindustrial elite housing.

[72] Flandrin, *Familles*, p. 92; Blunt, *Art and Architecture*, floor plans, pp. 369–371.

frowned upon such habits, but her very disapproval evokes the indifference of many employers to such bodily exposure:

> Let not one of your menservants enter your room in the morning before you are dressed, and do not uncover your bosom before them while you are dressing; for since you must hide it from strangers for fear that demons should lay traps for them, you should show the same consideration for your servants who are men and as fragile as the rest.[73]

Even late in the century, masters and mistresses felt no more qualms about stripping in front of their servants than did the kings in the presence of their courtiers. During the d'Entrecasteaux case in 1784, the chambermaid Marie Bal reported as a matter of course that she had entered to look for a handkerchief in the room where her master was dressing; Voltaire's friend Madame du Châtelet found it quite natural to have her valet pour water over her in her bath, and was surprised at the agitation that seized him.[74] There was more to these masters' attitudes than mere indifference. Within the codes of upper-class behavior prevalent in early modern Europe, prudery varied according to the social status of the person undressing and the spectator. In general, it was considered an affront to expose one's body to a person of equal or superior social status, while the same gesture in front of an inferior had the connotations of a favor.[75] One does not show one's back, one's rear, or other indecent parts to a friend, Della Casa explained in his sixteenth-century *Galateo*, but conversely, "If a great lord did such a thing in the presence of his servants or of a friend of inferior rank, he would not be showing vanity, but rather affection and sympathy."[76] Right up until the

---

[73] Liancourt, *Règlement*, p. 45.

[74] A.D.A. B 6270, June 1784; the anecdote about Madame du Châtelet was reported by Voltaire's secretary, Longchamp, and is quoted in Norbert Elias, *La Société de Cour*, p. 25.

[75] Norbert Elias, *La Civilisation des moeurs*, pp. 198–199.

[76] Ibid., p. 198.

LE BAIN.

De la Lettre ou du Chocolat   J'ai le cœur bien plus délicat
Que préfère Madame? Ah ma chère Justine,   Plus foible infiniment, hélas! que la poitrine

5. Domestic intimacy: *Le Bain*, after Romanet, late eighteenth century. (Phot. Bibl. nat. Paris)

end of the Ancien Régime, admittance to the *lever* or the *coucher* of the king was one of the highest honors to which a courtier at Versailles could aspire.

If masters were not loath to remove their clothes in front of their servants, they balked still less at direct physical contact with them. Sexual relationships between masters and maidservants were very common throughout the Old Regime. Early in the century, somewhere between one-tenth and one-third of all recorded illegitimate pregnancies occurred as a result of liaisons of this sort, though the real incidence was probably higher since wealthy masters could buy the silence of their servants or of the officials in charge of recording the *déclarations*.[77] Qualitative evidence suggests that many masters assumed their maids to be fair game, and probably willing as well. In some of the coarser popular songs and poems of the sixteenth century, it was taken for granted that the chambermaid would replace Madame in the bedroom if the latter were ill or away traveling.[78] The tone and terms unselfconsciously used by writers from Tallemant to Restif in describing real or fictional affairs of this sort suggests that the attitude of masters toward such involvements was, to say the least, very offhand. In Tallemant's chronicles we meet Monsieur d'Atis, whose relations with his wife were stormy for he "was always getting some servant with child." As for Monsieur de Monbazon, "he took a fancy to the doorman's daughter at Rochefort and it became absolutely necessary to put her in bed with him."[79] By the later eighteenth century, fictional characters like Mr. B

[77] Jacques Depaw, "Illicit Sexual Activity and Society in Eighteenth-Century Nantes," in Robert Forster and Orest Ranum, eds. *Family and Society*, pp. 165–167; Cissie Fairchilds, "Female Sexual Attitudes and the Rise of Illegitimacy: A Case Study," *Journal of Interdisciplinary History* 8:634–642.

[78] See "Chambrière à louer à tout faire," "Le Cacquet des chambrières," "Les Ruses et finesses des chambrières de ce temps," and "Arrêt Burlesque" in *Recueil de pièces rares et facétieuses anciennes et modernes*.

[79] Tallemant, *Historiettes*, II:64, 221. For a fictional illustration see Restif de la Bretonne, "La Belle bourgeoise et la jolie servante" in *Les Contemporaines*, III:128–147. For a striking example of similar attitudes across the Channel,

or Count Almaviva were depicted as villains. But just a few decades earlier the callous philandering of masters aroused little indignation.

Physical contact between master and servant also occurred daily in the guise of violence. Masters, as we have seen, were always ready to raise a hand against servants of either sex. But oddly enough, it was perhaps not common, but certainly not unheard of, that servants should fight back. Madame d'Amet's chambermaid took her revenge one day by beating her mistress, an episode which apparently cleared the air, leaving them the best of friends.[80] Legrain, Mirabeau's servant, recounted that he was attacked by one of his previous employers and defended himself with the chimney shovel. He stayed on another eighteen months, then left despite his master's entreaties that he remain in the job. And while in the service of Mirabeau, a violent quarrel with his master degenerated into blows: "He was very strong, but he saw that I was a fearless fellow."[81] The Cardinal de Retz himself is said to have fought with one of his stableboys who beat him to a pulp, and Vauvenargues, reporting the anecdote, insisted that this incident in no way wronged him in his honor.[82]

That some masters allowed servants to fight back when they beat them is an extreme—and no doubt rare—manifestation of their indifference to the formalities of the relationship. In both middle- and upper-class households, masters conversed freely with their servants.[83] They did not demand any special signs of deference, did not insist, for instance, as nineteenth-century masters would, that their servants address them in the formal third person. The fluid, unconstrained character of daily interactions between

---

see Miriam Slater, "The Weightiest Business: Marriage in an Upper Gentry Family in Seventeenth-Century England," *Past and Present* 72:39.

[80] Tallemant, *Historiettes*, II:291.

[81] Legrain, "Souvenirs," pp. 20, 107.

[82] The anecdote is reported by Vauvenargues in "Réflexions sur divers sujets," *Oeuvres complètes*, I:262.

[83] Ariès, *Centuries of Childhood*, p. 397.

masters and at least some of their servants is quite evident everywhere. It is visible in texts such as *Les Cacquets de l'accouchée*, which shows the maids gossiping at the mistress's bedside.[84] It appears in police records, in Monsieur de Saffray's troubled appeal to his coachman after the theft of his silver: "I hear the little beggar trusts you. I do not want to be his ruin; just try to get him to confess whether he stole my silver."[85]

Such informality was characteristic even of the highest-ranking masters in the realm: the Connétable de l'Esdiguières chatted with his servants every night in the kitchen, and the Duchesse du Maine played cards with her staff and passing tradesmen, hissing at her chambermaid: "I'm cheating, but then they are always robbing me."[86] Some upper servants were well aware of their masters' dependence on them, and could get away with liberties of speech that ranged from outspokenness to downright impudence. Both Madame de Staal and Legrain reprimanded their masters, and Cardinal Servient's valet one day stared at his master and blurted out: "A pox on you! I lost my bet: I had bet that you were blind in the left eye, and it turns out to be the right one!"[87] This freedom of speech and manners was essentially the privilege of upper retainers in wealthy establishments, and of the maidservants of middle-class families, of whom Audiger complained: "When you say anything to them they shout you down, try to bargain, and never fail to threaten to leave."[88] Lower servants could allow themselves no such extreme liberties.

But if not all servants were allowed total liberty of speech, most of them were granted a great deal of freedom of movement both inside and outside of the house. The whereabouts of servants

---

[84] "Les Cacquets de l'accouchée," cited in Jean-Louis Flandrin, *Les Amours Paysannes* (Paris, 1975), pp. 61–62.

[85] A.D.C. 2B 1049, May 1775.

[86] Tallemant, *Historiettes*, I:52.

[87] Legrain, "Souvenirs," p. 107; Marguerite de Staal de Launay, *Mémoires de Madame de Staal*, pp. 89–90; Tallemant, *Historiettes*, II:194.

[88] Audiger, *La Maison reglée*, p. 110.

were of little concern to the authors of domestic handbooks. Fleury suggested that domestics be given adequate amounts of food and wine at home rather than pocket money to spend in taverns; but he made it clear that he was concerned with their morals, not their mobility.[89] Nor do these handbooks mention specific areas of the house to which servants were to be confined. Presumably scullery maids and stableboys were not welcome in the masters' bedrooms, but employers were never sufficiently preoccupied over such matters to feel the need to consign ground rules to paper.

In wealthier households, upper servants, lackeys, and chair carriers were supposed to await orders in antechambers and *garde-robes* contiguous to the masters' living quarters. In practice, servants were well aware of the times at which they were to be on duty, and spent whatever free time they were allotted circulating freely both inside and outside of the house. In 1775 Pierre Perrée, who worked for the Marquis de Saffray, told the police of his actions in the two days before he was arrested for theft. He had spent Saturday afternoon drinking with various friends, first in a tavern and then at the house of a man named Perrette, and had left at eight to go serve his masters. The next day he returned to Perrette's after dinner between four and five in the afternoon, and the company repaired to a nearby tavern; at seven Perrée left them to join his master at the house of Monsieur de Couvert. On Monday morning he was back at Perrette's again, breakfasting with his friends.[90] The Marquis de Saffray may have been particularly easygoing, but while servants in other households were not necessarily given this much leeway, they always had opportunities to wander away from the house for drinks, walks, games, or shopping.[91]

---

[89] Fleury, *Devoirs des maîtres*, p. 231.

[90] A.D.C. 2B 1049, May 1775.

[91] In the d'Entrecasteaux household, Auguste Reynaud reported that on Sunday May 30, 1784 he was out walking in town between 5 and 9 P.M. At 10, various servants left the house to go fetch their respective masters from dinner parties. The coachman was out for a walk between 11 and 12 P.M. All of the

Masters and mistresses were not in the least bit inconvenienced by the close and constant presence of servants, nor, as we have seen, did they shrink from direct physical contact with them. Nor, apparently, did they feel threatened by certain manifestations of familiarity and independence, by the occasional outspokenness or impudence of their employees, or by their roving away from the household. All of this suggests that employers felt quite secure in their sense of social superiority. Imbued with the values of a rigidly hierarchical society, they saw their servants as creatures of another species, as half-witted children, animals, or objects. They could afford to let domestics share their intimacy for they felt totally shameless and guiltless in their presence. Such familiarity was but the corollary of objectification. Some vivid examples of the patronizing and degrading ways in which masters throughout the Ancien Régime handled their servants can be found in the letters of Madame de Sévigné. On a visit to the country the Marquise, who was abysmally ignorant of agricultural techniques, one day decided that the tedding of hay was a delightful occupation—for others: "Tedding is the prettiest thing in the world; you just toss hay and frolic in a field; if you know that much, you know how to ted. All of my servants set to it merrily." Unfortunately, the lackey Picard did not share her enthusiasm, and stoutly refused to go to the field, protesting that this was not his job. She continued her letter to Coulanges:

> It occurred to me that this was the hundredth naughty prank he had inflicted upon me, that he had no heart and no affection. . . . If you see him again, do not receive him, do not protect him, and remember that he likes tedding less than any boy in the world and is the least deserving of good treatment.[92]

---

servants were on duty the next morning, but before they started work at least three of them went to mass and one went shopping. A.D.A. B 6270, June 1784.

[92] Sévigné, *Lettres*, I:341–342; see also the letters of August 19 and 21, 1675,

Throughout her letters, she described the crises in her servants' lives as if these were the caprices of ill-behaved children. As for the servants whom she did not know—the objects of a great deal of trafficking between aristocratic households—they were stripped, under her pen, of any traces of humanity. To her daughter who was planning a visit to Paris she wrote: "Do not bring any pages; they are a provincial merchandise, and of no use around here."[93] On another occasion, discussing her new cook—a prized acquisition filched from another wealthy household and the one she was sending her daughter—she wrote:

> We are trying him out for dinner, and I will send you news of him. He seems clean. I would suggest that you have Surdet scrubbed; he is monstrously filthy. . . . His wages are of thirty louis, with no profits. Just see how he suits you. This is not a marriage.[94]

Such comments are not to be dismissed as just so many examples of Sévigné's notoriously nasty wit. Some seventy years later, in 1744, the letters that an obscure nobleman from Normandy sent his wife from the field contained similar instances of objectification. To Monsieur de Franval, lackeys were commodities to be bought, sold, or exchanged. "I will send you what you need to get a lackey," he wrote in December of 1744, "and I hope that you will not be sorry that you gave yours up to me or to our son. As for Monsieur La Jeunesse, I no longer wish that he salute [i.e., serve] you."[95] In a letter dated several months

---

I:814–817. On the latter occasion, the nurse who was feeding Madame de Grignan's child complained of being underfed. In the course of the ensuing quarrel, the woman felt it necessary to strip naked before Madame de Sévigné, to prove that she was not diseased, and her husband loudly protested this scandalous treatment of his wife. The Marquise wrote that the nurse was "la plus difficile, la plus méchante, la plus colère du monde," and that her husband had come up with "cent sottises."

[93] Ibid., I:696.

[94] Ibid., II:471–472.

[95] A.D.C. 2E 6645, Fonds Simon de Franval, letter of December 8, 1744.

later, in the midst of an epidemic of dysentery, Franval reported the ailments of his servants and his horse in the same breath, as an annoying series of inconveniences:

> Since I last wrote to you about that little scoundrel La Jeunesse, he has seemed to me somewhat more submissive; he was ill for two or three days, or pretended to be, then the other one in his turn had a bellyache, and just as he was recovering my horse strained its shoulder . . . in short we are suffering a whole chain of troubles and setbacks.[96]

No matter how much affection employers felt for their servants, no matter how genuine their concern for some members of their staff, it rarely crossed their minds that these men and women were beings like themselves. Masters and mistresses allowed their servants into their bedrooms, undressed before them, slept with them, confided in them, and often tolerated their impudence because domestics, in their eyes, were creatures of a different species. So firm stood the invisible barriers of status that this freedom and intimacy posed not the slightest of threats to the domestic and social hierarchy.

Such laxity and lack of self-consciousness are possible only in situations where virtual social equality is unthinkable. In the same way, masters and mistresses in the antebellum American South allowed their house slaves to sleep in their bedrooms, to circulate freely in the masters' quarters, and to express themselves freely upon occasion. Mistresses poured out their hearts to their black maids, but assumed that they were deaf and dumb when conversing in their presence.[97] In the latter case, the chasm between white and black had the same effect as the rigid stratification of Ancien Régime society: it removed all threat from intimacy, physical contact, and close emotional bonds. For the exact same reason did preachers and moralists throughout the

[96] Ibid., letter of June 13, 1745.
[97] Genovese, *Roll, Jordan, Roll*, pp. 335–353.

6. Taking liberties in front of the servant: *Le Toucher*, by Abraham Bosse, circa 1635. (Phot. Bibl. nat. Paris)

Old Regime incessantly remind their audiences and readers that master and servant were equal, that the inferior was in fact superior in the eyes of Jesus. They could afford to deliver such a message, and their readers could pay lip service to it because all concerned were well aware of how far removed from social realities were Christian notions of natural equality.

At bottom, employers were dependent upon their servants. They needed not merely to control and coerce them, but to secure their loyalty, dependency, and even affection. Fénelon admonished his readers:

> Therefore try to get your servants to love you, but without any vulgar familiarity: do not engage in conversations with them; but fear not to inquire often of their needs, affectionately, and without disdain. Let them find counsel and compassion in you; do not chide them too harshly for their faults.[98]

Even their crudest tactics for coercion—the manipulation of money, names, and clothing—were also forms of psychological control. By letting servants into their intimacy, by allowing them some freedom of speech and movement, masters did nothing more than place the final seal upon the covenant.

The high turnover rate of many servants reveals that masters had limited success in one of their goals, that of establishing long-lasting bonds with their household employees. But overall, both the ideology and the behavior of employers suggest that they more or less consciously sought to create relationships that were more than just contractual. Why, then, did they want their servants to identify with them, depend on them, maybe even love them? It may be that, as Hegel argued in his famous passage on Lordship and Bondage, a master can never rest assured of his domination unless he recognizes in some way the humanity of his bondsman. The dialectic notwithstanding, masters had very

[98] François de la Mothe Fénelon, *De l'Education des filles* (Paris, 1881), p. 71.

prosaic reasons for wanting to create such bonds. Servants performed crucial tasks for their employers outside of the household, in the world that escaped the master's direct control. In a society where patterns of patronage and deference came easily to most people, imposing authority within the household was a relatively easy matter. Masters were also well aware, however, that servants had their own interests, their own futures in mind. For this reason, they played on self-interest, on symbols, and on emotions in order to ensure that loyal and dependent workers would adequately represent their interests and their honor in the world beyond the boundaries of the household.

CHAPTER 5

The Uses of Loyalty

Some of the characteristics of seventeenth- and eighteenth-century service are so familiar to us from literary and artistic works of the age that we tend to take them for granted. Yet upon reflection they may strike us as singularly wasteful. Why did employers feel the need to surround themselves with as many servants as they could afford? Why did they insist upon unmarried live-in servants? Why did the wealthier among masters outfit their pages and lackeys in expensive liveries and allow them to remain idle for long stretches of the working day? And why the employment of so many expensive and troublesome men, when women could work just as hard, and for half the price?

The answer to these questions, broadly stated, is that many masters employed their servants not just to perform necessary chores within the household, but also as their representatives in the outside world. Under the Old Regime, the nature of domestic service was not simply defined by a two-way relationship between master and servant, but by a triangular one involving masters, servants, and "the public." The servants of wealthy masters were chosen, dressed, and trained to appear in public as living symbols of their employers' status. But they were also expected to behave actively as extensions of the masters. The roles that servants played outside of the household were often brutal, dangerous, or demeaning. But their behavior was crucial to the smooth functioning of a society in which masters, even those of mediocre status, systematically avoided direct contact and confrontation with the lower echelons of the urban populace.

This chapter will describe and interpret the public behavior of domestic servants in the towns of eighteenth-century France. It will suggest an analogy between the conduct of real servants in the public arena and the roles assigned to fictional maids and valets in the great comedies of France's classical theater. This analogy between reality and fiction may shed some light on the repercussions of the master-servant relationship on society at large, and thus help us to understand the real meaning and uses of *fidélité*.

No doubt, servants were first and foremost a practical necessity for most employers. Before the advent of more efficient forms of household management, the wealthy needed large numbers of servants to keep households of relatives, friends, and family living at a decent level of comfort. Even the more modest establishments of bourgeois or artisanal families could scarcely function smoothly without the services of women who drew water, scrubbed clothes, or kneaded dough. In this respect, the needs of eighteenth-century masters were no different from those of generations of their predecessors and descendants.

But in early modern France, employers who could afford such expenditure wanted servants who could be trotted out for display, domestics who would accompany them in each of their ventures outside of the house. That servants were used in public as emblems of their employers' wealth and dignity was universally recognized and widely accepted. Claude Fleury advised his readers to employ as few servants as possible, in order to avoid sloth and vanity. Nonetheless, he conceded:

> One must make allowances for propriety which does not permit a great lord to go alone on foot like a bourgeois, or a rich bourgeois to carry a heavy load on his shoulders. But

it seems unreasonable that a man of lower birth should have three or four lackeys following him just because he is rich.[1]

In *La Double Inconstance*, Marivaux, good bourgeois that he was, lampooned the social fetishism that made such troublesome escorts into signs of social standing:

ARLEQUIN   Incidentally, tell me something: I have spent an hour wondering what can be the use of those big gaudy ruffians who keep following us everywhere. Those are indeed strange fellows.

TRIVELIN   The Prince, who loves you, has done this to show you his benevolence; he wants these people to follow you as a mark of honor.

ARLEQUIN   Oho, so it's a mark of honor?

TRIVELIN   Assuredly.

ARLEQUIN   So tell me, who is following the people who follow me?

TRIVELIN   Nobody.[2]

Marivaux might well scoff, but many was the middle-class man who dreamed of buying himself such an honor.

From the Middle Ages to the early seventeenth century, retinues of *domestiques* usually included vassals, clients, or other dependents of the household, and reflected the master's real military and political power. As Fleury's comment suggests, however, by the late seventeenth century servants had become mere objects of conspicuous consumption.[3] The number and appearance of one's servants were primarily a function of wealth and taste, not necessarily of lineage or real power. Wealthy employers could

[1] Claude Fleury, *Les Devoirs des maîtres et des domestiques* in Alfred Franklin, *La Vie de Paris sous Louis XIV: Tenue de maison et domesticité*; pp. 211–212.

[2] Pierre Carlet de Marivaux, "La Double Inconstance," in *Théâtre complet*, I:271.

[3] Jean Louis Flandrin, *Familles: Parenté, maison, sexualité, dans l'ancienne société*, pp. 65–68; Marc Bloch, *La Société féodale*, I:223–241.

be extremely fastidious about the appearance of those servants most exposed to the public eye, a tendency that may have been reinforced in the eighteenth century by greater wealth and mobility among the elites. In 1787 the Chevalier de Miromesnil wrote a long and nagging letter to his mother in Caen, giving her advice on her servants' dress. He advised her to give her coachman a good pair of boots, and have him shine them, "otherwise he will look as if he is driving a hackney carriage." "Do not have your lackeys wear jackets," he added, "they always look scruffy." He went on to suggest cloth collars rather than velvet, and sky blue as the best color.[4]

This preoccupation with the appearance of the servants concerned not just their attire, but their height, stature, and even race. Béat Louis Muralt, a Swiss traveler who visited Paris in the 1740s, reported that in the capital fashions in servants were subject to the same whimsical variations as sartorial fads:

> Changes in fashion are no less frequent in other areas than clothes; but they can be far more inconvenient when they affect things that are harder to change. This person goes bankrupt changing his furniture which is still new but no longer a novelty; that one changes his dinnerware which is of good quality but no longer in fashion; another gets tired of his house before it is built because another way of building has come about. And yet another dismisses his servants though they serve him well, because they are no longer stylish. For even servants are subject to this law, even among womenfolk who it seems should not need to change them. Fashion allows them to be served by men, and gives them the pleasure of such changes. Sometimes one must have small lackeys, sometimes big ones, and sometimes pages. Some have wanted Moors to serve them. I heard it recently said that mutes would be a good idea and I have no trouble

[4] A.D.C. 2E 2862, Fonds Graindorge d'Orville, letter of November 8, 1787.

believing this, short of another sort of servant that French *politesse* will never allow them to introduce.[5]

Only the wealthy could afford to employ servants whose primary function was to display their masters' wealth and taste. There were two different types of servants, wrote the Abbé Collet in 1758. Most of those who worked in houses of the first rank were hired "pour la décence et pour la montre." These domestics, he explained, only put in a few hours' work in the morning and spent the rest of the day serving at their masters' tables and waiting for their orders in antechambers. More than any others, he added, they were exposed to the moral dangers that derived from idleness. Others, on the contrary, were expected to work very hard, "those who serve in the country, those of artisans or of the common bourgeoisie, but also many of those who, though employed in noble households, are only accepted on condition that they perform a fair share of work."[6] The servants who were used as status symbols were those whose functions placed them in the public eye, such as pages, lackeys, coachmen, and doormen. All of them were male. Not very many employers could afford the luxury of these male servants whose wages were twice as high as those of women, especially since they were left idle for half of the day. But the employment of male servants for reasons of prestige was an ideal assiduously imitated by all who aspired to gentility.

Though some urban artisans and tradesmen kept valets to help with the heavy work, in larger towns the great majority of menservants were in the employ of wealthy and prominent masters. As a rule, menservants were to be found in households that employed staffs of three or more servants. Of the 1,518 servants listed in Aix's *Capitation* list for 1710, 31 percent were male; 9 out of 10 of these menservants were employed by the clergy, the

[5] Béat-Louis Muralt, *Lettres sur les anglois, les françois et les voiages*, I:241–242.

[6] Abbé Pierre Collet, *Instructions et prières à l'usage des domestiques et des personnes travaillant en ville*, pp. 58–59.

aristocracy, and by noble and non-noble *parlementaires* and office-holders. The city's oligarchy of noble *parlementaires* employed a total of 510 servants (an average of 3.7 per household), over half of whom were male. The nobility of the sword averaged only 1.6 servants per household, a total of 223, one-third of whom were male. The families of non-noble lawyers and officeholders employed on average 1.4 servants per household; only 1 out of 4 of their servants were men.[7]

In Toulouse in 1698 the *parlementaires* were less firmly entrenched than their counterparts in Aix. In that city, the titled nobility had the more elaborate households and employed the most male servants, but they were imitated by social climbers in the city's administrative bodies and in the legal profession.[8] Lyon was a city without a *parlement*, but the officers of the Lyonnais *Cours des Monnaies* hankered after social and political promotion, and tried to pose as counterparts of neighboring Grenoble's *parlementaires*. It is telling that the proportion of lackeys among the menservants working for the officers of the *Cour des Monnaies* grew steadily from 59 percent in 1706 to 85 percent in 1759.[9] All over France *anoblis*, public officials, lawyers, and assorted Monsieur Jourdains emulated the old aristocracy by hiring unruly adolescents and decking them out in livery.

The specific ways in which aristocrats and all those who imitated them chose and used their servants are classic examples of the socioeconomic behavior that Thorstein Veblen once dubbed conspicuous consumption. As we have seen, many servants en-

---

[7] These figures were calculated from Aix's *Capitation* for 1701, A.C.A. CC13. Forty-eight employers listed as *bourgeois* employed one servant each; only four of these servants were men.

[8] Cissie Fairchilds, "Masters and Servants in Eighteenth-Century Toulouse," *Journal of Social History* 12:369–370.

[9] Maurice Garden, *Lyon et les lyonnais au XVIIIe siècle*, pp. 508–509; Bernard Fradin, "Domestiques d'établissement et domestiques de maison à Lyon au XVIIIe siècle" (Mémoire de Maîtrise, Univ. de Lyon, 1976), pp. 15–52.

joyed a number of highly visible benefits, such as fine clothes, material security, or long stretches of leisure. All of these advantages were in fact designed to show off the wealth and power of the men and women for whom servants worked.

The ideal aristocratic household was characterized by the employment of large numbers of men. According to Audiger's classic handbook, *La Maison Réglée*, the staff of a *grand seigneur* should comprise thirty to thirty-six servants, all of them male except for the scullery maid. The gentleman's counterpart, *la dame de qualité*, could content herself with fourteen servants, only three of whom should be women.[10] In reality only a tiny number of eighteenth-century employers had the money or felt the need to run a household on so lavish a scale. The richest members of the *Parlement* of Paris had staffs of twelve to fifteen servants, and the average *parlementaire* in the capital city employed about eight.[11] In Aix at the end of the seventeenth century, only eight employers kept more than ten servants, and in Bayeux in 1768 the largest household was that of the bishop, with a staff of seventeen.[12] But no matter what the size of their household, wealthy or status-hungry masters did their best to afford the services of men. The expensive *hôtels* of the Parisian Faubourg Saint-Germain were staffed almost exclusively by men,[13] but even middling officials and impoverished nobles in provincial towns like Aix or Bayeux managed to

[10] Audiger, *La Maison réglée*, in Franklin, *La Vie de Paris sous Louis XIV*, pp. 11–12, 68–69.

[11] François Bluche, *Les Magistrats du Parlement de Paris au XVIIIe siècle*, p. 341.

[12] Jacqueline Carrière, *La Population d'Aix-en-Provence à la fin du XVIIe siècle*, p. 73; Jean-Paul Coste, *La Ville d'Aix-en-Provence en 1695: Structure urbaine et société*, II:717; the data on Bayeux is from the *Capitation* of 1768, A.M.B. C 4538.

[13] Jean-Claude Goeury, "Evolution démographique et sociale du Faubourg Saint-Germain" in Maurice Reinhard, ed., *Contributions à l'histoire démographique et sociale de la Révolution Française*, 2nd series (Paris, 1965), p. 43.

include one lackey among their staff of three or four. In Ancien Régime towns, the highest proportions of menservants were always to be found in those districts inhabited by nobles or wealthy commoners.[14]

Masters did not choose their menservants indiscriminately. They often went out of their way to select men and boys whose appearance was in some way remarkable. At the very least they tried to secure the services of handsome, well-built youths: a good *physionomie*, a *belle figure* were topmost among the qualities required of prospective lackeys and pages.[15] When Madame de Franval wrote to her husband of the hiring of a young lackey, the first thing that she mentioned was that he was "jeune et d'une figure revenante."[16] Some employers, especially women, surrounded themselves with graceful young pages, while others on the contrary collected the tallest and sturdiest fellows they could find, preferably foreigners or even blacks. A Moorish page, explained the caption on a seventeenth-century fashion plate, was the ideal accessory for a lady who wished to show off a pale complexion.

In both Paris and Lyon, Swiss and German servants were much sought after, and usually installed as doormen at the thresholds of wealthy houses. Early in the century one author complained that most doormen in Paris were from Switzerland or other foreign

---

[14] Aix's *Capitation* of 1701 lists about one male servant to two females in the four wealthier central districts of Saint-Jean, Les Augustins, Bellegarde, and the Bourg Saint-Sauveur. Only in the artisanal Quartier des Cordeliers did female servants outnumber males by four to one (A.M.A. CC 13). In Lyon under the Revolution, one-third of the servant population of the town lived in the wealthy Section of the Federation, consisting of 36 percent of the town's male servants and only 15 percent of the females. By contrast, 18 percent of the women but less than a tenth of the men lived and worked in the popular Section of La Halle aux Blés. Garden, *Lyon*, p. 249.

[15] *L'Etat de servitude ou la misère des domestiques* (Paris, 1711), pp. 7, 16; Duchesse de Liancourt, *Règlement donné par une dame de qualité à M*** sa petite-fille pour sa conduite et celle de sa maison*, p. 117.

[16] A.D.C. 2E 6645, Fonds Simon de Franval.

7. Servants for display: A lady and her black page, fashion plate,
circa 1689. (Phot. Bibl. nat. Paris)

parts, that French doormen affected the appearance and manners of foreigners, and that all of them were extremely rude.[17] On the eve of the Revolution, Sébastien Mercier also noted this, tongue-in-cheek: "You should learn, sir, that only the bourgeois have doormen: gentlemen of quality have *suisses*"[18] In Lyon, if male servants were not foreign, they came from the northern and western provinces more frequently than did members of any other occupational group.[19]

In different ways, the appearance of male servants was meant to signal the social and economic power of their employers. If the employment of very young or very small boys suggested to the public the nurturing capacity of a rich family, the use of big, strong men was an extravagant display of their wealth. Be they German or Swiss, husky peasants from Normandy or the Massif Central, or even blacks imported from Africa, these sturdy men spent much of their time in conspicuous idleness waiting in antechambers and at doorsteps. The more powerful the servant, the more he displayed the waste of valuable male energy that his master could afford. Veblen himself pointed out that "the leisure of the servant is not his own leisure."[20] The physique, attire, and attitudes of servants all served to highlight their role as extensions of the master's household and vicarious consumers of his wealth.

We have already seen what the livery meant to servants and to others around them, and the role that clothes played in the relationship between master and servant. But these elaborate costumes were first and foremost designed to impress the outside world. An Italian traveler who visited Paris late in the seventeenth century was shocked at the luxury of servants' costumes, and speculated that the French capital must have been on the verge of ruin:

[17] *Devoirs généraux des domestiques de l'un et l'autre sexe envers Dieu, leurs maîtres et maîtresses*, p. 151.

[18] Louis-Sébastien Mercier, *Le Tableau de Paris*, X:141.

[19] Garden, *Lyon*, pp. 251–252.

[20] Thorstein Veblen, *The Theory of the Leisure Class*, p. 60.

Now that lackeys and coachmen have begun to wear scarlet and feathers, and that gold and silver have spread even to their clothes, it seems that excessive luxury should come to an end, since nothing can so effectively disgust noblemen from gold adornments as seeing such clothes on the backs of the most vile creatures in the world.[21]

The history of eighteenth-century fashion was to prove him very wrong indeed. Masters continued, right up to the eve of the Revolution, to outfit their servants in modish and expensive garb. The inventory of an army officer in 1788 listed a glittering wardrobe for his servant, complete with gold-braided hat, embroidered jackets, and velvet waistcoats.[22] Late in the century, writers continued to grumble at the elaborate costumes and swords sported by the servants of the rich.[23]

The dress of servants was meant to symbolize their allegiance to the master and household. In medieval times the main color and facings of the livery were those of the family coat of arms, and were worn by every subordinate member of the household, including noble followers and members of the clergy.[24] Up to the nineteenth century, the ceremonial dress of servants was often an elaborate version of the fashion of preceding times. Lackeys in the seventeenth century wore the ruffs and short bloomers of the previous century, just as nineteenth-century footmen were dressed on formal occasions in knee breeches and frock coats. The archaic styles of these costumes were no doubt visible reminders of the family's ancient lineage: pages and lackeys had to run around sporting sartorial advertisements of their employers' ge-

[21] Jean-Paul Marana, *Lettre d'un sicilien à un de ses amis*, pp. 26-27.

[22] A.D.C. 2E 2861. Fonds Graindorge d'Orville.

[23] Joseph Berthélé, ed., *Montpellier en 1768 et 1836, d'après deux documents inédits*, p. 69; Denis Turmeau de La Morandière, *Police sur les mendians, les vagabonds, . . . , les filles prostituées, les domestiques hors de maison depuis long-temps, et les gens sans aveu*, p. 141.

[24] Phillis Cunnington, *The Costume of Household Servants from the Middle Ages to 1900*, pp. 16, 44.

nealogies. Veblen, again, remarked that servants, like wives, have often worn ornate and uncomfortable costumes, clothes that were visibly expensive and inconvenient because they served no other function than to display the master's or husband's ability to pay and to keep servant or wife away from productive work.[25] Comfort matters little when clothes are worn on behalf of somebody else.

Nearly all servants, male and female, lived in the master's house, and as a rule they were unmarried. Coresidence and celibacy were required by most masters of all servants, male and female, and were characteristic of preindustrial service. Both declined in the nineteenth and especially the twentieth century.[26] There were of course obvious practical reasons for both these requirements, but they can also be interpreted as forms of ostentation. Feeding and sheltering an employee as well as having him wear clothes that he very obviously could not have bought for himself are all signs that point to where the wealth and power lie. The argument here again is Veblen's. When leisure and consumption are vicariously performed by servants, he argued, they must reside with their patron "so that it may be plain to all men from what source they draw."[27] A similar argument could apply to the unmarried status of servants. The masters' insistence on celibacy is maybe comparable to the vows of chastity demanded of postulants to monastic orders, since ideally all of a servant's energy and commitment were to be devoted to the service of his or her master, as those of the monk are to his God. The fact that servants were unmarried made it clear to the world, as did their costume and place of residence, that these were utterly dependent creatures whose only source of income and focus of allegiance was the master's household.

[25] Veblen, *Leisure Class*, pp. 181–183.

[26] On the requirement that servants be unmarried, see Flandrin, *Familles*, p. 67. The decline in proportions of unmarried servants was slow, however. In 1901, 56 percent of all male servants but only 21 percent of all females were married; see Marcel Cusenier, *Les Domestiques en France*, p. 268.

[27] Veblen, *Leisure Class*, p. 78.

For the benefit of the public, servants were cast into the role of extensions of their masters, a role that was specifically required of domestics hired for display, but which all of them, from stewards to scullery maids, were supposed to play. But how well and how willingly did they act out the script written for them? One may well wonder how many really identified with their masters' interests and reputations, like the ironically named Honour in Fielding's *Tom Jones*, whose

> pride obliged her to support the character of the lady she waited on, for she thought that her own was in a very close manner connected with it. In proportion as the character of her mistress was raised, hers likewise, as she conceived, was raised with it; and on the contrary she thought the one could not be lowered without the other.[28]

There can be no question that some servants actually internalized their masters' values to the point of self-consciously aping them. The delusions of grandeur of an Aixois valet named Louis Morard appear clearly in the letter he wrote to his sweetheart Isabeau Roubaud, the daughter of an attorney. Morard's missive may well have been dictated to a public scribe: the calligraphy is beautiful, the spelling near perfect, and the grammar barbaric. He informed Isabeau that since the arrival of the courier from Aix, he had been suffering the torments of Hell, "which joined to the indisposition I suffered as I was leaving Aix very nearly laid me in bed, nay even in the grave, since I learnt that the object of my affections was ill." After a long disquisition on Morard's yearnings for his friend, the letter ends on a perilous syntactic pirouette: ". . . begging you furthermore to remain convinced that not a soul in the world could be with more respect and attachment than I have the honor to be, my very dear lady, your very humble and obedient servant."[29] Morard, the son of a

---

[28] Henry Fielding, *Tom Jones*, p. 253.
[29] A.D.A. IVB 1168, June 16, 1711.

farmer, must have learned to compose in this style by imitating his master, the Baron de Viens. In this case the veneer was thin, for Morard's pretensions to gentlemanly elegance collapsed when Roubaud sued him for seduction. The lady was no better than a whore, he snapped, "and if she got pregnant at that time she's been working at it for a while."[30]

But few servants had such pretensions or delusions. They were well aware of the social gulf that separated them from their employers, and the feelings that they harbored in private toward them were often, as we have seen, anything but warm. But public life was a different matter. Contemporaries were quick to complain of the high-handed and affected behavior of the servants of the rich. The seventeenth-century moralist La Bruyère used it as a parable of misplaced human vanity: "Unless they have more wits than is usual for their sort, the doorman, the valet, and the liveried henchman do not think of themselves in terms of their low birth, but of the level of fortune of those whom they serve."[31] Around the same time, the traveler Marana professed outrage at the insolence of Parisian lackeys, and much later, in the 1760s, a police official echoed his complaint: "They often outshine their masters with their impudent and affected behavior which ill behooves their servile condition."[32] The novelist Mouhy complained that servants were so deeply impressed with the status of high-ranking masters that they looked down their noses at subsequent employers of lesser status: "Inflated by the imaginary honour of having served in better houses than our own, they chafe at the indignity of losing rank and of having to obey masters whom they consider so far below those whom they have previously served."[33]

---

[30] Ibid.

[31] Jean de La Bruyère, *Les Caractères*, p. 229.

[32] Marana, *Lettre d'un sicilien*, pp. 27, 32–35; Turmeau de La Morandière, *Police sur les mendians*, pp. 141–142.

[33] Charles de Fieux, Chevalier de Mouhy, *Mémoires d'une fille de qualité qui ne s'est point retirée du monde*, 4 vols. (Amsterdam, 1747), III:5–6.

Retainers of the wealthy and powerful were known to brag about their masters' status, and could be very fastidious about the consideration due to their employers in public. An episode of the Fronde in Aix, the Journée de Saint-Sebastien, was touched off by one of the Comte d'Alais's henchmen who attacked a lackey belonging to the Conseiller de Saint-Marc. The lackey had offended him by staring at the count without removing his hat.[34] Barbier's *Chronique* records many other such stories of servants bickering and fighting over the dignity of their respective masters.[35] Such demonstrations of solidarity and vicarious pride were by no means confined to the aristocracy of service. Domestics who worked for men and women of middling or mediocre status would also rise in angry defense of their employers' interest or honor. In 1717 the maidservant of Monsieur de Riquety, a bourgeois of Aix, picked a fight with an apothecary who had been filing suits against her master. She reportedly screamed at the man's wife that her husband was "a wretched *montagnard* with property only two days old, who wanted to get the better of people who had been rich for a hundred years."[36] As some historians of Ancien Régime urban society have remarked, servants almost always upheld their masters' interests when dealing with the outside world.[37] No matter what their private feelings, no

[34] Roux-Alpheran, *Les Rues d'Aix, ou recherches sur l'ancienne capitale de la Provence*, 2 vols. (Aix-en-Provence, 1846), I:117–118.

[35] One such story—no doubt apocryphal but revealing nonetheless—concerns the coachman of the Abbé Dubois. Its point is a pun that defies translation: "Son cocher se querelloit avec le cocher de M. l'Archevêque de Reims, qui est Mailly. Chacun d'eux s'échauffoit sur la qualité de son maître; le cocher de l'archevêque de Reims dit que son maître sacroit le Roi. 'Voila grand'chose, dit l'autre cocher, mon maître sacre Dieu tous les jours!' "; Edmond Barbier, *Chronique de la régence et du règne de Louis XV*, I:39.

[36] A.D.A. IVB 1172, June 14, 1717.

[37] Yves Castan, "Mentalités rurale et urbaine en Languedoc," in *Crimes et criminalité en France sous l'Ancien Régime* (Paris, 1971), p. 142; Jeffry Kaplow, "Sur la population flottante de Paris à la fin de l'Ancien Régime," *Annales Historiques de la Révolution Française* 39 (January–March, 1967):4.

matter who their employers were, they tended in the public arena to fulfill the role that was expected of them by behaving as loyal emissaries of their masters. If their behavior inside the house was often ambiguous, their public demeanor usually was not. Outside the household, servants almost unfailingly espoused their masters' interests and rose up in defense of their honor.

Servants were often accused of brutality and arrogance, especially in their dealings with the laboring poor. Even masters, or those who wrote in their behalf, deplored the ways in which servants victimized their alleged social inferiors. The Prince de Conty made a note in his handbook to put a check on the obnoxious behavior of stewards, maîtres d'hôtel, and other servants who tended to "vex and do violence" to paupers and debtors.[38] Another author, writing of valets, fretted to much the same tune:

> They must not keep outsiders from being admitted into the master's presence during the time reserved for such purposes; it is tyrannical indeed when for instance a poor worker, a merchant, or some other who wants to speak to the master is only admitted if he buys permission, so to speak, from the *valet de chambre*.[39]

These authors may have been well-intentioned, but viewed in the context of contemporary realities their disapproval rings hollow. Servants who harassed debtors and turned paupers away from the door were merely performing one of the tasks assigned to them by their masters. In a society where the elites avoided, whenever possible, direct contact with their social inferiors, servants were crucial intermediaries between the rich and the poor. As Yves Castan observes, the barrier of servants that stood between the master and the populace was a screen that filtered "relation-

[38] Prince de Conty, *Mémoires de Monseigneur le Prince de Conty touchant les obligations d'un gouverneur de province et la conduite de sa maison*, p. xix.

[39] *Devoirs généraux des domestiques de l'un et l'autre sexe envers Dieu, leurs maîtres et maîtresses*, pp. 132-133.

ships with the community, the choice of artisans and tradesmen, and the recommending and choice of new servants."[40]

The daily routines of servants put them in constant contact with the outside world. They performed all sorts of transactions which their masters could not engage in themselves for fear of jeopardizing their safety and dignity. The nature of these tasks did nothing to bolster the popularity of domestic servants in society at large. They bargained their way through the shopping duties, hired some menial laborers but denied others work, hounded debtors and slammed doors in the faces of creditors, turned visitors away from the threshold or the antechamber. Some were entrusted with important duties, and were expected to throw their weight around. In 1716 the valet of an important town official in Aix filed a suit against a mason who had executed a job improperly. The valet had clearly been in charge of the whole business: "He had asked surveyors to report on the state of the building, and they declared it necessary to effect repairs immediately, to which end he had given an estimate to [the mason] Brun."[41] Women, too, were entrusted with these sorts of responsibilities. Jeanne Sylvestre, the chambermaid of a wealthy *conseiller*, Monsieur de Valabre, was apparently put in charge of town-country liaisons: in 1714 she came before the police on behalf of one of Valabre's tenants who was owed eighteen livres by a carter in town.[42]

More commonly, servants were sent to collect debts, either directly or through legal channels. In August of 1718 the maidservant of Mademoiselle de Martin filed a complaint against two different parties, Jacques Saurin, who owed her mistress nine livres, and Mademoiselle d'Oulière, who owed her three.[43] If carried out directly, such missions were often attempted at the peril of life and limb. In 1762 Marguerite Boutier, who worked for the brothers Dreveton, was sent to collect a debt from a carter

[40] Yves Castan, *Honnêteté et relations sociales en Languedoc, 1715–1780*, p. 284.
[41] A.M.A. FF 70, fols. 91–92, September 3, 1716.
[42] A.M.A. FF 68, fol. 194, March 5, 1714.
[43] A.M.A. FF 71, fol. 83, August 4, 1718.

named Pierre Martin. She was thrown out the first time, but her masters sent her back. Martin greeted her with screams of *gueuse, foutue laide, mariasse,* dealt out a few kicks and slaps, threw her on the ground, and jumped on her. Boutier came before the police with a bruised cheek and several tufts of hair missing.[44] Anne Hermitte was treated in much the same way by the tenants of her master, a perfume merchant who sent her back again and again to draw water from their well, knowing perfectly well what was in store for her.[45] If servants acted in arrogant or brutal ways, if they invoked their masters' status and power, it was for very understandable reasons of self-protection.

In July of 1720 an angry Parisian mob lynched the coachman of the Scottish embezzler John Law. In September another crowd pelted his coach and servants with rocks and mud, to cries of "There goes the livery of that wretched scoundrel who won't pay the ten livre notes!"[46] Barbier, who reported these events, told a story thirteen years later of two very drunk Parisian rakes going to pick a quarrel with a certain Madame Hatte, who had offended their hostess, Madame de Saint-Suppli. Madame Hatte was out when they arrived at her house, and they took out their anger by raping her chambermaid as a "sacrifice."[47] These stories, the first of violence against the retainers of a public figure, and the other of the private dishonoring of an innocent chambermaid, are not unrelated. Similar but less dramatic incidents involving the victimization of servants occurred daily on the streets of eighteenth-century French towns. Servants were easy targets for all who resented their masters, and as such were frequently exposed to insults and attacks vicariously directed at their employers.

The employees of unpopular masters naturally suffered the most. In Aix in the early thirties, Joseph Augier, the valet of an English gentleman, was persecuted by a stridently anglophobic

[44] A.D.A. IVB 1227, September 1762.
[45] A.D.M. IIB 1235, November 6, 1786.
[46] Barbier, *Chronique,* I:49, 66.
[47] Ibid., II:412.

carpenter named Michel. The carpenter never missed an occasion to pour abuse on Augier, "reproaching him with being the servant of an Englishman, that one must have no honor to do such a thing . . . the English are scoundrels and it takes greater cads and rascals than they to serve them."[48] But most servants were exposed to attacks simply because they got caught in the midst of a crossfire of animosity between their masters and other towns-folk. They were treated as scapegoats by all of those who, for one reason or another, bore a grudge against their employers. In Bayeux in 1723 the merchant Etienne Le Maître filed a complaint against an unfriendly neighboring family, the Bethons. Yves Bethon had sent his sons to rough up Le Maître's maidservant, Elizabeth Gosset. A few days later, Madame Bethon cornered the girl in the courtyard and lashed out at her: "Go tell your master that I say he's a bankrupt, a thief and a forger."[49] Fifty years later in the same town, the innkeeper Denis Hardy complained of the jealousy of his next-door neighbor, the blacksmith Michel Le Guelinel. Le Guelinel and friends had spent part of the previous night beating a loud tattoo on the window of Hardy's maid, and had pounced on his valet when he came out to make them stop.[50] In Aix at mid-century, Monsieur de Bourges provoked the ire of Jean-Baptiste Cay by telling the police of Cay's illegal gambling parties. Cay trapped his enemy's housekeeper one day: "He hurled the most foul and heinous insults at her, called her a whore and the plaintiff's slut, that she had been on the galleys, and indeed only a vile creature like herself could work for the plaintiff."[51]

Servants took the brunt of much of the hostility that was in fact aimed at their masters in conflicts that were often shot through with social tensions, and opposed rich to poor, or commoner to nobleman. Such was the fate of Suzanne Vandry of Bayeux, the maidservant of an impoverished nobleman, François Le Vaillant

[48] A.D.A. IVB 1189, September 19, 1733.
[49] A.D.C. 2B 878, June 1723.
[50] A.D.C. 2B 1060, August 1779.
[51] A.D.A. IVB 1222, August 1758.

de Cabernon. The gentleman was having trouble with a cantankerous cotenant named Gouet who took out his resentment by leaving trash at Le Vaillant's doorstep, nailing abusive posters to his door, or setting off firecrackers under his window, and was in the habit of referring to Le Vaillant as the *gueux de gentilhomme*. The usual victim of the Gouet family's persecutions was, of course, the unfortunate Suzanne. Gouet's wife and daughters forced her to sweep up refuse in the courtyard, remove dirt from the well, and threatened to break her pitcher when she went to draw water. Le Vaillant scolded his maid for giving in to the Gouets' intimidation, and from his own secure vantage point waxed indignant before the police about "the vexation of being scorned in this way through his servants."[52]

Servants were not always the passive victims of verbal and physical aggression. They responded to attacks whenever possible with their own share of kicks, slaps, and violent abuse. But violence was dealt out just as it was suffered, within the codes dictated by domestic solidarity. If servants got into fights on their own behalf, their employers usually got involved in one way or another. In Aix in 1728 the maidservants of Madame de Meynier and Monsieur de Rians got into a tussle over some spilled oil. Insults were being exchanged as Madame de Meynier arrived on the scene. "What does that one want?" Rians's servant pointedly inquired, and got a slap across the face for an answer. "You boor!" screamed Madame de Meynier. "Boor yourself," answered the servant, who ran to take refuge in her master's kitchen where Monsieur de Meynier caught up with her and beat her with the stump of his sword.[53]

Most often, though, it was the masters who incited their servants to perform acts of aggression which they themselves would not carry out. The servants rarely hesitated to comply. In poorer

[52] A.D.C. 2B 1041, 1773.
[53] A.D.A. IVB 1182, March 9, 1728.

households, this could happen right within the family. Madame Bertot, the wife of an Aixois artisan, resented the presence of her father-in-law in the house and made no bones about insulting him. But she dared not lift a hand against him, and when a quarrel broke out one day she got the maid to hurl a stone at the old man's head.[54] More usually, masters pushed their servants to carry out violence against rival families. The most brutal instances of this sort of deferred violence took place in the countryside where masters used their valets and even their maids as thugs. In the small parishes around Caen and Bayeux, the standard reaction to the appearance of a stranger or an enemy was that of Michel Fontaine, who hounded his neighbor Le Garruel, "telling his servants to throw stones at that *bougre de malbourou*"; or that of the widow Gaussey who greeted an outsider by "calling her daughters and maids and saying kill me that dog."[55] But the same thing happened in town. Months or years of hostility would build up to violent encounters, of which servants were usually the protagonists and the main victims.

One such feud in Bayeux involved two families—that of Madeleine Le Mavois, a wealthy property owner, and her neighbors, the Acards. The Acards systematically undermined Le Mavois's household by terrorizing and attacking her maids and laborers. In 1715 she filed a complaint against her neighbors because their servant, Marie Constantin, egged on by her masters, had battered Le Mavois's maid over the head with a pitchfork.[56] In Aix in 1724 the bitter hostility between Gaspard Donneau and Joseph Clergue, innkeepers on the same street, was mainly acted out by their respective maids, who happened to be sisters. The two women were at each other's throats every time they met on the street, encouraged by their masters who remained at a careful distance. On one occasion Clergue's wife yelled at Donneau's wife

---

[54] A.D.A. IVB 1238, December 1767.
[55] A.D.C. 2B 859, October 2, 1716; A.D.C. 2B 857, June 16, 1716.
[56] A.D.C. 2B 856, June 1715.

that she was "an old slut and a fat whore," and handed her maid a distaff, urging her to "Hit that old slut with it!"[57]

The violence carried out by servants was often just an acting-out of their masters' resentments and hostilities. In these eighteenth-century towns, the threat of physical aggression was ever present. "I'll knock you out," "I'll strangle you," "I'll murder you" were the cries, recorded in police blotters, that punctuated the most trivial of quarrels. But masters who wanted to maintain a dignified appearance shied away from direct physical confrontation with one another or their inferiors, and servants could rarely allow themselves to raise a hand against a superior. Violence was therefore acted out vicariously.

Animals, for instance, were sometimes used as targets by those who wished to vent anger at their owners but did not dare initiate the physical clash. In Marseille, Rose Chapelein complained that the locksmith Argerot, who bore a grudge against her, had sent his maid out to mistreat her cat. When she reprimanded the servant, the latter dealt her a kick and Argerot, "delighted that his servant had taken advantage of this opportunity," came out and added a few insults to the injury.[58] Thus, feuds that erupted into violence usually involved not only whole families, masters, wives, servants, but even their animals.

But not all were involved in the actual fighting to the same degree. One such affair involved two families, that of the surgeon Marin and that of his enemy Ripert. Marin complained before the *Sénéchaussée* in June of 1719 that a beautiful hunting dog belonging to him had strayed into the Riperts' kitchen, where it was knifed by two of the house servants. Marin stormed over to the Ripert house accompanied by his wife and his valet Turrier. According to his account, Ripert's valet lunged at Turrier and began to pummel him, whereupon Madame Ripert descended to

[57] A.D.A. IVB 1179, March 29, 1724.
[58] A.D.M. IIB 1242, September 18, 1758.

the kitchen brandishing a stick, insulted Marin's wife, and also set upon the unfortunate Turrier.[59]

In the two cases cited, the central role of servants as initiators and targets in physical clashes is evident. In the Chapelein case, Argerot's maid physically attacked both the cat and its owner, while the master confined his intervention to verbal abuse. Wives and servants were the main actors in the clash between the Marin and Ripert households. The masters remained aloof, and most of the actual fighting involved the valets and maids. The servants were caught in the thick of a battle that had started as a feud between their employers and had been acted out mainly at the lower echelons of the domestic hierarchy.

Why did these masters and mistresses, most of whom belonged to the urban middle classes, expect and encourage their servants to endanger their physical safety for the sake of their employers? To be sure, masters were understandably reluctant to expose themselves directly to blows and insults when others could be pressed into doing so on their behalf. But it can also be argued that masters and servants in this milieu were more or less consciously imitating the attitudes of their social superiors. The use of servants as go-betweens and thugs, and the expectation that they would take up the cudgels for their masters were above all characteristic of the aristocracy. Pages and lackeys who worked for the very wealthy would often collide in brutal encounters. Some of this took the form of gang fighting between bands of rowdy adolescents. The Abbé Collet suggested as much: if one lackey is mistreated by another from a different household, he wrote, both will appeal to their comrades and a minor incident will lead to a murderous brawl.[60] But lackeys reacted in this way precisely because in public they felt bound to one another and to their master's household. They tended to attack the servants

[59] A.D.A. IVB 1174, June 4, 1719.
[60] Collet, *Instructions et prières*, p. 325.

of rival households, and fought while invoking their respective employers' names and status. These sorts of battles occurred everywhere on every scale, ranging from a mundane collision in 1712 between the servants of the Archbishop of Aix and those of the Prieur de Saint Jean, to a huge battle that broke out twelve years later in Paris between a hundred of the king's servants and an equal number belonging to foreign ambassadors.[61] Masters tolerated these skirmishes, and maybe even encouraged them, because such incidents afforded servants the opportunity to proclaim their loyalty in the public arena.

The codes of etiquette, both explicit and implicit, that governed the behavior of the well-to-do did not allow for the public display of emotion or brutality or of any sort of physical impulse. According to Della Casa's popular etiquette book, a man of stature was not to run in the street. That, explained the author, is the manner of lackeys.[62] At Versailles, where the standards for taste and good behavior were set for much of the Old Regime, courtiers cultivated self-control and rationality, and frowned upon impulsive reactions.[63] A man of quality would demean himself if he showed anger or raised a hand in public against anyone, especially a social inferior. The servants of the rich were therefore entrusted with the dirty business of settling their masters' scores for them. The proper reaction to an offensive inferior was that of the gentleman in Sorel's *Francion* who exclaims: "Faith, if thou wert not destined to die on the gibbet I would have thee fight with a cook's boy from my kitchen!"[64] Sending one's servants out to rough up an enemy was a way of demonstrating both superiority and contempt. It is well known that the Chevalier de Rohan responded to Voltaire's sarcasms by sending his lackeys to beat up the philosophe. From the aristocracy on down, masters in

[61] A.D.A. IVB 1167, June 14, 1712; Barbier, *Chronique*, I:117–118.

[62] Della Casa, *Galateo* (1558), chap. 4, sec. 5, quoted in Norbert Elias, *La Civilisation des mœurs* (Paris, 1973), p. 110.

[63] Norbert Elias, *La Société de cour* (Paris, 1974), pp. 98–110.

[64] Charles Sorel, *Histoire comique de Francion*, I:92.

every walk of life had their servants bear the brunt of personal and social conflicts that opposed them to their enemies, rivals, and inferiors. Employers kept their hands clean and their dignity intact by using domestics as buffers, as thugs, and as scapegoats. In doing so they sacrificed the physical safety of their employees; in some cases they sacrificed their servants' reputation as well.

The shielding of masters by their employees was moral as well as physical: servants often took the blame as well as the blows. Admittedly, this worked both ways, since masters occasionally went to court for their servants' misdemeanors. Employers were legally responsible for the offenses committed by servants acting upon their orders or in the exercise of their domestic functions.[65] In Aix, masters were routinely summoned before the courts when, as often happened, a careless domestic emptied the contents of a chamber pot out of a window and spoiled the clothes of a passer-by, or for more serious offenses like the shortchanging of a customer.[66] After some bickering, the master would grudgingly hand over some money as compensation, a sum that was subsequently deducted from the guilty servant's wages. Economic solidarity was a public matter, not a private one. Masters assumed legal responsibility for their servants' misdemeanors because custom and law obliged them to do so, and no doubt also because by doing so they once again publicly asserted their control over their servants' lives. But in matters where their own honor and reputation were involved, they did not hesitate to sacrifice the good name of the men and women who worked for them.

In 1699 there were complaints in Aix that the innkeeper Sauvaire was watering down his wine. Sauvaire came before the police spluttering with indignation at this attack on his integrity, and got his servant Thérèse to confess in public that it was she who

---

[65] Pierre-Jacques Brillon *Dictionnaire des arrêts, ou jurisprudence universelle*, II:723; Léon Hom, *De la Situation juridique des gens de service*, p. 23; Henri Richard, *Du Louage des services domestiques en droit français*, p. 37.

[66] See, for instance, A.M.A. FF 65, February 18, 1706; A.M.A. FF 94, February 16, 1774; A.M.A. FF 66, September 30, 1706.

had poured water into the wine barrel. Either this was in fact true or else Sauvaire had bought or terrorized his maid into telling the story in order to protect his trade. But whatever the case, the girl's reputation was ruthlessly sacrificed.[67]

In another case that occurred ten years later in the same town, a mistress and a tradeswoman were responsible for damaging the honor of a servant whom they both knew to be innocent. A woman butcher named Ailhaude had been accused in the marketplace of cheating on the amount of meat she had weighed for the maid-servant of Mademoiselle Gondard. Ailhaude rushed to Gondard's house, threw herself at the other woman's feet, and engaged in some loud histrionics until Gondard agreed to accuse her servant of using a device known as a *chouille* to falsify the weight of the meat. This was a very public matter. Ailhaude ran back to her bench in the market and shouted at whoever was around to listen that she had been wrongly accused by a servant who was carrying a *chouille* in her pocket. The truth eventually came out, thanks to a conscientious municipal official and a repentant Mademoiselle Gondard. They claimed that their object in publicizing the true story was to keep Ailhaude from further swindling, and the maid's reputation was never once mentioned.[68]

A servant's reputation was a negligible quantity which he or she, if properly loyal, would ideally renounce for the sake of an employer. The inexhaustible Barbier reported that a servant was arrested for begging in Paris in 1749, and that he confessed that he was doing so in order to support an impecunious master.[69] The story is perhaps apocryphal, for that sort of tale was not new. In a famous episode of the Spanish picaresque novella *Lazarillo de Tormes*, young Lazarillo goes out to beg crusts of bread for the starving and proud hidalgo he is serving. This story could be read as a parable of the role that masters in preindustrial Europe expected their servants to play.

[67] A.M.A. FF 63, February 5, 1699.
[68] A.M.A. FF 67, July 14, 1710.
[69] Barbier, *Chronique*, IV:403–404.

The world in which these masters and servants evolved was one in which notions of honor and shame were crucially important.[70] In this respect the small towns and neighborhoods of larger cities under the Ancien Régime are comparable to those present-day Mediterranean societies whose workings have been analyzed by anthropologists such as Pitt-Rivers, Peristiany, and Bourdieu. Both types of society are small-scale and exclusive, both lay great stress on face-to-face dealings, and in both the concepts of honor and shame are the motor elements of social interaction.[71] These are societies that Pierre Bourdieu calls "primary," in which relationships with others are more important than a private sense of selfhood, and "the being and truth about a person are identical to the being and truth that others acknowledge in him."[72] In the towns of eighteenth-century France, as in the villages of twentieth-century Greece, Algeria, and Andalusia, a person's identity and status were defined, for the most part, in the public arena. In these environments ceremonies, ritual games, and above all

[70] These concepts governed the lives of the middle and lower classes as well as the elites: see Castan, *Honnêteté et relations sociales*, passim. Historians of early modern France have recently begun to explore the culture of public life in urban society, focusing on the ways in which the values of different segments of society were expressed in situations of conflict. Besides Castan, see Natalie Davis's essays in *Culture and Society in Early Modern France*, and Arlette Farge, *Vivre dans la rue à Paris au XVIIIe siècle*. These studies, like my own, rely heavily on police records for evidence, with the inevitable result that the picture is skewed toward the violent side of life. Street life in the seventeenth and eighteenth centuries was indeed violent, but probably less so than this chapter might suggest. Police records, however, are the most reliable and voluminous source of information on these matters, and the major justification for using them in this way is that it is precisely in situations of conflict that people are driven to give expression to their values and beliefs. Some of the broad historical problems raised by the study of public life are discussed by Richard Sennett in *The Fall of Public Man*.

[71] See J. G. Peristiany, ed., *Honour and Shame: The Values of Mediterranean Society*, Introduction.

[72] Pierre Bourdieu, "The Sentiment of Honour in Kabyle Society," in ibid., p. 212.

quarrels and fights allow for the public affirmation of social values. They provide the opportunity for a public symbolic display of a person or family's claims to social recognition, and beyond that of the values and beliefs of the whole society.[73] This is one of the reasons, no doubt, why public fights between servants, whether they opposed the maidservants of artisans or the lackeys of the wealthy, were frequent and acceptable occurrences, encouraged by the masters themselves. The logic of the situation nearly always compelled servants to invoke the dignity of their employers, and thus to proclaim it to the outside world.

But servants could only attack one another or their inferiors. Within such a society, violence is only acted out between equals. An inferior must limit his attacks to persons of equal or inferior social standing since he does not, by nature, possess sufficient honor to resent the affront of a superior. Superiors, on the other hand, cannot respond directly to the insults of those who stand lower than they on the social scale, because in theory such attacks pose no threat to their own reserves of honor: one is only vulnerable to the attacks of a "conceptual equal."[74] In other words, eighteenth-century masters only asserted themselves personally vis-à-vis an antagonist of similar status, for instance by challenging him to a duel. If they wanted to get even with an inferior, or merely to signify the inferiority of a person who had attacked them, they were obliged to do so through their servants or risk losing face. That, ultimately, is why Rohan sent his flunkeys to beat Voltaire.

Servants, in sum, were used as scapegoats not just by their masters, but by all of society. Masters, trammeled by explicit rules of propriety and by society's implicit codes of honor, used their employees to vent hostility and carry out acts of aggression to which they themselves could not stoop. Enemies took out their frustration and anger at their wealthier neighbors by attacking

[73] Ibid., p. 203.

[74] Julian Pitt-Rivers, "Honour and Social Status," in Peristiany, ed., *Honour and Shame*, pp. 31, 57; Bourdieu, "Kabyle Society," in ibid., p. 197.

the maids and lackeys who worked for them. And the servants themselves, isolated and vulnerable creatures bound to their masters by the force of self-interest and self-protection, accepted to play the role that was assigned to them. In their quarrels and fights with other townsfolk or the servants of rival households, they publicly invoked, and thus reinforced, the dignity and power of their employers. The master-servant relationship, it has been argued, had an important impact outside of the household on society at large. Domestic servants performed crucial tasks as intermediaries between their masters and others, and in doing so took on the roles of recipients and bestowers of much vicarious violence. Much of the hostility that might otherwise have exploded between rich and poor, debtors and creditors, or simply between hostile neighbors was absorbed by the buffer zone formed by the presence of servants. If masters took advantage of their servants' vulnerability, left them standing at the doorstep, sent them out on business or to settle scores with enemies, this was not just a demonstration of their own wealth and power, but also a protection from direct confrontation.

That masters, and indeed much of society, saw and used servants as mediators and scapegoats is evident in the most popular image of domestic service produced and consumed by Ancien Régime society—the portrayal of servants in dramatic literature.

In the century and a half preceding the Revolution, the appeal of Parisian theaters increased steadily as they became the capital's centers for cultural creation and elegant social intercourse. The Comédie Française, founded by Louis XIV in 1680, provided the setting for much of the century-long succession of comic masterpieces that began with Molière and ended with Beaumarchais. Other institutions, such as the Théâtre des Italiens and the Opéra Comique, competed unsuccessfully with the Comédie, while popular theaters such as the Théâtre de la Foire and later the Boulevard theaters attracted a more plebeian audience by staging farces and vaudevilles.[75] The provinces followed suit more slowly but had come into their own by the second quarter of the eighteenth century, when newly erected theaters began to draw large audiences in prosperous commercial centers such as Bordeaux and Nantes.[76] In Paris all classes of society attended the theater. Even at the prestigious Comédie Française, where entry fees were relatively high, the middle classes were always strongly represented in the audience, and the presence of working people in the *parterre* is abundantly attested to in contemporary documents. In the course of the eighteenth century, theaters gradually became more class-segregated, as middle-class attendance increased and the more plebeian elements of the audience were pushed out of the *grands théâtres* into more popular playhouses.[77] But throughout the seventeenth and eighteenth centuries, aristocratic spectators were the most regular and influential patrons of Parisian theaters. It was essentially they whose money filled the coffers of the Comédie, and whose outlook and ideals imposed themselves upon French drama. Until the advent late in the eighteenth century of the *drame bourgeois*, the tastes of the aristocracy prevailed in the creation of entertainments that were performed for—and much appreciated by—a socially mixed audience.[78]

Servants were ubiquitous creatures in the comedies that were written and performed during the heyday of French classical theater, from the mid-seventeenth to the early eighteenth century. Out of 250 comedies published between 1610 and 1700, only 8 did not include at least one servant in the cast of major characters, and there were on the average three or more servants in every play.[79] Nor were servants minor characters in these plays: there

[75] John Lough, *Paris Theatre Audiences in the Seventeenth and Eighteenth Centuries*; Henri Lagrave, *Le Théâtre et le public à Paris de 1715 à 1750*.

[76] Lough, *Theatre Audiences*, pp. 164–165, 265–268.

[77] Ibid., passim.

[78] Ibid., pp. 107, 161–162.

[79] Jean Emelina, *Les Valets et les servantes dans le théâtre comique en France de 1610 à 1700*, pp. 17, 70.

was a major valet role in about 3 out of 4 of the most successful comedies performed between 1670 and 1730.[80] The very conspicuousness of stage servants demands some sort of explanation. Why should servants appear at all, let alone play such important parts in plays that were written about, and to a large extent directed at, their masters? More specifically, what dramatic role did servants play in these comedies, what psychological needs did they fulfill for the audience, and in what ways did their role on stage mirror the social role outlined in this chapter?

It may seem difficult to go looking for reflections of contemporary reality in characters that owed so much to tradition. Crispin, Frontin, Arlequin, and Pierrot, the great stage valets who dominated the French theater for much of two centuries, were characters directly derived from the Italian Commedia dell'Arte, and their literary ancestry can be traced all the way back to the slaves in Greek and Roman comedies.[81] What is more, there is a heavy, timeless quality to the literary image of master and servant. Over centuries, the protagonists of plays and novels in the Western tradition have had a sidekick of inferior status appended to them, the better to demonstrate the hero's wisdom or folly: Prospero needs Caliban, as Quijote needs Sancho Pança and Bertie Wooster needs Jeeves.[82] The archetypal servant in seventeenth-century French comedy was the *balourd*, a bumbling fool whose stupidity and physical clumsiness outweighed his occasional display of ingenuity in pulling his master out of a tight situation. In the eighteenth century the character of the stage valet evolved into a type known as the *fourbe*, a nefarious schemer ready to betray his master, if need be, in pursuit of his own

---

[80] Paul Kreiss, "The Valet in French Comedy, 1670–1730" (Ph.D. diss., Northwestern Univ., 1968), I:329.

[81] Emelina, *Les Valets et les servantes*, pp. 178–184, 440–446.

[82] Some critics have focused on the philosophical implications of the literary coupling of master and servant, most notably W. H. Auden, "Balaam and the Ass: On the Literary Use of the Master-Servant Relationship," *Encounter* 3 (July 1954):35–53.

interests.[83] Both types of character hark back to older literary types, the *balourd* to the traditional fool and the *fourbe* to wicked confidantes in the style of Iago.

Real servants apparently failed to recognize themselves in these characters. This, at least, is what the lackey author Viollet de Wagnon maintained. Commenting on the regulations that excluded servants in livery from the audiences of theaters, he surmised that this prohibition must have been demanded by the actors themselves who did not care for real servants to pass judgment on the shallow characters they portrayed:

> Everyone knows that no good play is ever performed in their theaters that does not include a lackey's role, and that if [servants] were granted easy access, one of them might jump onto the stage and challenge the actor with regard to the role of his character, while persons of every other condition and estate pretend to recognize it as true.[84]

Although these stereotypical figures of servants had little in common with their real counterparts, they unquestionably appealed to the theater-going public. For a quarter of a century, spectators flocked by the thousands to the Théâtre de la Foire to watch the legendary Raymond Poisson, clad in black clothes, white ruff, and tall boots playing the valet Crispin,[85] just as they crowded the Comédie Française to laugh at the antics of maids and valets in high comedy from Molière to Marivaux. During the heyday of classical comedy, from about 1670 to 1730, the French theater offered its public little more than stereotypes of servants. Yet their very success suggests that these distorted images must have been recognizable, appealing, and reassuring to the audiences that applauded them.

A closer look at the roles and characterization of servants in

---

[83] Emelina, *Les Valets et les servantes*, pp. 153–181.

[84] Jacques Viollet de Wagnon, *L'Auteur laquais, ou réponses aux objections qui ont été faites au corps de ce nom sur la vie de Jacques Cochois, dit Jasmin*, p. xlix.

[85] Emelina, *Les Valets et les servantes*, pp. 165–167.

8. The servant on stage: Raymond Poisson in the role of the valet Crispin.
(Phot. Bibl. nat. Paris)

these plays may help us to understand the popularity of such characters.[86]

The leading studies of servants' roles in French classical comedy suggest that the importance of these characters derived from three different functions. Servants were dramatic regulators and commentators, they embodied psychological and physical release, and they voiced or acted out dreams of social inversion. In many plays the first character to appear before the audience was a cranky valet who strutted around the stage bemoaning his fate and complaining of his master's quirky ways. Like dozens of others, Hector in Regnard's *Le Joueur*, Sganarelle in Molière's *Dom Juan*, and his descendant Leporello in Mozart and Da Ponte's opera opened the play by capturing the audience's interest and sympathy with their gossip and complaints. They introduced the main characters and made intermittent appearances thereafter, judging and commenting on the action. They were the only characters on stage to address the audience directly, appealing to their judgment and sympathy. Servants in seventeenth-century comedy, Jean Emelina has argued, were the direct descendants of the Greek chorus.[87]

Unlike the chorus, however, servants usually took a direct part in the development of the plot, regulating the comic tone by their burlesque appearances, and mediating between the forces in presence on stage. The maid Dorine in Molière's *Tartuffe*, for instance, provides constant comic relief in a potentially oppressive plot by noisily clashing with both her master and his devout

---

[86] Several literary critics have studied the role of servants in the hundreds of plays in which they figured prominently from the seventeenth century until the Revolution. Since it was impossible for me to envision reading even a reasonable sampling of these plays, I have confined my reading to the major dramatists, and relied heavily on the excellent and exhaustive studies by Emelina and Kreiss cited above. For more specialized studies see Jean Emelina, *Les Valets et les servantes dans le théâtre de Molière*, and Claude Rigault, *Les Domestiques dans le théâtre de Marivaux*. For the later period, see Maria Ribaric-Demers, *Le Valet et la soubrette de Molière à la Révolution*.

[87] Emelina, *Les Valets et les servantes*, pp. 132–133.

protégé, and also serves as a rallying point for the anti-Tartuffe elements in the household. In other cases, servants remained on the sidelines but voiced, like the chorus, the moral judgment of the audience. The maids in Molière's plays were redoubtable judges whose intimate knowledge of the family's every quirk and conflict gave them the freedom to speak their minds. The soubrettes in Marivaux's stylish comedies peeped through keyholes at their mistresses' antics before the mirror or at their flirtations with young men, and then treated the audience to venomous descriptions of their employers' foibles.[88] None of this criticism was really subversive, for servants remained powerless creatures who could be brought back to their senses with a slap across the face. But their harsh, down-to-earth judgments involved the spectators in the play, for they echoed the supposed reactions of the audience. Servants on stage mediated between the main characters and also cast a bridge between the protagonists and the audience. Their primary dramatic function was thus analogous to their principal social role: on stage, as on the street, servants were cast in the role of go-betweens.

If servants displayed some attractively commonsensical traits when acting as judges or mediators, they nonetheless constantly reminded the audience of their fundamental inferiority. The behavior and speech of servants was characterized by various forms of verbal and physical impropriety that marked them off clearly from the other characters. Servants on stage snapped back at their masters and abused their inferiors; they used popular forms of speech, clichés, and proverbs; their talk exploded into torrential loquacity, in tirades peppered with immoral or lewd suggestions and constant references to physical appetites.[89] No character but a servant could deliver a repartee like Dorine's stinging response to the hypocrite Tartuffe who asks her to cover her bosom:

[88] For instance, in Marivaux, *L'Île des esclaves*, scene 2.
[89] Emelina, *Les Valets et les servantes*, pp. 236–238, 259–278.

> Your soul, it seems, has very poor defenses,
> And flesh makes quite an impact on your senses.
> It's strange that you're so easily excited;
> My own desires are not so soon ignited,
> And if I saw you naked as a beast,
> Not all your hide would tempt me in the least.[90]

The physicality of servants was ready to surface in nearly every one of their repartees, in copious allusions to food, drink, lust, and laziness.[91] Unlike any of the other characters on stage—not to mention the statuesque protagonists of the tragic repertoire—servants had bodies and used them, tumbling, fighting, eating, and receiving blows.[92]

The motivations of stage servants were no purer than their speech. Male servants were almost invariably depicted as contemptible characters. Such was Sganarelle in Molière's *Dom Juan*, a hedonist who opened the play on a celebration of the virtues of tobacco, a man of infinitely elastic moral standards who applauded and assisted his master while covertly disapproving of his conduct, a coward whose fears, when faced with manifestations of the supernatural, were of a distinctly physical and not metaphysical sort. The immorality of female servants had a more insidious quality to it. They incited mistresses to rid themselves of aging husbands or to deceive them, and in many of Molière's great comedies they negated the moral standards of the age by scheming with children against their parents.[93] In the plays of the early eighteenth century, the immorality of servants became more pronounced and more threatening. The valets and soubrettes of Lesage, Dancourt, and Regnard often shunned petty deception for large-scale swindling.[94]

[90] The verse translation is Richard Wilbur's: Molière, *Tartuffe* (New York, 1963), p. 53.

[91] Emelina, *Les Valets et les servantes*, pp. 221–222.

[92] Emelina, *Les Valets et les servantes*, pp. 234–235.

[93] Ibid., pp. 242–243.

[94] Ibid., p. 228; Ribaric-Demers, *Le Valet et la soubrette*, pp. 61–140.

In tragedy as well as comedy, servants were often portrayed as villainous creatures. The tragic analog of the *fourbe* was the corrupt confidante, the evil nurse Oenone in Racine's *Phèdre* or Nero's flunkey Narcisse in *Britannicus*.[95] In both tragedy and comedy it was servants who enticed their masters into lying or deceiving, and in doing so they discharged the protagonists from the main burden of moral responsibility. Servants on stage, one critic contends, served as "moral and social scapegoats" within the play. By suggesting deceit to their superiors or carrying out impostures themselves, they acted out their masters' half-formulated wishes while taking upon their shoulders the whole burden of guilt. The servant, Emelina argues, was "a degraded double of the master," whose role was to confirm endlessly, by his very wickedness, the moral and social superiority of his betters.[96] Here again, servants on stage performed roles that were analogous to those which their real-life equivalents played in society. They released the pent-up tensions of others in the theater just as their counterparts did on the street. Playwrights used them as moral and social scapegoats, for that was one of the roles that real servants performed in contemporary urban society.

Seventeenth- and eighteenth-century plays are shot through with themes of abortive social inversion. Anyone who has seen Mozart and Da Ponte's *Don Giovanni* is bound to remember the opening scene in which the Don's servant Leporello thunders: "Voglio fare il gentiluomo, e non voglio più servir!" ("I want to be a gentleman, I no longer want to serve!"). Tirades of this sort,

[95] Emelina, *Les Valets et les servantes*, pp. 289–290.

[96] Emelina, *Les Valets et les servantes*, pp. 287–295, 446. Emelina offers a psychoanalytic explanation for the quasi-universal wickedness and physicality of stage servants. Servants who assist their young masters in crossing an old father are the agents of unresolved oedipal conflicts, he argues. On a broader scale, the physicality of servants makes them "the dramatic representation of the id" (p. 303), incarnations of the pleasure principle battling against, but ultimately defeated by, the reality principle (pp. 303–312). The explanation is attractive, but it does not account for the waning and ultimate disappearance of these servant types in the late eighteenth century.

in which a servant rhetorically challenged his fate and his master's authority, were standard dramatic fare in French comedy for well over a century. Since the 1630s at least, hundreds of servants had exclaimed on stage, as did the valet in Rotrou's *Les Ménèchmes*:

> Sous quel astre inclément le ciel m'a-t-il fait naître?
> Que n'est-il en ma place, et que ne suis-je maître?[97]

The message of Christian moralists came alive on stage: we are all of the same flesh and blood, only fate determines our station in life. Yet the respective characterizations of master and servant made it seem hollow and ridiculous. Entire plays revolved around the theme of social role reversal. Two of Marivaux's comedies, written between 1720 and 1730, *L'Ile de la Raison* and *L'Ile des Esclaves*, were set in utopian surroundings where masters, temporarily enslaved to their servants, were exposed to vitriolic criticism which resulted ultimately in their moral reform. But Marivaux took great care to place temporal and spatial limits on these didactic experiments: they were confined to three years and set in islands.[98]

The theme of social inversion pervades Marivaux's great comedies, the most famous of which is *Le Jeu de l'Amour et du Hasard*. In that play, two young people named Silvia and Dorante are engaged to be married but have never met. They independently decide on the same stratagem, that of changing places with their valet and maid for a day in order to observe their betrothed without being recognized. The inevitable sociosentimental complications ensue as they fall in love with one another in the guise of servants, and the play is happily resolved by the revelation of the true identities of masters and servants. But these games of imitation and role reversal on stage were always carefully con-

[97] Cited in ibid., p. 42. These lines translate into: "Under what unhappy star was it my fate to be born? Why is he not in my place, why am I not the master?" See also Regnard's *Les Ménèchmes* (1706), act IV, scene 2, and his *Le Joueur* (1695), act I, scene 1.

[98] Marivaux, *Théâtre complet*, vol. I.

trolled by the masters. Should servants take the game too seriously, they exposed themselves to ridicule like Mascarille in Molière's *Les Précieuses Ridicules*. Playwrights used the foolish and ephemeral pretensions of fictional servants to underscore and reassert the superiority of their masters.

Mimicry, dreams, and temporary inversion may have had, on a much reduced scale, the effect that is commonly attributed to carnivals in early modern societies. The servants' fantasies of social promotion must have appealed to the lower orders, while the failure of their dreams reassured the masters in the audience. The stereotypical figures of servants who buffooned their ways through French comedies for a century or so performed roles within these plays that were stylized reflections of the parts assigned to real servants by their masters in the drama of daily life. Fictional servants were mediators who involved the audience in the plot, yet at the same time protected the dignity and aloofness of the protagonists, their masters. Their indecency and physicality punctuated the play with comic release, made it accessible to the *parterre*, and united the audience in peals of laughter. At the same time, their wickedness and thwarted dreams of social promotion reminded the spectators where honor and superiority really lay. In a world still dominated, until midcentury at least, by the cultural values of the aristocracy, fictional servants, like real servants, were used as go-betweens and scapegoats to assert and protect the dignity and power of their betters.

The role of servants in dramatic fiction reflected in distorted fashion their real social role as crucial auxiliaries to the maintenance of authority by their masters. Authority itself was dependent upon a certain style of self-presentation by the elites. Edward Thompson has argued that in eighteenth-century England the ruling classes asserted their power through a cultural hegemony that was contingent on the adoption of theatrical modes of behavior. Real economic and physical power amounted to little, he argues, unless buttressed by the appropriate expressions of pomp, dignity, and aloofness.[99] The French elites acted no differently. They may in fact have been more prone to assert their power by means of theatrical stances because of the model that was offered to them by Versailles. At court, every moment of the king's day took the form of a carefully staged production acted out in the presence of throngs of courtiers. The influence of Versailles radiated throughout the realm, leaving a stamp of theatricality on the households of great princes and middling noblemen alike.[100] Aristocrats maintained social power by displaying their wealth in the public sphere. This explains why they paid such fastidious attention to the clothes, physique, and general demeanor of their servants. They used servants as objects of conspicuous consumption, but also as a supporting cast for their public appearances. Noblemen did their best to appear distant and theatrical; it is telling that until 1759 noble spectators at the Comédie Française were allowed to sit on stage chatting, joking, and occasionally trammeling the comings and goings of the actors.[101] The line between the world of the aristocracy and that of the theater was, in this way, deliberately blurred.[102]

[99] Edward P. Thompson, "Patrician Society, Plebeian Culture," *Journal of Social History* 7:387–390.

[100] Elias, *La Société de cour*, Introduction. Roland Mousnier, *Les Institutions de la France sous la monarchie absolue*, I:78–82.

[101] Lough, *Theatre Audiences*, pp. 115–117.

[102] Literary critics, more than historians, have been sensitive to the theatrical dimensions of aristocratic culture. They note, for instance, the standard use of the term *le public* to mean society at large. The center for propagation of this cultural model shifted in the eighteenth century from Versailles to private salons in town. See Eric Auerbach, "La Cour et la Ville," in *Scenes from the Drama of European Literature*, pp. 133–179; Peter Brooks, *The Novel of Worldliness: Crébillon, Marivaux, Laclos, Stendhal* Introduction and chaps. 1–2. Historians have very recently begun, in the wake of Thompson's work, to take an interest in the theatrical dimensions of political authority in preindustrial France and Britain; see Douglas Hay, "Property, Authority, and Criminal Law," in Douglas Hay et al., *Albion's Fatal Tree: Crime and Society in Eighteenth-Century England*, pp. 17–63; John Brewer, "Theater and Counter Theater in Georgian Politics: The Mock Elections at Garrat," *Radical History Review* 22 (Winter 1979–1980):7–

Wealthy and noble masters and all those who emulated them sought to maintain a distance between themselves and the rest of the world, and they could only do so by using their servants as a sort of screen. A benign demeanor was possible only if the public were held at bay by a barrier of scowling menials. Sébastien Mercier once complained that "The more a great lord affects a modest countenance, the more his valets take on poses which anywhere else would be the height of ridiculousness."[103] He might well have been thinking of Lebrun's famous portrait of Chancellor Séguier sitting erect atop a horse that is surrounded by a bevy of stately page boys (see illustration 9). The Chancellor's affable gaze descends obliquely from the top of the painting; it is counterbalanced by the haughty stare of the servant standing below him to the right, whose look confronts the viewer directly and repels him. Chancellor Séguier, one of the most powerful personages of the realm, was no ordinary master. What Lebrun captured in this painting was the ideal of aristocratic service, a model that was widely imitated by all who had pretensions to dignity and power.

Though servants did, of course, perform essential tasks for their masters inside the household, much of this aristocratic system based on ideals of mutual loyalty was aimed at the outside world. Only the wealthy could afford retinues of liveried pages and lackeys, but even middle-class masters sent their servants out on the street to settle their scores for them. Masters took advantage of their servants' vulnerability and did their utmost to coerce or cajole them into some sort of allegiance to the household. They did so because the loyalty of servants was indispensable to them in a world where power depended on dignified aloofness. On the street just as on stage, the primary role of servants was to convince the public of their masters' superiority. Ultimately, the system was geared to the maintenance of authority by the social elites.

40; Orest Ranum, "Courtesy, Absolutism, and the Rise of the French State," *Journal of Modern History* 52:426–451.

[103] Mercier, *Tableau de Paris*, IX:6.

9. Servants for display: *Chancellor Seguier and his Pages*, by Charles Lebrun, 1661 (Cliché des Musées Nationaux–Paris)

Throughout most of the Old Regime, masters demanded that their servants be loyal, and they did their best to impress upon domestics a sense of identification with, and dependence on, employer and household. The masters' insistence on loyalty did not derive from any doubts as to their own authority over their menials; inside the household, most employers were quite secure in their sense of social superiority. Rather, the loyalty of servants was necessary in order for masters to assert themselves in the world outside of the household. As Clifford Geertz has recently argued, the emblems and trappings of authority are not to be dismissed as mere "excrescences, mysteries, fictions and decorations"; in some societies they are the true stuff of power.[104] France of the Old Regime was one such society, in which the elites modeled their behavior on the elaborate theatricality of Versailles. But in order to impress the world with their wealth and to maintain a distance from their inferiors, the French elites needed their servants both as objects of ostentatious expenditure and as loyal auxiliaries who kept the public at bay.

The model for this use of servants was provided by the aristocracy, and by masters of lesser birth wealthy enough to keep several male domestics and influential enough to command easily the loyalty of their servants. But masters of lesser stature tended to imitate the rich. They aspired to the employment of male domestics, and they too expected their servants, male or female, to defend their masters' interests and reputations outside of the household. The fact that fictional servants were assigned similar roles as mediators and scapegoats in contemporary plays suggests that these assumptions concerning the proper function of domestics were shared by large segments of society. Pervasive as they were, these assumptions did not outlast the Revolution.

Nineteenth-century ideals and realities of domestic service differed markedly from those that had prevailed in the previous

---

[104] Clifford Geertz, *Negara: The Theatre-State in Nineteenth-Century Bali*, pp. 121–136.

century. Postrevolutionary domestic handbooks advised masters to hire women rather than men, and indeed by the mid-nineteenth century eight or nine out of ten domestic workers were female. Nineteenth-century servants were more numerous than their fore-bears, but far less conspicuous. Their masters outfitted them in drab uniforms, kept their work and leisure under tight control, and did their best to confine them to the house. It is perhaps revealing that after Beaumarchais the servant all but disappeared as a central character on the French stage. The Revolution must surely have played an important role in the redefinition of do-mestic service; but so basic a change in ideals and patterns of behavior is unlikely to take place over the course of just a few years, even years as tumultuous as were the 1790s in France.

In fact, several decades before the Revolution, enlightened writers began to express distaste for the wasteful and cruel ways in which masters used their servants. Some vented annoyance at the servants themselves for accepting to play so demeaning a role. In 1768 the anonymous chronicler of Montpellier protested, on humanitarian grounds, against the use of sedan-chair carriers:

> The custom of being carried by men is a great scandal. It offends nature itself, and nothing is more ridiculous than to see a canon, a bishop, an officer or a judge, in a word anyone who wants to act like a lord, have himself closed up in a box and carried on the backs of men who struggle through mud, ice, and snow, at the risk of being crushed if they miss a step.[105]

The custom was not merely cruel, he intimated, it was just plain silly. But it took a mind like that of Jean-Jacques Rousseau to strike right at the heart of the system:

> A bourgeois gets more service out of a single lackey than does a duke from the ten gentlemen who surround him. . . . A doorman and a footman make poor ambassadors. I would

[105] Berthélé, *Montpellier*, p. 69.

not want to have those people always interposed between myself and the rest of the world, or to go clashing around in a coach as if I were afraid of being accosted.[106]

Aristocratic service remained a powerful model for the rest of society, but its prestige was slowly undermined in the second half of the eighteenth century. Where, then, are we to find the forces of erosion? In the rise of middle-class employers, in the protestations of intellectuals, or in a change in the fortunes and attitudes of the servants themselves? Were the ideals and realities of aristocratic service undermined from below, or were they challenged from above?

[106] Jean-Jacques Rousseau, *Emile ou de l'Education* (Paris, 1964), p. 433.

Part Three

 ❧

BREAKING THE
COVENANT

CHAPTER 6

Aristocratic Service in the
Age of Enlightenment

In 1772 a man of letters named Jean-François Cailhava l'Estendoux published a treatise on the art of comedy. Two of its chapters
were devoted to plays in which servants led the action. Since
Molière and Regnard, he wrote, authors had lost all verve and
levity in their treatment of servants; playwrights had in fact
gradually banished valets from the stage, a development which
Cailhava himself deplored.[1] Cailhava was fighting a rear-guard
battle, and he knew it. He acknowledged that most contemporary
writers wished to dispense altogether with those *intrigans subal-
ternes* whose presence injected a measure of vulgarity into even
the best of plays. Fashionable theatergoers no longer saw the
necessity of having servants play such important parts within the
plot. "Do we not have as much spirit as our valets?" they would
ask. "Are we not capable of conducting our own intrigues in
town and at court?" If a playwright, he concluded, were to depict
servants on stage as Molière had in *Le Bourgeois Gentilhomme*, he
would only bring upon himself the scorn and indignation of most
persons of quality and taste.[2] In the century since Molière had
produced his comic masterpieces, the attitudes of playwrights
and the educated public toward the traditional roles of valets and

[1] Jean-François Cailhava L'Estendoux, *De l'Art de la Comédie*, I:33.
[2] Ibid., I:28–39.

maids had gone through a sea change. The apparent reasons for this change were esthetic and ideological, but in fact it was rooted in much deeper social and cultural transformations that took place over the course of the eighteenth century. The gradual repudiation by the public of the familiar *valet de comédie* was merely one of the repercussions of a series of concurrent changes in the relationship between master and servant, in the sociology of employers, in the fortunes of the servants themselves, and in the broader ideological climate of the age.

Most of Cailhava's fellow critics objected to the traditional role of servants on stage. Cailhava quoted the playwright Dorat as arguing that it was downright indecent to let these inferior beings carry out trickeries on behalf of their young masters and mistresses against parents, uncles, and guardians.[3] This sort of argument was by no means a new one in the 1770s. Some thirty years earlier similar objections had been raised by a more famous critic, Diderot himself. Diderot's *Entretiens sur le Fils Naturel*, published in 1757, was the first and most important manifesto in favor of a new style of play that was later dubbed *drame bourgeois*. In the *Entretiens* two characters, Dorval and "Moi," carry out a polite but earnest critical discussion of Diderot's own play, *Le Fils Naturel*. On the subject of servants, Dorval abruptly shifts gears from a hackneyed Christian-Stoic attitude to one more characteristic of his contemporaries. If real servants are capable of virtue and devotion, he first argues, why not depict this in drama?

> Moi   But if you were writing for the theatre?
> Dorval   I would dispense with moralizing, and would carefully avoid giving any importance on stage to beings who are worth nothing in society. . . . If the poet leaves them in the antechamber where they belong, the action taking place between the

[3] Ibid., I:29.

main characters can only be stronger and more
interesting.[4]

This fragment of Diderot's dialogue captures the playwright-
philosophe's ambivalence toward servant roles, a dilemma which
he shared with most other authors of *drames bourgeois*. The *drame*
purported to present an exact reflection of contemporary life, and
specifically to rehabilitate the middling and lower levels of society
that had been neglected or mistreated in the high comedy of the
classical age. As a result, the decades before the Revolution witnessed a flowering of works by Diderot, Mercier, Falbaire, Sedaine, and others, whose personae included upright merchants,
honest innkeepers, high-minded artisans, and toiling indigents,
all of them much prone to delivering speeches about virtue,
charity, or hard work.[5] From the plays of Nivelle de La Chaussée
at midcentury to those of Sedaine in the 1790s, via those of
Mercier and Diderot himself, servants lost much of the truculence
and spirit that had endeared them to earlier generations of theatergoers. They became honest, loyal, and colorless.[6] Little wonder
that the stage valet was ultimately doomed to disappearance when
he was made to deliver lines like those of Gervais in Desforges's
La Femme jalouse:

C'est assez. Viens ma fille, en quelque asile obscur.
On est riche partout quand on a le coeur pur.[7]

---

[4] Denis Diderot, *Paradoxe sur le comédien précédé des entretiens sur le fils naturel*,
pp. 32–33.

[5] The classic work on the subject is Felix Gaiffe, *Le Drame en France au XVIIIe
siècle*; see part 3, chap. 3. John Lough has argued that these plays were by no
means as successful as Gaiffe suggested, and that their portrayal of the lower
orders of society in particular was received with much sarcasm and disbelief;
see his *Paris Theatre Audiences in the Seventeenth and Eighteenth Centuries*, pp. 249–
268.

[6] Gaiffe, *Le Drame en France*, pp. 386–390; Maria Ribaric-Demers, *Le Valet
et la soubrette de Molière à la Révolution*, pp. 172–190.

[7] Quoted in Gaiffe, *Le Drame en France*, p. 389: "Enough! follow me, daughter, to some humble retreat/ One is rich anywhere when one's heart is pure."

For all of their professed compassion toward servants, the authors of these early melodramas were in implicit agreement with Diderot's final word on the subject, since for the most part they kept domestics away from center stage, or dispensed with them altogether. In all twenty-eight of Sedaine's plays, only eleven servants appeared, and at that only to play minor roles.[8]

Yet the ideological ambivalence and literary shortcomings of Diderot and his successors were not alone responsible for the decline of servant roles in eighteenth-century drama. As early as the first decades of the century, dramatists had begun to push servants out of the limelight. Paul Kreiss, who has studied servants in 150 plays published between 1670 and 1730, finds that in the thirty years before 1700 only one or two plays per decade contained no servant role; by the 1720s, the proportion of plays in which no servant appeared had increased to over 25 percent. In the early decades of the century, many plays still included a major valet role, but the number and importance of minor servant roles declined sharply between 1690 and 1730.[9]

As the numerical importance of servants in comedies began to wane, the traits attributed to them also changed. The Regency and the first years of the reign of Louis XV were, to all appearances, a golden age for servants on stage. In comparison to the noisy maids and bumbling valets of Molière's comedies, the servants created by writers like Dufresny, Regnard, and Dancourt seemed worldly, articulate, and poised.[10] But the increasing sophistication of these characters was counterbalanced by their cynicism and wickedness. The amoralism which traditionally provided comic relief in a play now reached levels that made it downright threatening.[11] In the plays of the first third of the century, servants were as shrewd and roguish as ever, but their

[8] Ribaric-Demers, *Le Valet et la soubrette*, pp. 78, 104, 140, 211.

[9] Paul Kreiss, "The Valet in French Comedy, 1670–1730" (Ph.D. diss., Northwestern Univ., 1968), I:39.

[10] Ribaric-Demers, *Le Valet et la soubrette*, pp. 78, 104, 140, 211.

[11] Ibid., pp. 76–78, 90–104, 119–140.

ambition reached new heights and was sometimes crowned with success. This new and threatening image of the servant can be traced back to very early plays such as Lesage's *Turcaret*, first performed in 1709. *Turcaret* is a cruel comedy of manners that portrays a wealthy and vulgar parvenu, Turcaret, the dupe of three unscrupulous aristocrats who in turn are hoodwinked by a couple of scheming servants, Lisette and Frontin. Turcaret, we learn, is a former lackey who has elbowed his way up the social scale. By the last act of the play, Turcaret, the Barònne, and her two noble cronies have ruined and ridiculed one another, and the servants are collecting the spoils. The world of the masters collapses amidst financial disaster and grotesque recriminations, and Frontin has the last word: "The reign of Monsieur Turcaret is over; mine is about to begin."[12]

The transformation of servants from the good-natured *balourds* of Molière's plays to the grasping cynics of Dufresny, Dancourt, and Lesage has usually been explained with reference to the unscrupulous financial speculation and rapid social mobility that characterized the last years of Louis XIV's reign and the Regency that followed.[13] It is also probable that new canons of taste came to forbid the suggestion on stage of bodily functions and baser instincts, so that playwrights had to find new ways of demonstrating the moral inferiority of domestic servants. At any rate, the new traits of stage servants sounded their death knoll, as if playwrights had scared themselves and their public with their own creations. By the middle of the century, servants were rapidly becoming insipid characters. It was left to the *drame bourgeois* to deal them the last blow.[14]

The old fictions died a slow death, however, For all of the superficial differences, the servants who appeared in the plays of Lesage or Marivaux had much in common with the fools and scapegoats of earlier fiction. The comedies of Molière and his

[12] Alain-René Lesage, *Turcaret*, act V, scene 14.
[13] Ribaric-Demers, *Le Valet et la soubrette*, pp. 99–104.
[14] Ibid., pp. 172–182.

contemporaries were frequently performed, with great success, right up to the end of the century.[15] Finally, although servant characters were edulcorated by the *drame bourgeois*, the reign of the great stage valets ended not on a whimper but on a bang. Five years before the outbreak of the Revolution, the protagonist of Beaumarchais's controversial and immensely popular *Mariage de Figaro* took on his master equal to equal: "Nobility, fortune, rank, position! How proud they make a man feel! But what have you done to deserve such advantages? Put yourself to the trouble of being born—nothing more!"[16] The role of Figaro marked an important departure from traditional literary images of servants because, like many servants in subsequent fiction, Figaro demystified the world of his masters instead of confirming it. Yet he was the last servant to occupy center stage in the French theater. Despite exceptions such as Victor Hugo's Ruy Blas, servants were never to regain their prominent role on the French stage.

The change that came about was a slow one, but by the end of the century it was clear that neither authors nor the public wanted to see servants cast in their traditional role as scapegoats and buffoons on stage. If, as we have argued, the traditional literary roles of servants were a reflection of those which masters expected their real servants to play, does this slow change in literary taste point to a change in social relationships? In a world still by and large dominated by traditional values of loyalty and deference, did any changes nonetheless affect the relationship between master and servant over the course of the century?

[15] Kreiss, "The Valet in French Comedy," I:330–333. *Tartuffe*, for instance, was performed 675 times between 1711 and 1793, *Le Médecin malgré lui* 885 times in the same period. The plays of Regnard and Dancourt were almost as popular as those of Molière, even at the height of the Revolution.

[16] Pierre Caron de Beaumarchais, *Le Mariage de Figaro*, act V, scene 3; translation by John Wood in *The Barber of Seville and the Marriage of Figaro* (London, 1964), p. 199.

Social attitudes are never monolithic, nor are they usually subject to irreversible changes over the course of a few years or even decades. In eighteenth-century France the relationship between master and servant was paternalistic and brutal, sometimes very close, and often quite informal, at least by nineteenth-century standards. It rested upon the objectification of domestics by their masters, and the dependency and loyalty of the servants themselves. In many respects, these attitudes persisted right up to the Revolution. The informal and erratic quality of the financial tie between master and servant, for instance, changed little over the course of the century. Masters continued to pay their servants at irregular intervals, and servants continued to draw advances on their wages.[17] Yet other signs point to a very slow erosion of the traditional pattern of domestic relations.

As we have seen, throughout the Old Regime proximity in space and frequent physical contact between master and servant were characteristic features of life in many households. Yet in the eighteenth century employers tended more and more to maintain a certain distance from their employees. Wealthy residences in the seventeenth century had been very open and public places where family, servants, and visitors mingled freely in large undifferentiated rooms that opened onto one another. Over the course of the next century, domestic architecture underwent a series of changes that were aimed at allowing individual members of the family greater amounts of privacy. The interior of patrician dwellings exploded into a multiplicity of smaller rooms connected by halls and corridors, and the first signs of a systematic concern as to the whereabouts of servants began to appear. Domestics were more carefully confined to the kitchen, the hall, or the

---

[17] Cissie Fairchilds has been able to document a change in patterns of remuneration in Toulouse, where masters were more likely to pay their servants with greater regularity after mid-century; see her "Masters and Servants in Eighteenth-Century Toulouse," *Journal of Social History* 12:377–378. In Aix, no such change is clearly discernible.

antechamber, and for the first time masters equipped themselves with bells and pulleys in order to summon them from a distance.[18]

This growing need for a physical segregation between master and servant affected domestic architecture more visibly in England than in France. As early as the seventeenth century, the servants of large country houses in England were banished from the main hall where they had previously eaten and slept, and were confined to the basement. Backstairs, closets, and separate servants' quarters eventually became common features of eighteenth-century domestic architecture. As the century progressed, servants' quarters were pushed further and further underground, and eventually the whole staff was removed to a separate wing of the house.[19] Because the dwellings of the French upper classes were more exiguous than those of their English counterparts, such segregation was of necessity less drastic, and probably also came into effect at a later date. Yet a growing concern with privacy is evident, even—or especially—among masters of lesser rank.

When Madame Simon de Franval of Caen hired a live-in tutor for her son in July of 1742, she was faced with a serious organizational problem, and wrote to her husband in disarray:

> We must pay heed that we have three maids and five children sleeping here; we can put two [children] in the little room upstairs but with difficulty because of the closet that gives onto the big room. That leaves two in the small room with the three maids; if the tutor were put in the small room with the two older children, that leaves the three younger ones upstairs, where we should also have one maid sleep since we do not have space for all three of them; well, I am getting tangled up in all of these details that are hard to

[18] Philippe Ariès, *Centuries of Childhood: A Social History of Family Life* (New York, 1962), pp. 398–400; Jean-Louis Flandrin, *Familles: Parenté, maison, sexualité dans l'ancienne société*, p. 92.

[19] Mark Girouard, *Life in the English Country House*, pp. 136–138, 206–208, 218–219, and floor plan, p. 230.

explain from afar, but I want to be free to go to my children's rooms at any time and arrange things as I please, and want the maids to be able to do the same. I cannot say more than that.[20]

The complications created by the addition of a male servant to a household already living at close quarters would have caused no such anxiety to a seventeenth-century mistress. Madame de Franval's closing remarks about wishing to circulate freely in her children's rooms suggest that in this household at least stricter rules of propriety were beginning to prevail. While many masters and mistresses, especially those of higher social standing, were still casual about undressing in front of their servants, the authors of new handbooks took them to task for doing so. "Did you undress in front of your servants in immodest or indecent fashion?" was one of the questions that Antoine Blanchard asked of his readers in a confessional guide published in 1736.[21]

Within the confines of the household, the attitudes of employers toward their servants were changing, albeit slowly. Not only were eighteenth-century employers more concerned about the whereabouts of their servants, they also began to avoid physical contact with them. The illegitimate pregnancy records of Aix and Nantes show a decline in the proportion of pregnancies that resulted from sexual encounters between masters and servants. In Nantes, the proportion of master-servant relationships among all recorded illegitimate pregnancies stood at 36 percent in the 1740s and fell to 9 percent in the 1780s.[22] In Aix the decline was much less dramatic, but followed the same track: affairs between masters and servants accounted for 4.5 percent of

---

[20] A.D.C. 2E 6645. Fonds Simon de Franval, letter of July 20, 1742.

[21] Antoine Blanchard, *Essai d'exhortation pour les états différens des malades*, II:219; see Flandrin, *Familles*, p. 141.

[22] Jacques Depaw, "Illicit Sexual Activity and Society in Eighteenth-Century Nantes," trans. Elborg Forster, in Robert Forster and Orest Ranum, eds., *Family and Society*, p. 167.

all pregnancies in the first half of the century, and 3.6 percent in the second half.[23] The decrease is slight in this case, but its significance is confirmed by evidence of broader changes in sexual mores. Both Jacques Depaw and Cissie Fairchilds, the authors of these studies, have demonstrated that in Nantes and Aix alike sexual relationships between upper-class men and working-class women were on the wane in the eighteenth century. They dropped from 29 to 19 percent of all recorded cases in Aix, and from 40 to 10 percent in Nantes, while the percentage of encounters between men and women of similar social standing (working-class couples for the most part) increased proportionally.[24]

The causes and meaning of this overall shift in patterns of illegitimate encounters have been variously interpreted.[25] The hypothesis most germane to our argument is that of Jacques

[23] Cissie Fairchilds, "Female Sexual Attitudes and the Rise of Illegitimacy: A Case Study," *Journal of Interdisciplinary History* 8:635, 649.

[24] Fairchilds, "Female Sexual Attitudes," pp. 635, 649; Depaw, "Nantes," p. 178.

[25] Edward Shorter opened the debate in the early 1970s by arguing that the rise of illegitimacy in the eighteenth and nineteenth centuries was due to a change in sexual attitudes among the laboring poor. According to Shorter, the eighteenth century witnessed the beginnings of a sea change in attitudes toward sexuality and courtship among the poor, from the traditional "instrumental" attitudes that were characteristic of premodern society to more "expressive" and "spontaneous" attitudes toward sex that were to triumph finally in the twentieth century. The most noteworthy responses to Shorter's work have come from Cissie Fairchilds, Joan Scott, and Louise Tilly, who argue that women's attitudes toward courtship, sex, and marriage changed very little in the eighteenth and nineteenth centuries. The rise of illegitimacy, they believe, was due to the persistence of traditional patterns of courtship—which very often included premarital sex—in societies that were subject to rapid economic and demographic change. See Edward Shorter, "Illegitimacy, Sexual Revolution, and Social Change in Modern Europe," *Journal of Interdisciplinary History* 2 (1971):237–272; "Female Emancipation, Birth Control, and Fertility in European History," *American Historical Review* 78 (1973):605–640; and *The Making of the Modern Family*. See also Cissie Fairchilds, "Female Sexual Attitudes"; Joan Scott and Louise Tilly, "Women's Work and the Family Economy in Nineteenth-Century Europe," *Comparative Studies in Society and History* 17:36–64.

Depaw, who links the decline of master-servant and other socially unequal relationships to changing norms of family morality. In the second half of the century, he argues, the middle-class family began to close in upon itself. Before mid-century in Nantes, extramarital sex was most often a domestic business, involving the master and his maidservant. Later in the century, upper-class men were less likely to carry on such affairs, or at least more inclined to conceal them. If they did want a mistress, they more often went looking outside of the family circle, and secured the affections of working-class women whom they installed in furnished rooms in town. These new standards of behavior, more delicate or more hypocritical than those of old, were, according to Depaw, among the first signs of the emergence of the nuclear family and the concomitant emphasis on conjugal fidelity and "decent" behavior within the home.[26] The sexual exploitation of maidservants by their masters by no means disappeared in the eighteenth century. Such occurrences were to survive well into the twentieth century as one of the uglier realities—and myths— of upper-class life. But beginning in the eighteenth century the visibility of these sorts of affairs began to wane. They became less overt and acceptable because they threatened the harmony and intimacy of a new style of family life.[27]

The physical contact between master and servant that occurred daily in the form of blows and beatings seems also to have declined over the course of the century. In most households, admittedly, brutality probably abated little. Instances of violence perpetrated by masters are recorded in police blotters right up to the end of the century. Yet society's norms of behavior were changing in this respect as well. A police regulation issued in Paris in 1778

---

[26] Depaw, "Nantes," 165–169, 189–191.

[27] The most comprehensive recent discussion of the eighteenth-century evolution of family life toward a more intimate and "companionate" style is in Lawrence Stone's *The Family, Sex, and Marriage in England, 1500–1800*, chaps. 6–9, 13; see also Randolph Trumbach, *The Rise of the Egalitarian Family*, and Flandrin, *Familles*, chap. 3.

contained a new sort of injunction: "Masters are urged to treat [servants] with kindness and humanity, and are forbidden to hit them, abuse and mistreat them, while reserving the right to demand of Justice what they cannot obtain themselves."[28] By the end of the century, violence against servants had become more typical of lower-class than upper-class households. The author of a handbook published in 1785 remarked that masters of lower social standing "usually treat their servants with extreme harshness . . . the lesser the distance between master and servant, the more mistreatments the latter has to suffer."[29] The same author categorically condemned such violence: "As for beating any person, whether he be a servant or any other man, never forget that blows are assaults upon his life and existence, and as many insults to his Maker."[30] The use of the masculine pronoun in this text is ambiguous, but may well suggest that the beating of grown men provoked more comment and uneasiness than did the mistreatment of maidservants. It is likely that middle- and lower-class masters and mistresses continued to punch and slap their maidservants into their household duties. Wealthier employers, by contrast, became more reluctant to resort to physical punishment, especially when dealing with menservants.

These three trends—greater spatial segregation within the home, the waning of sexual relationships between master and servant, and the new objections to corporal punishments—suggest that the attitudes of masters toward their servants were going through a transformation. On the one hand, employers came to feel the need for greater privacy from their servants, and some were coming to shun the casual, intimate, or brutal forms of contact that had previously characterized the relationship. On the other hand, they began to show more respect for their servants as autonomous human beings. Sexual and physical violence perpetrated against

[28] F.-A. Isambert et al., *Recueil général des anciennes lois françaises*, XXV:447.
[29] *L'Art d'être heureux sur la terre mis à la portée du peuple de toutes les nations*, p. 137.
[30] Ibid., p. 139.

servants were much less acceptable at the end of the century than at the beginning, at least in theory. These two facets of the change in employers' attitudes were, of course, intimately connected, and are visible both in the new attitudes of masters and in the new norms of domestic relations they adopted.

Many employers no doubt continued to objectify their servants, and to look upon them as rather troublesome but unfeeling commodities. But eighteenth-century masters were far more aware of the presence of their servants than their predecessors had ever been. The signs of this new sensitivity are difficult to discern in such cryptic, formulaic sources as legal documents or police blotters. But a change of attitudes is evident in some of the more penetrating works of fiction of the age. In seventeenth-century novels, servants were such familiar and unobtrusive presences that they were hardly ever mentioned unless they happened to appear as protagonists. Eighteenth-century novelists, by contrast, began to write of them as intruders, spies, alien elements within the household. Marivaux's Marianne, plagued by doubts about her own social origins, flinches when she feels the look of a servant upon her:

> The sight of that servant standing there reawakened my sensitivity to what had happened, and made me blush again. . . . That valet mortified me, for those people are more scornful than any others in their baseness, and delight in despising those whom they have respected by mistake.[31]

Elsewhere Marianne records as a personal triumph her ability to act like a true lady in the presence of her new chambermaid.[32] Another of Marivaux's heroines, Silvia in *Le Jeu de l'amour et du hasard*, is similarly aware of the judgment of her servants. When the maid Lisette suggests that her mistress might be in love with a mere valet, Silvia's reaction is one of acute embarrassment and

[31] Marivaux, *La Vie de Marianne*, pp. 94–95.
[32] Ibid., p. 247.

hostility: "I am still shaking from what I heard her say: with what impudence do servants not treat us in their minds? How those people degrade one!"[33]

Marivaux himself, of course, was hypersensitive to questions of status and behavior and his plays amply demonstrate his obsession with the complexities of the master-servant relationship. But his characters' awareness of the presence of servants was by no means exceptional. In the works of lesser novelists such as Robert Chasles and Charles de Mouhy, masters and mistresses react in much the same way. One episode of Mouhy's *Mémoires d'une fille de qualité* recounts a loud quarrel between the masters which attracts the household servants. Immediately a lackey is called in and the masters affect loud hilarity in order to save face before the staff. The chambermaids in this novel are evil creatures whose power derives from their access to the family's secrets. Madame de Saint Preuil is plagued by fear and guilt in the presence of her maid Louison, who knows that little Agnès is not Monsieur de Saint Preuil's child. Agnès confides the secret to her own maid Babet, and is later haunted by dreams in which her mother admonishes her: "How can you sleep soundly when you do not know what has become of Louison and Babet?"[34]

These examples are fictional, but they do suggest a new sensitivity to the presence of servants. Even more convincing, perhaps, are the totally unselfconscious asides that punctuate eighteenth-century fiction: "We sent the lackey out," "We dismissed the servants," "In order to get rid of my chambermaid I sent her out to make coffee," and so on.[35] These cryptic notations imply that masters no longer felt it possible to hold intimate or important discussions in the presence of the servants. At least one contemporary observer, Turmeau de la Morandière, admitted frankly to the discomfort that employers felt around domestics.

[33] Marivaux, *Le Jeu de l'amour et du hasard*, act III, scene 8.

[34] Charles de Fieux, Chevalier de Mouhy, *Mémoires d'une fille de qualité qui ne s'est point retirée du monde*, 4 vols. (Amsterdam, 1747), I:9–13, 214–220, III:238.

[35] Ibid., II:7; *Suite des illustres françoises* (Lille, 1780), pp. 276, 328.

LA TOILETTE.

Papillon voltigeant de toilette en toilette,   Et la maîtresse & la soubrette ;

L'Homme à la mode veut captiver à la fois   Et ces amans du jour se tromperont tous trois.

10. Eighteenth-century mistress and chambermaid: *La Toilette*, 1774.
(Phot. Bibl. nat. Paris)

He advised his readers to keep fewer servants: "To the advantage of earning from your inferiors the esteem, friendship, and respect that they owe you for your rank and qualities, you will add that of ridding yourself of the pack of domestic enemies that surrounds you and watches you."[36] Comments such as these suggest, as do changes in domestic architecture and in standards of behavior, that eighteenth-century employers were more aware of the presence of their servants than their predecessors had been, and that they felt increasingly uncomfortable with that awareness.

This gradual change in feelings and behavior was accompanied by a shift in the emphases of the handbooks that set the standards for domestic relations. In the classic handbooks of the late seventeenth and early eighteenth centuries, such as those of Fleury, Audiger, and Madame de Liancourt, the central themes were those of loyalty and responsibility. Though they repeatedly drew attention to the servants' moral duties, the authors of these handbooks were explicitly writing for the masters. And it was upon the masters that they placed the onus of ensuring that servants be materially and morally provided for. They insisted that any servant who was not fundamentally corrupt could and should be set upon the path to salvation by his master. In return, the servant was enjoined to demonstrate his gratitude and live up to his end of the covenant by repaying his master with absolute loyalty and submission.[37]

These ideals continued to govern much of the rhetoric of later handbooks, but over the course of the eighteenth century these ideals of responsibility and loyalty gradually lost their place as organizing principles in normative texts. It was still recommended that masters keep close track of their servants' behavior, but as early as the 1730s the stress on religious and secular instruction had dwindled to a much more limited concern about

---

[36] Turmeau de la Morandière, *Police sur les mendians, les vagabons, . . . , les filles prostituées, les domestiques hors de maison depuis long-temps, et les gens sans aveu* (Paris, 1764), p. 147.

[37] See Introduction.

manners.[38] According to Jean-Louis Flandrin, mid-century employers—or those who wrote for them—were more concerned with preventing servants from corrupting the children of the household than with the educational and moral reform of the servants themselves.[39] Over the course of the century, the high-minded principles of moral responsibility that once set the tone of domestic handbooks were gradually whittled down to a much narrower expression. At the same time, the loyalty demanded of servants was defined in more restricted terms than before. To the Abbé Collet, whose handbook for servants was published in 1758, *fidélité* mainly consisted in keeping one's mouth shut at the appropriate times in order to protect the family's secrets.[40] Collet expected little in the way of gratuitous loyalty from servants. The sort of spontaneous devotion to the master's interests that his predecessors took for granted became, under his pen, an exemplary and unusual demonstration of attachment: "Your love will be generous if it carries you so far as to defend your masters against those who attack them either in their reputation or in their possessions."[41]

New concerns with material details and the formalities of the relationship made their way into eighteenth-century handbooks. In Blanchard's 1736 confessional guide, some of the questions asked of masters concerned salary, contract, and fair remuneration. Employers were asked whether they had ruined their servants' reputations or slandered them out of vindictiveness in order to hinder their chances of future employment.[42] If writers like Blanchard began to intimate that employers ought to respect the professional autonomy of their servants, they also suggested that the loyalty that servants owed their masters was better demon-

---

[38] Flandrin, *Familles*, pp. 140–142.

[39] Ibid., p. 142.

[40] Abbé Pierre Collet, *Instructions et prières à l'usage des domestiques et des personnes travaillant en ville*, pp. 40–41.

[41] Ibid., pp. 40–41.

[42] Blanchard, *Essai d'exhortation*, II:219; Flandrin, *Familles*, p. 141.

strated by efficiency and hard work than by silence and probity.
"Did you work for yourself or for others instead of giving all
your time to your masters?" asked Collet of the servant.[43] Late
in the century, another author expressed this with even greater
clarity: "The loyalty of the servant does not only consist in not
stealing, but also in devoting all of his time to the profit of the
household that pays and feeds him."[44] By 1785, it seems, loyalty
was measured in hours and minutes well spent. Religious paternalism lived on, and continued to govern much of the rhetoric
of the standard handbooks; but the petty concerns of ninteenth-
century bourgeois society were already rearing their ugly heads.

Writers were beginning to acknowledge the moral independence of servants, as well as their professional autonomy. Seventeenth-century handbooks were directed at the masters alone, but
many of those published in the eighteenth century were wholly
or partially aimed at the servants themselves.[45] The extension of
literacy among the lower classes no doubt partially accounts for
this change, but the questions asked and the advice offered to
servants in these handbooks suggest that servants themselves were
now expected to demonstrate some moral autonomy in their choice
of households and masters and in their general behavior. Collet
began his handbook by urging servants to choose households and
employers carefully, and to avoid those establishments "where
salvation is impossible." Elsewhere he lined up instances of situations in which a servant was morally bound *not* to obey his
employer: when his master tried to secure his services for fraud,

---

[43] Collet, *Instructions et prières*, p. lv.

[44] *L'Art d'être heureux*, p. 112.

[45] In the 1730s some handbooks were destined for both masters and servants:
Blanchard's *Essai d'exhortation* of 1736, for instance, or Toussaint de Saint Luc's
Le Bon laquais, ou la vie de Jacques Cochois, dit Jasmin. By the second half of the
century, most handbooks were aimed either at masters *or* at servants. The Abbé
Collet, for instance, wrote one for servants that was published in 1758 (*Instructions et prières*) and six years later another for employers (*Traité des devoirs des gens
du monde et surtout des chefs de famille*).

usury, or criminal intrigue, attempted to swindle customers, or ordered a servant to work on a Sunday or other holy day.[46] According to Collet, servants who toadied indiscriminately to their masters were just as guilty as those who cheated, stole, or disobeyed.

Servants were urged to use their own moral judgment because moralists now realized that masters were no longer willing to devote much of their time and energy to the religious and moral supervision of domestics. In fact, the discussion of the master-servant relationship was gradually pushed to the periphery of handbooks and confessional guides whose authors concerned themselves more and more with the relationship between husband, wife, and children, and much less with the bond between master and servant which earlier had formed the core of these handbooks.[47]

Thus, changes in the content and emphases of prescriptive literature took place alongside the changes that were affecting the master-servant relationship both in reality and in fiction. In the eighteenth century, servants lost their pivotal role on stage. Within the household, they were gradually excluded from close and constant proximity to their masters. In normative texts, the paternalistic ideal slowly gave way to a more limited view of the relationship between domestics and their employers. As the century progressed, employers felt the need for greater amounts of privacy and excluded servants from certain areas of the household, just as in their fiction and ideals they pushed servants to the periphery of their interests and concerns. They did so in part because the relationship as it was traditionally defined and experienced now presented new problems. A new awareness of servants as autonomous workers and as beings possessed of their own faculties of judgment made employers increasingly uncomfortable in their presence. Thes signs of a growing diffidence on the part

[46] Collet, *Instructions et prières*, pp. 3, 12–13, 120–122.
[47] Flandrin, *Familles*, p. 152.

of masters can be linked to the emergence in the eighteenth century of a more intimate and affectionate style of domestic life, one which tended to exclude foreign elements from the midst of the new "companionate" family.[48]

But if, as we have seen, the master-servant relationship had always been shaped by forces that were external to the family, it is outside of the domestic sphere that we must go looking for the reasons behind these eighteenth-century changes. The traditional master-servant relationship, which rested upon reciprocal duties of responsibility and loyalty, was contingent upon the economic vulnerability and social isolation of servants. Masters took advantage of their servants' vulnerability because they needed their loyalty in order to maintain appearances and authority outside of the household. But over the course of the eighteenth century the bond between master and servant slackened considerably. As the century progressed, masters began to shun intimate contact with domestics, to lower their standards of responsibility toward them, to wax nervous at their presence within the household and impatient at their antics on stage. They reduced their expectations considerably, and came to demand hard and honest work from their servants instead of gratuitous loyalty. But why? Was it no longer possible to command such loyalty, or no longer desirable to secure it?

The ideal of the master-servant relationship that prevailed throughout most of the Old Regime was formulated by and for the aristocracy. Right up to the Revolution, members of the first two estates made up the dominant servant-holding group in most localities in terms both of the number of servants they employed and of the style of servant holding they adopted. Until the end of the century, the employment of a large staff of male domestics remained a coveted ideal for up-and-coming employers. But a

---

[48] Stone, *The Family, Sex, and Marriage*, chaps. 6–9.

look at the servant-holding classes of the population in the eighteenth century will show that the preeminence of the first two estates as employers was being slowly eroded.

Changes in the social distribution of employers are visible in some towns as early as the first half of the century. In Aix between 1695 and 1755 the proportion of households employing servants grew from 14 to 20 percent of those listed in the *capitation* tax rolls (see tables 6.1 and 6.2). Nobles of the sword maintained their position as servant holders, accounting for about 15 percent of all employers throughout the half century, while the proportion of servants they employed grew from 15 to 21 percent. Nobles of the robe similarly maintained or even increased their rank as employers over the course of those fifty years. Although they made up 15 percent of all masters in 1701 and only 12 percent in 1756, they employed more of the town's domestics (over a third) by mid-century than ever before. Traditional servant-holding groups in Aix therefore declined in percentage relative to the overall servant-holding population, but the proportion of servants they employed remained the same or increased. In other words, by the middle of the century relatively fewer noble families employed as many or more of the town's servants. A similar trend spanned the entire century in Toulouse, where noblemen kept larger staffs in 1789 than in 1698.[49]

Yet if aristocrats still clung to their expensive habits, they nonetheless lost ground relative to other groups, for servant holding was spreading among other segments of the population. Some groups were clearly on the decline in Aix, notably the clergy and employers belonging to the *petite robe* (lower level royal officials) and other administrators. In other words, some of the employers who had traditionally emulated the aristocracy were beginning to cut back on their staffs. The same was true in Toulouse where *parlementaires* kept their valets and maids throughout the century

[49] Fairchilds, "Toulouse," p. 378.

TABLE 6.1.

Distribution of Servants among Employers, Aix, 1701–1756

	1701		1715–19		1755–56	
	Number	Percent	Number	Percent	Number	Percent
Regular clergy	20	1.3	8	0.4	37	2.5
Secular clergy	43	2.8	74	3.4	53	3.6
		4.1		3.8		6.1
Nobles of the Sword	223	14.7	430	19.7	312	21.0
*Grande Robe**	510	33.6	579	26.6	363	24.3
Subtotal		48.3		46.3		45.3
*Petite Robe**	230	15.2	254	11.7	93	6.3
Other administrative	96	6.3	125	5.7	72	4.8
Subtotal		21.5		17.4		11.1

Professionals	119	7.9	149	6.8	165	11.0
Merchants	55	3.7	68	3.1	89	6.0
Bourgeois	48	3.2	155	7.1	51	3.4
Subtotal		14.8		17.0		20.4
Army and police	13	0.9	32	1.5	23	1.5
Finance	11	0.8	28	1.3	12	0.8
Single women	23	1.5	75	3.4	98	6.5
Urban services	73	4.8	133	6.0	85	5.7
Artisans	38	2.5	68	3.1	31	2.0
Rural workers	11	0.8	4	0.2	10	0.6
Subtotal		11.3		15.5		17.1
Total servants	1,513	100.0	2,182	100.0	1,494	100.0

* The category *Grande Robe* includes *Présidents* and *Conseillers*; all of them were noble. The category *Petite Robe* includes *avocats*, *procureurs*, *secrétaires*, and *audienciers*, most of whom were commoners.

Sources: *Capitations for Aix.* 1701:A.M.A. CC13; 1715–1719:A.M.A. CC 52–55, 57, 59; 1755–1756:A.M.A. CC68, 69

TABLE 6.2.
Social Distribution of Employers, Aix, 1701–1756

	1701		1715–19		1755–56	
	Number	Percent	Number	Percent	Number	Percent
Regular clergy	11	1.2	9	0.7	4	0.5
Secular clergy	35	4.0	48	3.7	36	4.0
Subtotal		5.2		4.4		4.5
Nobles of the Sword	133	14.8	223	17.0	140	15.9
Grande Robe	137	15.3	172	13.2	108	12.3
Subtotal		30.1		30.2		28.2
Petite Robe	161	18.0	167	13.0	80	9.1
Other administrative	64	7.1	86	6.6	50	5.7
Subtotal		25.1		19.6		14.8

	1701		1715–19		1755–56	
Professionals	104	11.5	133	10.2	110	12.5
Merchants	55	6.1	63	4.8	89	10.1
Bourgeois	49	5.5	140	10.7	50	5.7
Subtotal		23.1		25.7		28.3
Army and police	12	1.4	19	1.4	11	1.3
Finance	9	1.0	11	1.3	7	0.8
Single women	22	2.5	73	5.6	91	10.4
Commerce and urban services	59	6.6	98	7.5	64	7.3
Artisans	38	4.2	53	4.0	30	3.4
Rural workers	8	0.8	4	0.3	9	1.0
Subtotal		16.5		20.1		24.2
Total employers	897	100.0	1,299	100.0	879	100.0
Total heads of households	6,380		5,385		4,385	
Percent of employers		14.0		22.4		20.0

Sources: *Capitations for Aix.* 1701:A.M.A. CC 13; 1715–19:A.M.A. CC 52–55, 57, 59; 1755–56:A.M.A. CC 68, 69

while barristers doffed some of their social pretensions and began to employ fewer male servants and more women.[50]

At the same time, other groups were gaining importance as servant holders. In Aix, petty-bourgeois masters such as artisans and shopkeepers still counted for little, but solidly middle class employers were gaining ground. Professionals, merchants, and bourgeois together employed 14.6 percent of the town's servants at the beginning of the century and 20.5 percent by the 1750s. By mid-century these three groups still held less than half as many servants as the aristocracy, but they represented the same proportion of the town's employers (28 percent) as nobles of the sword and robe combined. The group whose numerical importance as servant holders increased most markedly over this period was that of single women, who accounted for 2.5 percent of the town's employers in 1701 and 10.5 percent in the 1750s. These women were commoners, usually middle-class widowed *rentières* who almost invariably employed a single maid. They were, in short, the female equivalents of the professional and rentier masters whose importance was also on the rise.

In Aix the surviving records cover only the first half of the century. In Bayeux the documents we have pertain only to the last thirty years of the century. Despite the chronological disparity, similar trends are discernible at the end of the century in the Norman town, an administrative and residential center in many ways comparable to Aix (see tables 6.3 and 6.4). In Bayeux, as in Aix and Toulouse, aristocrats consolidated their position as the town's principal servant holders. On the eve of the Revolution they amounted to a third of all employers and held just under half of the town's servants. The clergy, far more prestigious and wealthy in Bayeux than in Aix, lost some ground but still employed over 12 percent of the town's servants on the eve of the

[50] Lenard Berlanstein, *The Barristers of Toulouse in the Eighteenth Century*, p. 60.

TABLE 6.3.

Distribution of Servants among Employers, Bayeux, 1768–1796

	1768		1787		1796	
	Number	Percent	Number	Percent	Number	Percent
Clergy and former clergy	84	15.5	83	12.5	6	1.5
Nobles and former nobles	197	36.5	324	48.5	70	14.5
Professionals and administrators	69	13.0	60	9.0	56	11.5
Rentiers, bourgeois, unspecified commoners	21	4.0	57	8.5	83	17.0
Single women	59	11.0	48	7.0	119	25.0
Retailers	51	9.0	55	8.0	57	12.0
Innkeepers	21	4.0	23	3.5	35	7.0
Artisans	37	7.0	21	3.0	18	4.0
Rural workers	—	—	—	—	16	3.5
Independent servants	—	—	—	—	20	4.0
Total servants	539	100.0	671	100.0	480	100.0

Sources: A.D.C. C 4538:Capitation des Bourgeois, 1768; A.D.C. 4547:Capitation des Bourgeois, 1787; A.M.B. 1F 27:Dénombrement de l'an IV

TABLE 6.4.

Social Distribution of Employers, Bayeux, 1768–1796

	1768		1787		1796	
	Number	Percent	Number	Percent	Number	Percent
Clergy and former clergy	45	12	54	13.0	4	1.5
Nobles and former nobles	99	28	134	33.0	23	8.0
Professionals and administrators	56	16	49	12.0	36	13.0
Rentiers, bourgeois, unspecified commoners	17	5	50	12.0	59	22.0
Single women	46	13	43	10.5	81	29.5
Retailers	46	13	49	12.0	32	12.0
Innkeepers	10	3	10	2.5	19	7.0
Artisans	37	10	21	5.0	14	5.0
Rural workers	—	—	—	—	5	2.0
Total employers	356	100	410	100.0	273	100.0

Sources: A.D.C. C 4538:Capitation des Bourgeois, 1768; A.D.C. 4547:Capitation des Bourgeois, 1787; A.M.B. 1F 27:Dénombrement de l'an IV

Revolution.[51] The preeminence of the first two orders of the realm as servant holders in Bayeux was not challenged by what might be termed the "active" segments of the Third Estate. Artisans, tradesmen, professionals, and administrators had on the whole fewer servants in 1787 than twenty years earlier. In Bayeux the new masters were not shopkeepers, doctors, or lawyers, but the idle commoners designated as *bourgeois*, many of whom lived off revenues from investment in landed property.

Ten years later the social distribution of employers in Bayeux had been drastically reshuffled by social and political upheaval. The aristocracy and clergy, ruined or banished by the Revolution, accounted for less than a tenth of all employers. Trends that were barely perceptible a decade earlier had clearly come into their own. The productive and professional categories of the population did employ a greater proportion of the town's servants, but they were far outdistanced by the town's *rentiers* and bourgeois. In the Year IV of the Republic, nonworking commoners and single women together made up half of the town's employers and kept 43 percent of the town's servants.[52]

In Aix and Bayeux, which were typical of Ancien Régime society with their top-heavy administrative and ecclesiastical bodies and their stagnant economies, the overall trends were similar despite differences in detail. In both towns—as in Toulouse— noblemen showed no signs, before the Revolution, of relinquishing their costly habits. If anything, they employed more servants as the century progressed. Other groups among the traditional

[51] On the economy and society of prerevolutionary Bayeux, see Olwen Hufton, *Bayeux in the Late Eighteenth Century*, chaps. 1–5.

[52] Bérénice Grissolange, "Aix-en-Provence sous la Révolution: Structures sociales et familiales" (Mémoire de Maîtrise, Univ. de Provence, 1974), I:263. It is unfortunately impossible to compare my own statistics from the Ancien Régime *Capitations* with Grissolange's classification of employers under the Revolution, since her classification is based on a breakdown into categories of production (primary, secondary, tertiary, and *oisifs*), and mine on status and occupation. Her tables do not reveal, for instance, how many nobles and ecclesiastics continued to employ servants in Aix under the Revolution.

elites, however, were cutting back on their staffs: lower-level officeholders in Aix, clergymen and administrators in Bayeux. In both towns the employment of servants was becoming more socially widespread, though in Bayeux the preeminence of the first two estates was not really overhauled until the Revolution. In both sites the employers who gained ground most steadily were from the upper crust of the Third Estate: merchants and professionals in Aix, rentiers in Bayeux, and single commoner women in both towns.

In sum, the aristocratic model of servant holding lasted until the Revolution because noblemen continued, as a group, to employ more servants than any other segment of the population. But the dominance of the aristocracy was being undermined by the rise of new groups of masters who would not really come into their own until the Revolution.

These new masters had, on the face of it, much in common with the old aristocracy. The *bourgeois* of the Old Regime, many of whom became the *notables* of postrevolutionary society, derived their income from landed property and shunned productive occupations. Many of them, as we have seen, hankered after the ostentatious style of the aristocracy, and imitated them by hiring male domestics and dressing them in livery. But the growing importance of this group, and the overall extension of servant holding in the population to include larger numbers of professional and petty-bourgeois masters as well, ultimately contributed to the reshaping of the master-servant relationship.

One of the factors contributing to the redefinition of the master-servant relationship, then, was the extension of servant holding among the middle classes. The demographic explosion that took place in the later eighteenth century probably played a major part in bringing this about. As we saw in chapter 1, population growth pushed large numbers of rural youths out of the countryside onto the road to town. The urban middle classes, be they merchants, professionals, single women, or the ubiquitous *rentiers*, had probably always wanted servants. By the later eighteenth century, abundant supply was at last available to meet a built-in demand.

Though the aristocracy maintained its numerical supremacy until the Revolution, more middle-class households had access to the employment of servants than ever before. Of necessity this was slowly to affect the nature of domestic service and to change society's perception of what it meant to keep servants. More specifically, the proportion of single-servant households was on the rise, as was the employment of women instead of men. In Aix in 1701, 555 families out of the 897 who employed servants, or 61 percent, had only one employee. By 1796 the proportion had risen to 84 percent. In Bayeux, 69 percent employed one servant in the 1760s, and 75 percent in the 1790s.[53] At the same time, the proportion of women among the servant population rose slowly before the Revolution and rapidly thereafter. Up to the middle of the eighteenth century, one-third to one-half of the servant population in most towns was male. By the 1790s eight or nine servants out of ten were female, a proportion that was to remain constant throughout most of the nineteenth century.[54] In Aix, for instance, 70 percent of the town's servants

[53] A.M.A. CC13 (*Capitation* for 1701); Grissolange, "Aix-en-Provence sous la Révolution," I:263; A.D.C. C4538 (*Capitation* for 1768); A.M.B. 1F 27 (tax roll for the Year IV).

[54] In Lyon in 1702, 51 percent of the town's servants were female. According to Messance and Moheau, there were equal proportions of male and female servants in Paris in 1754, while the servant population of provincial towns such as Tours, Riom, Lyon, and Rouen was just over 50 percent female in the second half of the century. But their figures for male *domesticité* are probably too high, for they seem to have made little distinction between male servants, apprentices, and clerks. Under the Revolution the proportion of female servants stood at 75 percent in Bordeaux, and 90 percent in Marseille; see Maurice Garden, *Lyon et les lyonnais au XVIIIe siècle*, p. 250; Messance, *Recherches sur la population des généralités d'Auvergne, de Lyon, de Rouen, et de quelques provinces et villes du royaume*, p. 186; Moheau, *Recherches et considérations sur la population de France*, p. 116; Francois Pariset, ed., *Bordeaux au XVIIIe siècle*, p. 367; Thérèse Reynaud-Lefaucheur, "Les Femmes dans la population marseillaise en 1793" (Mémoire

were women in the 1700s, 90 percent in the 1790s, and 88 percent in the 1850s.[55] Female servants had always been more numerous than their male counterparts, but only in the later eighteenth century did they begin to outnumber menservants by a vast majority. The trend toward the feminization of service began to take shape concurrently with the extension of servant holding among new segments of the population. By the end of the century, a great majority of employers contented themselves with the services of a single maidservant.

The feminization of domestic service in the latter half of the eighteenth century was an unprecedented development. Throughout the Old Regime, masters of middling status had scraped and saved in order to afford the luxury of keeping a couple of lackeys whom they could outfit in flashy clothes and parade before the public. Now, it seems, some masters were shrinking from such unnecessary expenses. In Montpellier an observer noted in 1768 that the traditional paraphernalia of aristocratic service was viewed with distaste in some circles:

> For some time now many have rejected the ridiculous luxury that consisted in filling one's household with servants bedizened in gaudy liveries. Nowadays people prefer to hire only those that are necessary, and to keep them as busy and productive as possible.[56]

Makers of lace and ornaments in Montpellier were facing a crisis, he wrote, since masters were now increasingly loath to invest in

---

de Maîtrise, Univ. de Provence, 1975), p. 96. The figures cited for the nineteenth century are from Theresa McBride, *The Domestic Revolution: The Modernisation of Household Service in England and France 1820–1920*, p. 45.

[55] Jean-Paul Coste, *La Ville d'Aix-en-Provence en 1695: Structure urbaine et société*, II:959; A.M.A. CC13; Grissolange, "Aix-en-Provence sous la Révolution," I:259.

[56] Joseph Berthélé, ed., *Montpellier en 1768 et 1836 d'après deux manuscrits inédits*, p. 68.

expensive liveries and were coming to prefer simple uniforms to "those ponderous heaps of silk braid that cost so much."[57]

These new masters were no longer quite as willing to invest large amounts of money into the upkeep of a staff for display. They wanted fewer men, simpler uniforms, more productive servants. Though many of those who acceded to servant holding in the eighteenth century were prosperous professionals and *rentiers*—men and women who traditionally had emulated the aristocracy—these new employers were less likely, as the century progressed, to invest their hard-earned fortunes into hiring and equipping male servants. But was this change in social aspirations a matter of choice or of necessity? No matter how attractive the old ideals, they would be hard to attain if the services of male domestics were becoming prohibitively expensive.

The wages of servants in both sexes increased substantially in the eighteenth century. According to d'Avenel's classic history of wages and prices in France, the nominal salaries of servants went into a sharp decline in the second half of the seventeenth century, but from the 1720s until the end of the eighteenth century they increased steadily, those of women by 40 percent and those of men by 67 percent.[58] Recent local studies provide more detailed information, but on the whole d'Avenel's conclusions stand confirmed. All over France, the wages of servants escalated in the latter part of the century, usually by 40 to over 100 percent. The rate of increase naturally varied a great deal among different categories of servants, depending on sex and level of qualification.

In Toulouse the yearly wages of maidservants were 40 percent higher in the seventies and eighties than in the first half of the century, while those of unskilled men increased by 46 percent over the same period. In the eighties and nineties the salaries of both men and women soared to about double their prerevolu-

[57] Ibid., p. 103.

[58] Georges d'Avenel, *Histoire économique de la propriété, des salaires, et de tous les prix en général*, III:574–575.

tionary level.[59] In Aix the data cover only the second half of the century, but also show very substantial increases between the early 1740s and the late 1780s (see figure 6.1 and appendix 2). The wages of unskilled maids rose somewhat faster than in Toulouse, by 44 percent over a shorter time span. By contrast, the higher salaries of skilled women such as chambermaids, governesses, and female cooks only augmented by 17 percent. Lackeys fared little better. Their wages remained compressed below one hundred livres a year for most of the century, then increased by barely one-fifth. Those among Aixois servants who reaped the greatest benefits from the rise in wages were skilled menservants. In the twenty years before the Revolution, the salaries of cooks rose by 66 percent while those of valets more than doubled. In Aix, as in Toulouse, salaries shot upward in the late 1780s. Rates of increase, as might be expected, were not identical everywhere. In the Gosselin de Manneville household in Caen, the servants whose wages increased most between the 1740s and the 1770s were unskilled maids, whose wages were subject to a 90 percent increase. The salaries of male cooks rose by half and those of other skilled menservants by 42 percent. Lackeys did more than tolerably well, with increases of about 50 percent, whereas chambermaids fared even worse than in Aix (see appendix 3).

Despite the differences, some overall conclusions may be drawn from these examples. Employers, it seems, were reluctant to raise substantially the wages of either unskilled men or skilled women. The salaries of lackeys remained compressed at very low levels throughout the second half of the century—usually less than 100 livres—and the wages of chambermaids increased hardly at all. Unskilled maidservants earned substantially more in the seventies and eighties than they did in the fifties. But their salaries were so low to begin with that even when their wages were doubled this did not represent a great expenditure for their masters. By the 1780s most maids still earned at best 40 or 50 livres a year.

[59] Fairchilds, "Toulouse," pp. 375–376.

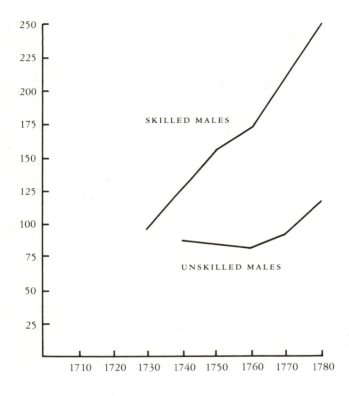

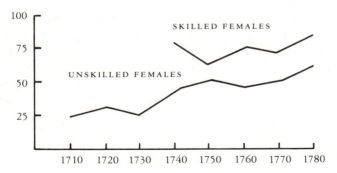

Figure 6.1. Nominal Wages of Servants in Aix, 1710–1790 (in livres tournois)

In the end, the only substantial benefits came the way of skilled menservants. A cook or a valet in a wealthy household might earn 100 or 150 livres a year in the 1750s. By the 1780s he could expect wages of 200 to 250 livres. At a time when the average worker still earned between 1 and 2 livres a day,[60] wages of that order with food, lodging, and sometimes clothes provided represented an enviable income.

In short, the figures suggest three simultaneous trends in the second half of the eighteenth century: the wages of female servants became more uniform, with chambermaids earning less and unskilled maids earning more; the incomes of unskilled males were debased to the point, perhaps, of rendering the occupation very unattractive; and the services of skilled menservants became extremely expensive. But how substantial were in fact the financial rewards of service at a time when prices were soaring upward?

If the wages of servants increased by 40 to 60 percent on the average over the course of the century, they were just barely keeping up with the rising cost of living, since prices all over the realm rose by over 60 percent between the 1720s and the 1780s. On the face of it, servants fared worse than other workers in town. In Caen, for instance, the salaries of skilled and unskilled workers rose faster than those of domestics in the second half of the century, by 55 and 66 percent, respectively, as against 40 to 45 percent for servants.[61]

Nonetheless, the better-paid among servants were in a position to reap substantial benefits from the particular economic conditions of the later eighteenth century. Overall, the century was one of expansion. The baneful effects of the late seventeenth-century recession continued to play themselves out in the early eighteenth century, but by the 1720s the economic tide had

[60] Camille Ernest Labrousse et al., *Histoire économique et sociale de la France*, II:668–670.

[61] Jean Claude Perrot, *Genèse d'une ville moderne: Caen au XVIIIe siècle*, II:1383–1384.

turned. Climatic conditions improved, famines and plagues re-
ceded, and the death of Louis XIV brought a long succession of
dynastic wars to an end.[62] Yet the era of economic expansion that
followed and lasted into the nineteenth century was also to know
its dark moments. In the second half of the eighteenth century,
recurrent agrarian crises periodically sent the price of foodstuffs
skyrocketing and brought urban trades to a temporary standstill.
The most severe of these crises occurred in the late 1740s, in
1770, and on the eve of the Revolution, but many others swept
the provinces at different times in the intervening years. No
matter how substantial the increase in their wages, workers in
both town and country were always vulnerable to the devastating
repercussions of crises that wrought havoc in their budget by
driving up the price of bread. Under these circumstances, servants
were likely to come out ahead.

Though their nominal wages may have stagnated or even slumped
in times of crisis, servants nonetheless had bed and board provided, and were therefore protected from the worst effects of these
crises. The economic fate of an unskilled maid earning 30 to 50
livres no doubt inproved little under these circumstances. But
the combination of rising wages and economic immunity worked
to the advantage of the better paid among servants, especially
men, allowing them to amass substantial sums of money and to
shore up their economic status by means of investments and loans
to other workers.

Marriage contracts in both Lyon and Aix show that by the end
of the century the fortunes of male servants at marriage were
superior to those of unskilled workers. In Lyon the marriage
settlements of unskilled *affaneurs* and servants were about equal
in the 1720s; by the 1780s, 31 percent of the servants settled
deeds involving more than 1,000 livres, as against 7 percent of

[62] This sketch of eighteenth-century economic conditions is based on Labrousse's *Histoire économique et sociale* (vol. II), especially part 3, chap. 6.

the *affaneurs*.[63] In Aix late in the century, servants were wealthier at marriage than unskilled workers. The median sum recorded in servants' marriage contracts in the 1770s was of 600 to 1,200 livres. On the average they were as wealthy as journeymen, if not quite as rich as master artisans (see appendix 4).[64]

Other financial transactions recorded in the logs of Aixois notaries offer a glimpse of the enviable fortunes of some menservants in that town. In the years 1705 and 1706, only nine documents— other than wills and marriage contracts—carried the names of servants. These were paltry receipts and settlements of minor accounts, none of which involved very large sums of money.[65] A random gathering of fifty-two such documents in the second half of the century offers a very different picture. In eleven of these cases, servants were involved in substantial dealings in real estate.[66] The cook François Jean, for instance, sold a house to one Henry de Ferry in 1760 for 3,400 livres; three years later the servant Charles Aubin purchased a farmhouse from the widow of a *conseiller* for 1,200 livres; the doorman of the Président d'Albertas bought a house in town from the widow of a glove maker; yet another manservant employed by the Conseiller de Brégançon spent 2,000 livres on a house in 1776.[67] Some servants purchased annuities for themselves for sums ranging from 100 to 2,000 livres, while others drew up apprenticeship contracts for their sons with master artisans. Sixteen of the documents concerned loans of substantial sums of money granted by servants to other townsfolk.

[63] Garden, *Lyon*, pp. 245, 263. In the 1720s, 96 percent of the *affaneurs* and 87 percent of the servants settled deeds involving less than 1,000 livres. In the 1780s, 93 percent of the servants married with less than 1,000 livres.

[64] A.D.M. IIC 236 (Contrôle des Actes).

[65] A.D.A. 301E 367, 368; 302E 1266; 303E 473; 305E 140; 306E 944; 307E 1265, 1266; 308E 1480, 1481; 309E 1392, 1403.

[66] A.D.A. 301E 394–398; 306E 971–975; 307E 1307, 1308.

[67] A.D.A. 306E 971, fol. 760; 306E 974, fol. 556; 306E 975, fol. 94; 307E 1307, fol. 215.

After midcentury, servants were frequently in a position to lend money to other workers. Only two such transactions surfaced in the records of Aix's *Bureau de Police* before 1750, whereas eight were recorded between 1763 and 1770.[68] The money was sometimes lent to artisans, but more often to destitute day laborers who came to plead poverty before the police. Claude Achard, who owed the cook Davin 15 livres, entreated them that "he was in no condition to pay them now, begging the Bureau to grant him time until the grape harvest." Similar pleas were heard from a worker named Louis who begged for more time, and from Ricard, an apprentice stocking maker, who assured the police that he was expecting money from back home. Both owed substantial sums of money to servants.[69] Only in two of these cases were pawning and usury explicitly mentioned, but one can easily imagine that most servants did not part with their hard-earned savings for the sake of charity alone.

Those among servants who invested in real estate while still in service evidently did so with the intention of augmenting their income by renting out rooms. Again, it was not until late in the century that evidence of such wealth was recorded. In 1771 a servant named Joseph Turcan brought suit against his own tenant, a Mademoiselle Blanc, on the grounds that she was serving white wine in her apartment and that her clients and children were satisfying their *besoins naturels* in the courtyard. Three of the five other tenants who testified on Turcan's behalf were former or unemployed servants who also rented from him.[70] Nine years later Emilie Le Comte, an actress from Brussels, complained that her landlord, a brutal and arrogant domestic known as Saint-Jean, had broken into her room, rummaged through her possessions, and beaten her when she dared to complain. She was paying 15 livres a month for a room in the house that he owned.[71]

---

[68] A.M.A. FF 93, fols. 109, 189, 197, 208; FF 94, fols. 6, 7, 14, 190.
[69] A.M.A. FF 93, fol. 189; FF 94, fol. 190; FF 93, fol. 109.
[70] A.D.A. IVB 1246, June 1771.
[71] A.D.A. IVB 1260, January 24, 1780.

In sum, the evidence from Aix suggests that some servants, most of them skilled men, were in a stronger economic position in the late eighteenth century than ever before. Reaping the rewards of a century-long rise in wages, yet protected from the worst effects of periodically soaring prices, they were able to save sizable sums of money which they invested in real estate or annuities, or increased by means of loans or rents. This surely did little to endear them to other townsfolk, either working class or middle class, and no doubt contributed to the discredit into which male service was falling. But it also rendered them less economically vulnerable, and hence probably less docile. For rising numbers of middling masters, the employment of skilled or even semiskilled men became not only prohibitively expensive, but perhaps downright unattractive as well.

Rising wages and high food prices were by no means the only causes, nor even the main ones, for the decline of male service. But they probably contributed to the evolution of domestic work into an occupation heavily dominated by women. On the one hand, the increased wealth of skilled menservants afforded them new measures of self-confidence and independence, which may indeed have influenced their poorer brothers in service. It would be difficult for parvenu masters, even wealthy ones, to deal with a group of menials whose fortunes—and no doubt pretensions— were on the rise. On the other hand, the vertiginous rise in the price of foodstuffs must have created serious budgetary difficulties for all but the most wealthy among masters. If food was expensive, high wages were out of the question. As a result, the wages of skilled menservants and the purchase of costly liveries became too great a financial burden for many who acceded to servant holding in the later eighteenth century, no matter how anxious they were to imitate their betters.

At first, masters sacrificed convenience to the need for display by hiring more lackeys and fewer valets, while they compressed the wages of skilled women such as chambermaids. This was the pattern for officers of various administrative bodies in Lyon in the first half of the century. In 1706, 59 percent of their men-servants were lackeys; by 1759 the proportion had risen to 85 percent, while that of valets dropped from 11 to 1 percent. They employed more women at mid-century, many of whom were maidservants who could double up as cooks.[72] Eventually the rise in wages and prices was such that many employers gave up this sign of social standing and stopped keeping menservants alto-gether. Eighteenth-century economic conditions thus contributed to the feminization of service by forcing some masters to cut back on their expenditures. In the last decades of the century, the rising cost of servant holding and the aura of wealth and inde-pendence that surrounded the upper crust of male service probably made the employment of men much less attractive to families who had access to servant holding for the first time. Figaro might be a hero on stage, but few middle-class masters, one suspects, would have cared to introduce him into the sanctuary of their own homes.

For noblemen and the wealthiest among social climbers, how-ever, cutting back on sumptuary expenditures remained out of the question. The ultimate effect of eighteenth-century social and economic change was to widen the gap between an elite of wealthy masters who held on to their large, male-dominated staffs, and the growing ranks of more modest employers for whom the ex-clusive use of female servants was not only a necessity but, in-creasingly, a self-conscious assertion of their own way of life.

New demographic and economic trends certainly undermined the traditional master-servant relationship. And yet, I would suggest, they merely accentuated and accelerated a transformation of cultural ideals that gathered momentum in the second half of the eighteenth century. The feminization of service and the ex-tension of servant holding to growing numbers of middle-class families did not occur on a massive scale until society was trans-

[72] Bernard Fradin, "Domestiques d'établissement et domestiques de maison à Lyon au XVIIIe siècle" (Mémoire de Maîtrise, Univ. de Lyon, 1976), pp. 49–51.

formed by revolutionary upheaval in the 1790s. Yet as we saw in the opening pages of this chapter, the ideals, realities, and fictional representations of the master-servant relationship had been changing very slowly, even among the elites, throughout the entire century. Demographic and economic change no doubt precipitated the demise of aristocratic service. But the rationale for the traditional mode of service, a system based on wasteful display, was ideological rather than economic. It is therefore to ideology that we must turn in order to understand why in the course of the eighteenth century that system lost its coherence and its justification.

Complaints about servants had always been widespread. Chroniclers, police officials, and disgruntled *honnêtes gens* of all sorts had always been ready to brand them as liars, troublemakers, and two-faced sycophants. Such criticisms, as we have seen, had a great deal to do with the uneasiness provoked by the ambiguous position of servants within a society whose organizing principle was the clear definition of rank and status. These sorts of complaints persisted, but as the century progressed they were more often subsumed under the broader criticism of the Old Regime that flowed from the pens of the philosophes and their followers.

The major writers of the French Enlightenment had little affection for servants. Voltaire disliked them as a result, perhaps, of his drubbing at the hands of Rohan's henchmen. "Valets are no different than courtisans," he snapped, "they do nothing but ape their masters."[73] Rousseau once worked as a lackey, but his writings contain many an acid comment on the subject of "those perennial job-seekers who . . . make it their business to serve everybody and attach themselves to nobody."[74] Diderot also pro-

---

[73] Voltaire, *L'Echange* (1734), in *Oeuvres complètes*, III:263.
[74] Jean-Jacques Rousseau, *La Nouvelle Héloïse*, p. 333.

fessed contempt for men who of their own volition had opted for a servile occupation. Service, he wrote,

> is the most abject of occupations, and it is always sloth or some other vice of character that causes one to hesitate between the livery and hard labor. If a man with broad shoulders and strong legs chooses to empty chamber pots rather than to carry loads, he necessarily has a vile disposition.[75]

Writers such as Diderot despised servants for choosing to subjugate their will to that of another, yet none of the philosophes ever questioned the existence of domestic service as an institution. To begin with, their comments were nearly always directed at male servants, for they saw nothing wrong in a woman's engaging in a servile occupation. But neither did they object to domestic service on egalitarian grounds. After all, with the possible exception of Rousseau, none of the major thinkers of the French Enlightenment ever nurtured visions of a truly egalitarian society. They did not object to the principle of service in itself, but to the roles that servants played in public and private life. They criticized the traditional functions of servants for three different but related sets of reasons: domestics, as they saw it, served as unnatural intermediaries between parent and child; male service was a drain on the economy and an obstacle to population growth; and personal servants were used as cogs in an outmoded system of social and political relations.

In the seventeenth and eighteenth centuries, writers customarily cautioned parents against allowing their children to spend large amounts of time with servants, especially lackeys. The argument of Christian moralists like Alexandre Varet or the Abbé Castel de Saint Pierre was simply that lower servants would introduce children to reprehensible pastimes or would ruin their

---

[75] Denis Diderot, *Réfutation suivie de l'ouvrage d'Helvétius intitulé l'homme* (1773–1774), in *Oeuvres complètes*, II:429.

characters by exposing them to deceit, dishonesty, or flattery.[76] But as a new system of familial values emerged in the later eighteenth century, writers carried these objections much further. To the likes of Rousseau and Mercier, the problem went deeper than the simple possibility that servants might corrupt the master's offspring. Even the most commendable wet nurse, tutor, or governess was a venal creature engaged in a lucrative business. What would become of children, they asked, whose first emotional experience was that of a relationship based on money? "How can one imagine," mused Sébastien Mercier, "that for twelve hundred francs a year some mercenary will bring up a real man?"[77] Rousseau raised the same point in the opening pages of *Emile*: "Venal soul! Do you think that money will buy your son another father? Be not deceived, you are giving him not a master but a knave!"[78]

Rousseau's well-known advocacy of maternal breast feeding over the employment of wet nurses derived in part from similar considerations. To Diderot as well, a wet nurse was nothing but "a hired woman whose only incentive is the hope of a mercenary reward."[79] The effects on a child's system of values of this early exposure to a mercantile relationship could only be detrimental. The demographer Moheau also argued against wet nursing on the grounds that it impeded population growth. Children entrusted to wet nurses grew up in total ignorance of family ties, he argued. If the only relationship they knew was that of debtor and creditor, how could they develop any commitment to the propagation of the species?[80]

Employers had always been fully aware of the "mercenary"

---

[76] Alexandre Varet, *De l'Education chrétienne des enfants selon les maximes de l'Ecriture Sainte*, p. 145; Charles-Irenée Castel de Saint-Pierre, *Avantages de l'éducation des collèges sur l'éducation domestique*, p. 14.

[77] Louis-Sébastien Mercier, *Le Tableau de Paris*, XII:132.

[78] Jean-Jacques Rousseau, *Emile ou de l'éducation* p. 23.

[79] Article "Nourrices" of the *Encyclopédie* of Diderot and d'Alembert.

[80] Moheau, *Recherches et Considérations*, 102–104.

motives that governed their servants' behavior. But in the later eighteenth century the recognition that such a financial bond existed within the domestic setting was more likely to provoke uneasiness. A major trend in both values and behavior, culminating in both England and France in the decades after 1750, transformed the family into a more confined environment in which ties between a small number of family members took on greater intensity. The ideal of the Western family became that of a warm and private environment, increasingly segregated from the cold and competitive world of the marketplace.[81] Under these new circumstances, the constant and conspicuous presence of servants became a problem, for domestics might hinder the direct flow of affection between family members, especially parents and children. More generally, the presence of salaried workers could subvert this new ideal of family life, for it introduced the stark realities of the marketplace within a realm that was to be one of pure affectivity. The logical consequence of these concerns was that within the household, just as in the theater, servants should be banished from center stage.

Criticisms of the traditional use of servants concerned public as well as private life. The most systematic denunciation of the characteristic features of aristocratic service was articulated by the Physiocrats and their followers in the decades after 1750. The Physiocrats' concern with national prosperity and population growth and the emphasis they placed on the agrarian sector are well known.[82] To economists of this school and their disciples, domestic service was the antithesis of productive work. Writers like Quesnay and Turgot rejected the traditional division of society into orders or estates and instead drew up social classifications based on productivity and proximity to the source of all wealth,

[81] Stone, *The Family, Sex, and Marriage*, chaps. 6–9. The increasing demarcation between public and private life in the eighteenth century is discussed extensively by Richard Sennett in *The Fall of Public Man*, chaps. 1–6.

[82] The best recent work on the Physiocrats is Elizabeth Fox-Genovese, *The Origins of Physiocracy*.

the land. Within such taxonomies, servants were always relegated to the lowest rank, among the "sterile" or "disposable" categories of the population.[83]

Physiocrats and demographers denounced male service on the grounds that the employment of men for sumptuary purposes robbed workers from the productive sectors of the economy. To Messance, servants were "hands made useless to agriculture, manufactures, and commerce."[84] Or, as Moheau put it, "The existence of servants is vicious in that their work is devoted to personal utility and their masters' pleasures rather than to an increase in national prosperity."[85] Private employers, these writers argued, had no right to keep men away from the productive sector, for in doing so they sacrificed the public good to private, selfish interests.

Ideas of this sort had gained popularity even before they were systematically expounded by economists and demographers. As early as 1743, the lawyer Barbier alluded to "the idea that seems to be circulating nowadays of repopulating the countryside by decreasing the number of servants in Paris."[86] From mid-century on, enlightened observers frequently complained of the effects of service on the local and national economy. In the 1760s the anonymous chronicler of Montpellier grumbled about the scandalous addiction of cooks and chambermaids to *café au lait*. These people, he wrote, preferred a life of slovenly refinement to the useful toils of the countryside. "In sum," he concluded, "everything to do with service costs Montpellier a great deal."[87] In the capital city around the same time, Turmeau de la Morandière echoed these grievances. Service, he wrote, "depopulates the towns, the provinces, the countrysides . . . robs workers from the arts

[83] Institut National d'Etudes Démographiques, *François Quesnay et la Physiocratie*, 2 vols. (Paris, 1958), II:793–794.

[84] Messance, *Recherches sur la population*, p. 105.

[85] Moheau, *Recherches et considérations*, p. 113.

[86] Edmond Barbier, *Chronique de la régence et du règne de Louis XV*, III:428.

[87] Berthélé, *Montpellier*, pp. 68–69, 149.

and crafts." It was evil, he added, to have society bear the burden of these parasites whose only function was to serve as props to ruinous and ill-advised extravagance.[88] Some twenty years later, Sébastien Mercier held the very same opinions. To Mercier the very sight of a group of lackeys conjured up a mournful image of deserted countrysides: "When you see a group of them in an antechamber, you must reflect that a void has been created in some province."[89]

The employment of male servants was detrimental to the public good in that it depopulated not just the countryside but the nation as a whole. In the minds of these critics, the baneful effects of male service could all be summed up in one word: sterility. The conspicuous celibacy of servants, especially men, was a slap in the face of the physiocratic-minded, who believed that population growth as well as agricultural productivity were the wellsprings of national wealth. Diderot believed that celibacy was contrary to the laws of nature, and downright antisocial as well. Marriage was "a debt that every man must pay to society." To Moheau, who pondered in his chapter on luxury the castration of animals and eunuchs as well as the celibacy of servants, marriage and reproduction were "the first duty of the citizen."[90] These writers usually pointed out that masters were more at fault than their servants. It was the vanity and selfishness of employers, they claimed, that coerced healthy men into unnatural barrenness.

As Physiocrats and philosophes saw it, the characteristic features of aristocratic service—male servants, celibacy, conspicuous idleness—were geared to the interests of private employers and worked to the detriment of the public good. This distinction between the interests of the nation and those of private individuals is also implicit in their criticisms of the roles that servants traditionally played in society.

[88] Turmeau de la Morandière, *Police sur les mendians*, pp. 143–145, 155.

[89] Mercier, *Tableau de Paris*, II:122–123.

[90] Diderot, *Le Prosélyte* in *Oeuvres complètes*, II:80; Moheau, *Recherches et considérations*, p. 79.

The philosophes and their followers disapproved of the ways in which affluent masters used their servants for display. They poured scorn on the custom of surrounding oneself with a following of liveried flunkeys. As one critic pointed out, such ostentation was available to anyone who had money and bore no relation whatsoever to the master's real social standing or moral stature: "Real greatness comes from birth or moral elevation, and does not consist in a numerous escort of valets; this pomp signifies nothing but a false and borrowed grandeur."[91] Mercier, as we have seen, ridiculed this use of a barrier of menials, and Rousseau similarly asserted that he would never want such people interposed between himself and the rest of the world.[92] Remarks such as these fit into a much broader repudiation of a whole system of social relations and political behavior based on personal bonding and the public display of wealth and power.

At the core of the matter was the question of theatricality, of the self-conscious role playing which, according to critics, characterized social life in town and especially at court. The most famous of these critics was of course Jean-Jacques Rousseau himself, who argued in a long letter to d'Alembert against the establishment of a theater in Geneva. To Rousseau the theater stood for all that was corrupt in the genteel urban society of his day. Far from bringing the spectators together, it was a place of mimicry and deceit in which one learned to posture and play roles. Much of the philosophe's ire was directed against actors, whom he denounced for teaching the public to play such roles. It is interesting that he accused actors of precisely those dispositions which he and his contemporaries attributed to servants: mimicry, conceit, and venality.

> What is the talent of the actor? It is the art of counterfeiting himself, of putting on another character than his own, of appearing different than he is . . . What is the profession

---

[91] Turmeau de la Morandière, *Police sur les mendians*, p. 134.
[92] Mercier, *Tableau de Paris,* IX:6; Rousseau, *Emile*, p. 433.

of the actor? It is a trade in which he displays himself for money, submits himself to the disgrace and affronts that others buy the right to inflict on him, and puts his person publicly on sale. I beg every sincere man to tell if he does not feel in the depths of his soul that there is something servile and base in this traffic of oneself.[93]

Though Rousseau never drew an explicit parallel between actors and servants, it is clear that within his system of references these groups were liable to similar sorts of criticisms. Both actors and servants adopted identities that were not their own, sported names and clothes that were given to them, and put their selfhood "publicly on sale." And spectators were taken in by the artificial world represented on stage as they were, on the street, by the illusion of moral and social authority created by retinues of lackeys.

If the theatre was one archetypal world of display, the court was another. To a critic like Sébastien Mercier, Versailles was a foreign land whose inhabitants spoke a different tongue, moved differently, and were strangers to the world of feelings: "One sees nothing there but surfaces . . . characters that seem to be little more than tapestry motifs."[94] Mercier objected specifically to the strict code of etiquette that prevailed at court, on the grounds that it erected barriers between different groups and stifled all spontaneous expressions of feeling. Worse still, this code of behavior had left its mark on social circles outside of the court, opening up a chasm between the elites and their inferiors: "This protocol has been disseminated and imitated in all houses of distinction and has served as a barrier to keep a multitude of unwelcome persons at bay."[95]

This code of courtly etiquette precluded the open expression

[93] Jean-Jacques Rousseau, *Politics and the Arts: Letter to M. d'Alembert on the Theatre*, trans. Allan Bloom, p. 79.

[94] Mercier, *Tableau de Paris*, IX:8.

[95] Ibid., IX:8, 48.

of feeling because any courtier who betrayed his emotions would make himself politically vulnerable. At Versailles the key to survival and success was a combination of psychological acuity and strict emotional self-control: "He who knows how to penetrate the minds of others without giving them access to his own thoughts has attained the pinnacle of artistry."[96] But there were people at court who had constant and intimate access to the secrets of the high and mighty, and could use their knowledge to go shooting up the social and political hierarchy. These were, of course, none other than the servants: "Valets circumscribe the princes in the manner of ivy that spreads over a tree-trunk so that it can no longer be distinguished, so that the eye confuses its foliage with that of the tree."[97]

The idea that servants could take over the households of princes was clearly an exaggeration, partly fueled by very old fears of the power of upper male servants. Yet Mercier had also put his finger on the very essence of court politics, a system that rested upon the confusion of private and public functions. Courtiers, after all, were nothing but glorified valets who vied with one another for the honor of attending the *lever* and *coucher* of their master, the king. The underlying message in Mercier's denunciation of Versailles was that court politics were corrupted by the invasion of the public political sphere by private domestic interests.

To prerevolutionary critics of society and government, the ties of loyalty that bound master and servant were, on a reduced scale, an example of that which they resented most in the old order—the system of privilege. In his *Essai sur les privilèges*, published in 1788, the Abbé Siéyès wrote of privilege in its etymological sense, as a system of private law which fostered divisions within the nation, creating social and political castes attached only to the pursuit of their own interests: "Enter, for a moment, the mind of a *privilégié*. He considers himself, along with his col-

[96] Ibid., IX:11.
[97] Ibid., IX:9.

leagues, as a member of a separate order, a chosen nation within the nation."[98] In this sense, servants who endorsed the interests of their masters were *privilégiés* whose very existence threatened national consensus. The increasing distaste with which enlightened writers and their public viewed aristocratic service was therefore a spinoff from much broader criticisms of a sociopolitical system which, through such bonds of personal allegiance, promoted private interests over the public good.

The repudiation of aristocratic service was by no means a major theme in the social criticism of the philosophes. Nor were these ideas, which emerged for the most part in the second half of the century, singlehandedly responsible for the demise of aristocratic service as a social ideal. As we have seen, changes affected the reality and image of the master-servant relationship in the household, in fiction, and in advice literature as early as the 1720s and 1730s. In all of these areas, employers began slowly to push servants to the periphery of their lives. All of these changes amounted to an implicit and as yet incomplete repudiation of the ties of loyalty that traditionally bound master and servant.

Demographic, economic, and cultural changes that spanned the century contributed to the erosion of these bonds. The influx of migrants into eighteenth-century towns made servants available to wider and less wealthy segments of the population; a sharp increase in the wages of menservants contributed to the growing unpopularity of male service; a broad transformation in the tenor of family life excluded servants from the close and constant proximity of their masters. These developments did, in the long run, contribute to the transformation of domestic service into a heavily feminized, private occupation increasingly associated with the middle classes rather than the aristocracy. And yet, aristocratic service survived right up to the Revolution. Noblemen anxious to maintain their status and parvenus enriched by the century's

[98] Emmanuel Siéyès, *Qu'est-ce-que le Tiers-Etat? Précédé de l'Essai sur les privilèges*, p. 9. See also William H. Sewell, Jr., *Work and Revolution in France: The Language of Labor from the Old Regime to 1848*, chap. 4.

increasing prosperity continued to spend large amounts of money on the maintenance of numerous and well-paid menservants. It was precisely the endurance and even the strengthening of these habits of conspicuous consumption that touched off much of the criticism articulated by enlightened writers after midcentury.

Coaches and sedan chairs, liveried pages and lackeys, and all of the traditional trappings of upper-class service survived as long as did the Old Regime itself. More specifically, they endured as long as did the court, the *maison* which continued to serve as a blueprint for the households of the wealthy. Enlightened critics paved the way for the ultimate rejection of aristocratic service by denouncing it as a symbol of economic irrationality and political corruption. But its real demise only came about when the Revolution swept away all such archaic but powerful symbols of the old order.

Even though it was accelerated by the social and political upheaval of the 1790s, the transition from aristocratic to bourgeois service was a slow and tentative one. The men and women who were ascending the social scale in the decades before 1789 and those who were promoted to social preeminence during and after the Revolution were not, for the most part, proud and self-confident bourgeois equipped with full-blown ideals and firm rules of conduct. Most of them were *rentiers*, merchants, and professionals, still unsure of their own status, many of whom felt threatened by the presence of menials within their homes at a time when democratic ideas were spreading in society. In the wake of the Revolution, the public display of social power became obsolete. But new masters still had to prove their social status to themselves, and the new system of domestic relations that began to take shape after the Revolution was geared to that end. At the height of the Old Regime, employers and their servants, locked in uneasy partnership, asserted themselves over the urban world. Later generations of masters would have to grapple directly and more cautiously with that world, confining their most crude displays of tyranny to their homes.

CHAPTER 7

The Domestication of Service

Very little in the way of prescriptive literature on domestic service was published in the decades immediately preceding the Revolution. The temporary eclipse of the genre may reflect a confusion in the minds of masters as to what standards should govern the relationship between master and servant. Could the traditional paternalistic ethos still be salvaged now that master and servant had drifted so far apart? In the age of *encyclopédisme* and reform, what norms could replace the precepts of Fleury, Fénelon, Audiger, and Madame de Liancourt? One writer, however, did suggest an ideal that masters might emulate in their search for new answers to old problems. That writer was none other than Jean-Jacques Rousseau, and his suggestions were widely read.[1]

In *La Nouvelle Héloïse*, the lengthy sentimental novel he published in 1762, Rousseau sketched out his vision of an ideal household. In Book Four of the novel, the hero Saint-Preux returns to the estate of the Baron d'Etange at Clarens, where he had served as a tutor to the baron's daughter several years before. His former pupil and lover Julie is now married to the benign Monsieur de Wolmar, and the spouses have settled down to a peaceful and virtuous life in the heart of the Swiss countryside. Impressed by their domestic arrangements, Saint-Preux describes

[1] On the popularity of *La Nouvelle Héloïse*, see Daniel Mornet, *Les Origines intellectuelles de la Révolution Française* (Paris, 1933), pp. 95–96, and the Introduction to Mornet's edition of *La Nouvelle Héloïse* (Paris, 1925).

life at Clarens in a lengthy letter to his English friend Milord Edouard. This letter has remained famous as the most detailed and suggestive piece of writing by a major figure of the French Enlightenment on the subject of household management.[2] Rousseau's description of domestic relations at Clarens reflects, in its many contradictions, the ambivalence that plagued employers of his generation in their search for a new solution to their problem. In many ways it is also a prophetic vision of a new style of domestic relations that was to come into its own only after the Revolution.

On the face of it, Rousseau's portrayal of the Wolmar household amounts to an updated secular version of the earlier Christian paternalism. The Wolmars are aristocratic masters, blue-blooded local squires who can exploit local society to their advantage in their choice and use of domestic servants. Julie and her husband do not hire experienced servants—"fully formed rascals," as Saint-Preux puts it—but very young boys and girls from the surrounding countryside who can be trained over the years into identification with the household and masters.[3] The respect and affection of these servants is secured by means of a careful balance of strict discipline and loving concern. Julie de Wolmar is forever intervening in the lives of her servants:

> Workers, servants, all those who have served her, be it for a day, become her children. She takes part in their pleasures, their grief, their lives; she inquires after their business, their every interest is hers as well; she takes care of them in a thousand ways; she offers them advice; she mends their quarrels.[4]

---

[2] Jean-Jacques Rousseau, *La Nouvelle Héloïse*, part IV, letter 10, pp. 329–352. For different readings of this text, see Jean Starobinski, *Jean-Jacques Rousseau: La Transparence et l'obstacle*, 1957; chap. 5, and Marshall Berman, *The Politics of Authenticity: Radical Individualism and the Emergence of Modern Society*, pp. 246–255.

[3] Rousseau, *La Nouvelle Héloïse*, pp. 331–333.

[4] Ibid., p. 332.

The Wolmars thus obtain of their servants not just obedience, but affection and loyalty as well. Though religion is hardly mentioned in the letter, Rousseau's idyllic picture seems not too far removed in its essentials from the paternalistic ideal that prevailed in the seventeenth and early eighteenth centuries.

Despite the picture of affectionate reciprocity that Rousseau sketches out in the first few pages of the letter, his attitude toward the master-servant relationship is at bottom deeply cynical. The Wolmars' apparent kindness toward their servants is in reality an artful and self-conscious manipulation of their menials. Rousseau candidly admits as much:

> In a republic, citizens are restrained by customs, principles, and virtue; but how can one contain servants, who are mercenary creatures, other than by restraint and coercion? The very art of the master lies in concealing that coercion under a veil of pleasure, so that servants will imagine that they actually want to do things which are in fact forced upon them.[5]

Nowhere does Rousseau allude to the masters' duties toward their servants. Their control over domestics is achieved not through reciprocity but by means of artistry (*l'art du maître*), by a successful manipulation of incentives and a strict enforcement of rules. Rousseau ostensibly denies that the relationship between masters and servants at Clarens is based on a monetary transaction: "[The servants] are not looked upon as mercenaries hired to perform some exact amount of work, but as members of the family."[6] Nevertheless, money is implicitly recognized as the alpha and omega of the masters' power. The authors of earlier normative texts hardly discussed the question of wages, still less did it occur to them to suggest steady monetary increments as an incentive for servants. But at Clarens servants are promised a five percent

[5] Ibid., p. 339.
[6] Ibid., p. 333.

raise every year, and are set back to their original salary if they misbehave or are temporarily dismissed. "This," explains Saint-Preux, "prevents the older servants from becoming insolent since their caution increases with the amount they stand to lose."[7]

The Wolmars also structure the lives of their servants in such a way as to obtain efficient work from them and keep tight control over their behavior. They run a large household with a staff of only eight: this understaffing is designed to save domestics from the dangers of idleness, but also works to the advantage of the masters. The fewer servants one employs, explains Rousseau, the better the services they will provide.[8] The servants' mobility is tightly controlled. Their every need, both material and social, is provided for within the household, and they are actively discouraged from seeking company or diversion elsewhere. And woe to the black sheep to whom this confinement might not appeal!

> If one of our people, man or woman, does not adapt to our rules and prefers the freedom to run off here or there under different pretexts, he is never refused permission to do so; but we look upon this taste for license as highly suspect, and we are not long in parting with those who show such predispositions.[9]

Finally, contacts between servants are reduced to a minimum, ostensibly in the interests of morality. The Wolmars insist upon a strict segregation between the sexes at all times, a rule that is only relaxed on Sundays and winter evenings when the staff and workers are brought together for dances or evenings by the fireside under the eye of their employers.[10] But the masters also resort to psychological pressure in order to separate their servants from one another. The Wolmars' acknowledged aim is to break up any threatening complicity or camaraderie that might undermine their

[7] Ibid., pp. 334–335.
[8] Ibid., p. 332.
[9] Ibid., pp. 340–341.
[10] Ibid., pp. 336–343.

authority. Domestics at Clarens are urged to help one another, and gratuitous calumny is frowned upon. But the masters will have none of "that servile and criminal behavior, that mutual tolerance at the expense of the master which a bad valet will not fail to preach to others under the guise of charity."[11] Hence, servants are pressured into reporting any actions committed by their peers that might go against the masters' interests.

The traditional paternalistic ethos that survived in eighteenth-century handbooks was based on a reciprocity of obligations between masters and servants. It was optimistic in that it assumed that servants could demonstrate gratuitous loyalty and affection and be reformed under the guidance of their masters. Rousseau's arcadia, though cast in the same mold, is deeply pessimistic. His attempt to resurrect the old paternalism under a new secular guise suggests that the urge to control the hearts and minds of servants remained strong in his day. If iconography is any clue, his ideal of sentimental paternalism did indeed appeal to some of his contemporaries (see illustration 11). But the Wolmars' relationship to their menials, as Rousseau describes it, is tense and contrived. Their authority ostensibly derives from closeness and moral influence, but in fact they are distant and calculating. Their methods for maintaining control over their servants prefigure those advocated to masters in nineteenth-century handbooks: keeping servants continually and efficiently occupied, separating them from one another, and restricting their mobility both inside and outside of the household.

Only gradually did masters come to the recognition that they could have little influence over the minds and feelings of their servants. Only in the early nineteenth century was it openly acknowledged that rules and schedules were more effective than gifts and sermons, and that authority was better maintained through distance than through closeness. This recognition became possible only after the revolutionary upheaval had precipitated a redefi-

[11] Ibid., p. 347.

11. Sentimental paternalism: *"C'est un fils, Monsieur!"* by Moreau Le Jeune, 1770 (Phot. Bibl. nat. Paris)

nition of domestic service by sweeping away some of the vestiges of the Old Regime.

In 1789 a pamphlet appeared in Paris, allegedly written by a servant, calling upon domestics to rally with the Third Estate.[12] *Avis à la livrée par un homme qui la porte* is a fiery and lucid tract that sums up the grievances of male servants. It suggests that in some quarters at least discontent and restlessness among men-servants had reached a peak in the first year of the Revolution. Some of the old themes reappear, such as the male servants' long-standing discomfort with the livery and its implications: "The bedizened costume we wear makes us into a class apart," intoned the author.[13] But unlike any previous spokesmen for the liveried population, he also pointed out the ways in which masters sacrificed their lackeys and pages to the public ire. And he resented it: "If an accident occurs, it is [the master's] fault since he is driving. No matter, the angry populace takes out its wrath on us; though we are innocent, our very situation exposes us to their blows."[14] Servants should recognize the Third Estate as their natural allies, he pursued, if only for reasons of self-protection: "You are the victims [your masters] will sacrifice to the people's vengeance."[15]

The author of the pamphlet ("born to the livery, and wearing it for thirty years") assured his readers that his aim was not to bring down the barriers between domestics and their *patrons*, nor to disseminate "a spirit of independence and rebellion."[16] But was it not preaching independence to dwell, as he did, upon the helplessness and dependency of masters? Nobles or commoners, he wrote, our masters are grown men who must be dressed, fed, and driven around like three-year-old children; we could do with-

[12] *Avis à la livrée par un homme qui la porte.*
[13] Ibid., pp. 3, 11.
[14] Ibid., p. 5.
[15] Ibid., p. 30.
[16] Ibid., p. 35.

out them, but they could hardly do without us.[17] And was it not calling to rebellion to conclude as he did: "Therefore, my friends, when our masters sound us out we must tell them frankly that we are of the people and will not abandon the people for them."[18]

We do not know how many servants read this pamphlet, or how they responded to it. Given the greater economic and professional autonomy of male servants in the latter part of the eighteenth century, it is not at all unlikely that such ideas were circulating in Paris on the eve of the Revolution. But whatever the case, the author of this pamphlet was fighting a rear-guard battle. Within a few years the wearing of liveries was to be made illegal, and *la livrée* as a symbol and a social category was all but destroyed by the social and political ferment of the 1790s.

The servants themselves apparently took very little part in the Revolution on either side. The many whose livelihood was jeopardized by recurrent economic crises and the emigration of wealthy masters can hardly have greeted the new order with enthusiasm. But vulnerable as they already were, domestics were unlikely to take a public stand against the Revolution and offer themselves as sacrificial victims to the people's wrath. The more loyal or docile among them followed their employers abroad, only to be hauled before the courts on charges of emigration or counterrevolution when they returned. Most of them loudly protested their ignorance and innocence.

Pierre Lefebvre was arrested in Caen in 1794 for having followed his master, an Irishman, to Belgium and Saxony. Was he not aware, they asked him, of the law that ordered emigrants to return before May 9, 1792? "I was on enemy ground," he replied, "and I never knew of the law that ordered me to return; I was not interested in politics, only in my duty as a servant."[19] Jean Corbrion left for Portugal in 1786 with Monsieur de Chateaufort,

[17] Ibid., pp. 4, 35.
[18] Ibid., pp. 12–13.
[19] A.D.C. 2L 172/1, Year II.

the French consul in Lisbon. His master, he explained, wanted to keep him in his service, and never informed him of the law on émigrés. But Corbrion was anxious to get home. Having changed employers, he negotiated a passage to England and from there crossed over to Hamburg disguised as a sailor. He was arrested in Normandy in 1795.[20]

Other servants were accused of corresponding with émigrés, and it is indeed likely that some of them were involved in counterrevolutionary intrigue. Some such cases were discovered by the police in the area around Caen. Eustache Porcher, for instance, a sixteen-year-old servant, was accused of corresponding with an exiled curé and another émigré. Marie Mallet, the maidservant of a non-juror priest, was used as a link in a counterrevolutionary network in the heart of rural Normandy.[21] On the whole, though, servants were as law-abiding during the revolutionary decade as they had been for the rest of the century. In this area of Normandy, they accounted for only 6.5 percent of the women indicted on criminal charges between 1792 and 1799, and 3.4 percent of the men.[22]

Those who lost their jobs did sometimes get into trouble for complaining imprudently about the new state of affairs that had robbed them of their livelihood. The cook Eugène Gervais was arrested in Paris in the summer of 1790 for inciting servants and workers against the bourgeois National Guard. He was accused of having declared that "there were sixty thousand servants in Paris who could unite with workers from different trades, and then one would see all those j.f. [*jean foutres*] go hide away at home with their f. uniforms."[23] In Aix that same year one Louis Blanchet was cross-examined by the police after he held forth in

[20] A.D.C. 2L 182/1, 3 Prairial, Year IV.

[21] A.D.C. 2L 170/5, Year IV; A.D.C. 2L 191/3, Year V.

[22] Philippe Hommeril, "La Criminalité dans le Calvados de 1792 à 1700" (Mémoire de Maîtrise, Univ. de Caen, 1973), pp. 117–118.

[23] George Rudé, *The Crowd in the French Revolution*, p. 65, note 5.

a tavern against the National Assembly. He had allegedly said that

> it was high time that things got better because servants and workers were the worst off under these circumstances . . . that if this went on, jobless servants and unemployed workers would have to take to the roads.[24]

These two servants railed against the revolutionary bourgeois whom they considered responsible for their depressed situation, and spontaneously identified with other jobless workers. But in Paris at least, many of them clamored for integration into middle-class revolutionary institutions. In August of 1789 and again in the summer of 1790, servants demonstrated to request full citizenship and the right to attend District Assemblies and to enroll in the National Guard.[25] In any case, they proclaimed their allegiance to the Revolution.

But whatever their political sympathies, servants were never conspicuous in the great revolutionary and counterrevolutionary *journées* that shaped the course of the Revolution. Out of 1,536 participants in Parisian riots and uprisings between 1787 and 1795 whose occupations have been identified, only 3 were servants.[26] In Marseille, not a single servant enrolled in the National Guard claimed to have participated in the siege of the Fort Notre-Dame (the local Bastille), or joined the local Jacobin Club. There were only 21 servants among the 433 volunteers who marched up to Paris and took part in the siege of the Tuileries, and only 8 were numbered among 1,400 persons arrested after the Federalist uprising.[27]

[24] A.D.A. IVB 1275, July 3, 1790.

[25] Rudé, *The Crowd*, p. 65; Theresa McBride, *The Domestic Revolution: The Modernisation of Household Service in England and France 1820–1920*, p. 15.

[26] Rudé, *The Crowd*, pp. 246–248.

[27] Dominique Radiguet, "Foules et journées révolutionnaires à Marseille, Août 1789–Août 1793," 2 vols. (Mémoire de Maîtrise, Univ. de Provence, 1968), II:25, 29, 39, 46, 53.

If domestics were not conspicuous among the actors of the Revolution, neither were they singled out as its victims. Servants accounted for a mere 3 percent of those executed under the Terror, or a tenth of all victims from the lower classes; these proportions are significantly inferior to their numerical weight in society.[28] Finally, servants were far less numerous among the émigrés than one might suspect. True, they did make up the largest category among emigrants from the urban laboring classes, 12 percent of the males in that category and 13 percent of the females. But in the overall count their representation was insignificant: whereas one-fifth of those who emigrated were peasants, less than 2 percent were domestics.[29] Servants and former servants no doubt knew better than to draw attention to themselves at such a time. Menservants, who were the most likely to lose their jobs and the most exposed to suspicion and resentment, quietly drifted into other occupations or else enrolled in the new armies of the Republic. In Caen, for instance, the number of male servants decreased by two-thirds between 1760 and 1792, while other types of unskilled labor increased sixfold and the military soared up to eight times its initial size.[30] Domestic servants played no great role in the redefinition of their occupation during and after the Revolution. The main challenge to the old idea of service came from above, not from below.

The legislators of the Constituent Assembly and those of the National Convention formally announced that domestic service no longer existed. A series of piecemeal decrees in 1791 and 1792 culminated in one of the articles in the Preamble of the Constitution of 1793: "The law does not recognize the existence of domestic service [*domesticité*]: there can only exist an exchange of

[28] Donald Greer, *The Incidence of Terror during the French Revolution*, pp. 156–160, 163.

[29] Donald Greer, *The Incidence of Emigration during the French Revolution*, pp. 132–138.

[30] Jean-Claude Perrot, *Genèse d'une ville moderne: Caen au XVIIIe siècle*, I:339–340.

services between the man who works and the person employing him."[31] On the new playing cards issued in 1793, King, Queen, and Valet were replaced by Genius, Liberty, and Equality.[32] But of course domestic service did not disappear, not even temporarily. The men who sat on the benches of the revolutionary assemblies employed domestics themselves, and had no intention of dispensing with their services. Nobody was ever forbidden to employ servants, nor were domestics themselves ever outlawed. What, then, did the legislators of the Revolution have in mind when they officially repudiated *la domesticité?*

The revolutionaries of the 1790s did not abolish domestic service, but rather continued and accelerated the process of re-definition begun in the later eighteenth century. Revolutionary legislators quite naturally recast their definition of servants and service within the terms defined by the philosophes. In January of 1790 a proposal for a mutual aid society for servants was drafted by the Paris police department. The preamble of the document stated that "The class of domestics [*la domesticité*] which under an arbitrary government is by turns tyrannical and oppressed takes on, under the reign of liberty, its true role as a useful part of the family."[33] This quote perfectly captures both the terms of the problem and the solution that was envisioned. Domestic service as it existed under the Old Regime was unacceptable because servants were "by turns tyrannical and oppressed," because they had too much power and too little dignity. This plan for a servants' mutual aid society was indeed aimed at giving servants more dignity and security, but it was initiated by the servants of Paris themselves. The legislators who sat in the assemblies had

---

[31] Paul-Ernest Vêtu, *De la Domesticité en France et dans l'ancienne Rome*, pp. 25, 38; Robert Sauty, *De la Condition juridique des domestiques*, p. 12; Louis Duguit et al., *Les Constitutions et les principales lois politiques de la France depuis 1789* (Paris, 1952), p. 63.

[32] Abbé Henri Grégoire, *De la Domesticité chez les peuples anciens et modernes*, p. 187.

[33] *Réimpression de l'Ancien Moniteur*, III:63.

little interest in the welfare and dignity of the mass of servants. They were far more concerned with redefining the occupation in the abstract and reducing *la livrée* from arrogant and influential bondsmen to "a useful part of the family."

On June 19, 1790, the Constituent Assembly formally destroyed the old nobility. In the course of the same memorable session, the deputies voted to remove from the monument to Louis XIV on the Place des Victoires the statues representing four provinces in chains—these were symbols of "humiliation and servitude"—and they also moved to make the wearing of liveries illegal.[34] The three issues were raised separately, but the ensuing discussion brought them together. The deputies spontaneously made the connection between aristocracy, absolute monarchy, and servitude. The most outspoken opponent of the motions, the Abbé Maury, went to the heart of the matter in his defense of the livery:

> No one is unaware that this usage goes back to the institution of the crusades, and that except for certain families not even the mayor of Paris is allowed his own livery. You are therefore attacking the nobility in its very essence.[35]

Ironically enough, the man who responded to Maury was a member of one of France's oldest and most powerful aristocratic families, the Duc de Montmorency. The livery, he said, was "one of those anti-social distinctions which, no matter how vain and childish they may seem, go against your deepest principles"; he exhorted his colleagues to outlaw a costume which he described as "one of the most striking reminders of the feudal system and the spirit of chivalry."[36] In the end, the question of the statues was voted on separately, but nobles and liveries were thrown together in a single motion which received enthusiastic support from most of those present. Hereditary nobility was completely

[34] Ibid., IV:676–679.
[35] Ibid., IV:677.
[36] Ibid.

abolished along with titles, aristocratic surnames, coats of arms, and liveries.[37] Since liveried henchmen had for so long aided their masters in the exercise of authority, it seemed fitting, no doubt, that both should be felled by the same blow.

The leaders of the Revolution were well aware of the social implications of a certain type of service which they rejected as a prop to the benighted "feudal" system they were destroying. But they were just as concerned with the political as the social implications of aristocratic service. In every constitution drafted or actually implemented in France from 1791 to 1817, the only occupational category systematically denied the right to vote or be elected was that of domestic servants. Until the Bourbon Restoration, domestics were barred from participation in political life along with bankrupts, criminals, women, and, in many instances, the poor.[38]

The overt justification for this arbitrary measure was that servants could be influenced by their masters and therefore could not be expected to express an autonomous political choice. But why did the legislators continue to assume that this would be the case, when they had officially redefined domestic service as a purely contractual relationship between employer and employee? The most likely explanation is that the men who drafted the revolutionary constitutions were acting upon old fears and long-standing grudges. As we have seen in earlier chapters, male service had always had connotations of privilege and political intrigue. Servants were liminal beings whose social marginality had long provoked fears of power and social inversion. In the decades before the Revolution, the male retainers of the aristocracy had become symbols of personal and arbitrary government, of the favoritism and intrigue that allegedly governed politics at Versailles. To the members of the Constituent Assembly debating, in June of 1791, the motion to exclude servants from the vote, the transition from

[37] Ibid., IV:678.
[38] Duguit, *Constitutions*, pp. 8, 63, 77, 109.

the issue at hand to wider questions of political corruption was an easy one. Pétion wanted it made clear that the prohibition would also apply to the King's servants who might be agents of the executive branch as well. And d'André argued that in a nation where some persons enjoyed considerable wealth, it was imperative to exclude from the assemblies men who were in the pay of influential personages:

> I ask whether it is not possible for the wealthy to form a coalition in order to fill the legislature with their men. If they have the means to employ talented men . . . could they not use sedition, intrigue, and even corruption in order to get them elected? I ask therefore that all salaried dependents be ineligible.[39]

The real issue debated in this session was not whether some middling master might exert influence over his valet. D'André, Pétion, and their colleagues in the Assembly were defining new standards of political behavior that required the symbolic exclusion of servants from the body politic.

Revolutionary legislators concerned themselves far more with the broad social and political connotations of a certain style of service than with the indignities suffered by the servants themselves. They were no more concerned than were the philosophes with female service. They made liveries illegal, for these were the symbols of hereditary social distinctions, and they neutralized the political connotations of service by excluding domestics from political life. In short, they struck the last blows at a dying institution, aristocratic male service.

The greatest effect of the Revolution on domestic service was, in the end, indirect. Whatever else the Revolution did or did not accomplish, most would agree that it discredited the aristocracy and destroyed the court. For all of the artificial glitter of the Napoleonic Empire and of the spluttering Restoration that

---

[39] *Ancien Moniteur*, VIII:623.

followed it, these institutions never really regained their power as models for the rest of society. As a result, the traditional use of servants became obsolete as the public display of power, whether at court or in town, lost its legitimacy. Very soon, neither upper- nor middle-class masters would feel the need for a system of domestic relations based on loyalty and mutual dependency and geared to public display. To be sure, many *notables* carried the banner of aristocratic service well into the nineteenth century. But the Revolution had swept away most of the justification for the aristocratic model of service. In the early nineteenth century, masters evolving in a new world had to redefine their relationship with their household employees and to find ways of using and controlling their servants that were better suited to their own needs and fears.

The nineteenth-century domestic workforce differed markedly from its eighteenth-century counterpart in that it was overwhelm- ingly composed of females. Whereas less than two out of three urban servants had been women under the Old Regime, the proportion of females among domestic workers reached 70 percent by the mid-nineteenth century, and 90 percent at century's end.[40] But the economic situation and behavior of these women appar- ently changed very little, if at all. Nineteenth-century maids, just like their earlier counterparts, were nearly all migrants to the city. With the advent of the railway, their area of recruitment expanded significantly, but most were still drawn from the same impoverished regions that had long supplied servants to the larger French towns: the Alps, the Massif Central, and especially Brit- tany.[41] One-half to three-quarters of the women who worked as servants still came from peasant families, and their careers fol- lowed much the same course as in the previous century. If suc-

[40] Marcel Cusenier, *Les Domestiques en France*, pp. 9, 17; Madeleine Auger, *Condition juridique et économique du personnel domestique féminin*, p. 17; McBride, *Domestic Revolution*, p. 45.

[41] McBride, *Domestic Revolution*, chap. 2.

cessful, they gathered a dowry and married rather late and rather well. But the weak and the unlucky still formed the largest group among unwed mothers, and were likely to turn to petty crime or prostitution if employment failed.[42] The financial contract between master and servant remained on the whole as informal as it had been in the eighteenth century, and trade unions protecting the rights of domestic workers were not formed until the early twentieth century.[43] Men had massively deserted the occupation for less confining employment in the growing sectors of a nascent capitalist economy.[44] With the dismissal or defection of its richest and most independent male elements during and after the Revolution, the social category of domestic service lost its only potential source of strength and cohesion. Nineteenth-century employers could impose their wills upon a group now essentially composed of women, of workers as isolated and vulnerable as they had ever been.

The most popular handbooks for employers published in the early nineteenth century—those of Jean-Charles Bailleul, Madame Pariset, and Madame Celnart, for instance—were clearly written for the well-to-do, but not for very rich or for aristocratic households. Even the aristocratic Comtesse de Genlis, the author of one of these handbooks, expressed satisfaction at the reduction in the size of household staffs: "The number of *gens de livrée* has been considerably reduced," she wrote, "and most people confine their staffs to only the necessary servants, which makes it easier to maintain order within the household."[45] In the 1820s both Madame de Genlis and her middle-class counterpart, Madame Pariset, advised their readers to keep a staff of three servants, two women and one man. The male servant was anything but a luxury item. Madame de Genlis thought that a house would be well

---

[42] Ibid., chaps. 5–6.

[43] Ibid., pp. 57–60; Auger, *Personnel domestique*, p. 103.

[44] McBride, *Domestic Revolution*, p. 39.

[45] Comtesse de Genlis, *Manuel de la jeune femme, ou guide complet de la maîtresse de maison*, p. 13.

staffed with a chambermaid, a female cook (skilled in the art of *une bonne cuisine bourgeoise*), and only if necessary a male servant considerably older than the women.[46] Madame Pariset's advice was exactly the same. A male servant was necessary, in her opinion, for certain heavy tasks that women were unable to perform. But she too believed that female servants could take on many of the duties previously assigned to men, and no doubt carry them out much better. Female cooks, she wrote, "are usually much cleaner than men, and also more willing to suffer inspections by the mistress." And, she added, female cooks could be assigned other chores in their spare time, whereas men usually refused to take on anything that fell outside of their official competence.[47]

This call for thrift and modesty in setting up one's household was an implicit repudiation of the old standards of luxury still prevalent among the very rich. Some writers were quite explicit, however, in their denunciation of aristocratic service. Louis Fouin, for instance, writing in the 1830s, was as sharp-tongued as Rousseau had ever been on the subject, but a great deal more class-conscious. He compared the servants of *grandes maisons* to those of the bourgeoisie. The former, he wrote, "have always been the most vicious and brazen . . . they are grotesque reflections of vanities whose absurdity cannot always be concealed by high birth, good manners, and opulence."[48] The livery had come back into usage, but it was "a false object of pride," and a sign of degradation. The servants of the bourgeoisie, he concluded, were far better behaved than those of the aristocracy because their masters controlled them much more effectively.[49]

Middle-class masters did indeed control their servants, but in different ways than did seventeenth- and eighteenth-century em-

[46] Ibid., pp. 71–74.

[47] Madame Pariset, *Manuel de la maîtresse de maison, ou lettres sur l'économie domestique*, pp. 164–165.

[48] Louis Fouin, *De l'Etat des domestiques en France et des moyens propres à les moraliser*, pp. 21–22.

[49] Ibid., pp. 22–25.

ployers. Earlier domestic handbooks had urged their readers to
treat servants strictly, but also to show kindness and compassion
toward them. In real life, masters were often brutal with their
domestics, but at the same time were secure enough in their sense
of social superiority to tolerate and even encourage closeness and
familiarity. Nineteenth-century employers were far less confident
in dealing with their menials. Unlike their predecessors, they
established strict rules governing the work and whereabouts of
servants, and fastidiously insisted on small signs of deference.
They did their best to widen the physical and psychological gap
between their servants and themselves. Whereas earlier employers
had controlled their servants by encouraging closeness, nineteenth-century masters established their authority by maintaining
a careful distance from their employees.

It was universally recognized that servants had become a problem to the widening middle-class constituency at which these
handbooks were aimed. Such was, very often, the authors' opening
statement: "How many complaints, how many recriminations do
we not hear from masters? They can obtain neither submission
nor respect," intoned the Abbé Bléton; to Madame Celnart, the
presence of servants was "usually considered a troublesome necessity"; to Madame Pariset, they were "a necessary and inevitable
evil that will be the bane of your existence unless you learn to
get the better of it."[50] Gone was the comforting assumption that
master and servant were born to their respective fates. The master's authority was no longer taken for granted: it had to be
skillfully and self-consciously asserted.

Since the late seventeenth century, the master-servant relationship had been losing most of its overtones of paternalism and
deference and was evolving into a far more openly contractual
arrangement. Yet the authors of early nineteenth-century hand-

[50] Jean-François Bléton, *Des Devoirs des serviteurs, des maîtres, des enfants, des
parents et de tous les hommes envers Dieu, l'Eglise et l'Etat*, p. 9; Madame Celnart
(Elizabeth Bayle-Mouillard), *Manuel complet des domestiques, ou l'art de former des
bons serviteurs*, p. v; Pariset, *Manuel*, p. 162.

books did not perceive the cash nexus as the root of the problems faced by new employers. Unlike their predecessors, they did acknowledge the financial side of the relationship as fundamental, and advised their readers to give servants fair wages: Madame Pariset briefly noted the proper wages for chambermaids and cooks; Madame de Genlis and the Abbé Bléton warned their readers not to skimp on their servants' wages for fear of losing both their employees and their reputations.[51] But the issue of remuneration still did not loom large. Masters still had control over that aspect of the relationship, and if they chose to pay their servants a decent salary it was only in order to protect their self-interest and their good name. Evidently, servants were not yet in a position to bargain over the level of wages with their employers. As a result, middle- and upper-class writers perceived the problem as deriving from the decline of deference rather than the rise of the cash nexus: domestics, as they saw it, had become unruly and intractable. Some writers fell into idealizing the Old Regime when, they claimed, servants were part of the family, when there were no hard feelings, no thefts, no disloyalties. The Revolution, of course, was responsible for the current debacle: "They all want, they say, to live at liberty," complained Bléton, "they might as well say that they want to live as libertines. The Revolution told them that they were all our equals."[52]

It may indeed have been the case that in an age of nascent democracy, servants, even females, became less submissive and harder to manage. But the evidence suggests that the problem was more a function of the masters' insecurities than of the servants' unruliness. To begin with, the primary responsibility for running the household for the first time lay with mistresses rather than masters. With a few exceptions, eighteenth-century moralists had written their treatises on domestic economy for the

---

[51] Pariset, *Manuel*, pp. 170–174; Genlis, *Manuel*, p. 24; Bléton, *Devoirs*, pp. 46–47.

[52] Jean-Charles Busson, *Etude sur les rapports des domestiques et des maîtres et sur les moyens d'améliorer ces rapports*, pp. 15–19; Bléton, *Devoirs*, p. 33.

male head of household, or for both masters and mistresses indiscriminately. But as early as the 1820s, the most popular household manuals were entitled *Manuel de la jeune femme* or *Manuel de la maîtresse de maison*. Many young women who were to employ servants had never been taught the basics of household management. As Madame de Genlis dryly observed, some of them compensated for their ignorance by making general nuisances of themselves:

> Among the classes in which women, before the Revolution, made a point of completely neglecting household affairs, one finds some these days who pretend to universal ability. They weary their servants with continual interference, and claim to know better than their cook or their steward.[53]

The problems arose in part, then, from the inexperience of middle-class families, and especially women, in dealing with servants; they were nervous and harsh because they were new to the game.

More generally, the petty tyranny over servants that is suggested in these handbooks appears to be a form of compensation for the restraints imposed on masters in the daily run of social life. At least one writer, the Abbé Busson, declared as much: "Do [masters] not compensate with the unbridled liberties they take at home for the constraints that public decency imposes on them in the run of daily affairs?"[54] This was the problem in a nutshell. Here were men and women of property and stature, most of them recently risen in the world or yet on the rise. They were living in a society that had repudiated the public ostentation of wealth and power as dangerously reminiscent of the old aristocracy. Theirs was a world in which much stricter standards of public behavior prevailed and physical violence of any sort—even vicarious—was increasingly associated with the "dangerous classes."[55] The employers for whom Madame Pariset and Madame

---

[53] Genlis, *Manuel*, p. 15.

[54] Busson, *Etude sur les rapports*, p. 22.

[55] Louis Chevalier, *Classes laborieuses et classes dangereuses*, book 3, part 2.

Celnart wrote their handbooks were anxious to set themselves off from their social inferiors, and to prove that in at least one realm of their existence they could exert complete, untrammeled authority. The advice given to masters and mistresses in early nineteenth-century handbooks was not aimed at securing the loyalty, affection, or dependency of servants, but at controlling their work and behavior and maintaining a distance between employer and employee. Many of the rules recommended in these manuals were reminiscent of those suggested by Rousseau in *La Nouvelle Héloïse*; but the remnants of paternalism that Rousseau had tried to salvage had now been completely discarded.

Just as Clarens was a world unto itself, the houses and apartments in which nineteenth-century middle-class families resided were, ideally, to be the servant's entire universe while he or she was in the family's service. Eighteenth-century employers complained loudly that servants were never at hand when they were needed but, as we have seen, it never occurred to them to restrict systematically their employees' mobility inside or outside of the house. All of that changed as early as the first two decades of the nineteenth century. Madame Pariset did acknowledge that servants were forced to venture into the outside world upon occasion for their master's business or even their own. But she suggested that employers carefully record the times at which their servants left and returned. She added, "In general it would be best that a servant only be occupied inside the house." The job might demand excursions for shopping and other business, but "they must be as carefully restricted as possible, and their duration strictly limited."[56] Jean Charles Bailleul expressed this most clearly in the conclusion of his handbook: "To the servant, the household in which he works is the whole universe: if his masters are happy with him, he needs nothing beyond it; he is lacking in nothing, and should therefore be satisfied."[57] These principles were indeed

[56] Pariset, *Manuel*, p. 15.
[57] Jean-Charles Bailleul, *Moyens de former un bon domestique*, pp. 252–253.

enforced by most employers in the nineteenth century. Typically, a housemaid was given a half day off to go out every other week. Except when the job demanded it, or by special, hard-won permission, no other outings were normally allowed.[58]

Even within the household, the servants' freedom of movement was drastically reduced. Once again, Rousseau's vision had been prophetic. Early nineteenth-century employers were advised to keep their servants as isolated from one another as possible. Just as Rousseau had denounced "that mutual tolerance at the expense of the master," so Madame Pariset, over half a century later, alerted masters to the dangers of allowing servants to develop a dangerous complicity with one another. These people were uneducated and narrow-minded, she wrote, and their gathering together could only breed gossip, quarrels, and calumny. The wise mistress would make sure that domestics were kept busy in different parts of the house. The chambermaid could work in her bedroom, for instance, while the cook did her share of sewing in the kitchen.[59] All servants were to be kept apart, but segregation between the sexes was to be especially rigorous. In the interests of decency and propriety, the areas of competence of men and women were to be carefully defined so as to keep contacts between them at a minimum. If the family employed a male servant, he would be in charge of the heavy housework, but only women should be assigned to the making of beds for it was "more decent that only women should carry out this task."[60] By a curious reversal of earlier customs, male servants were now put to work behind the scenes, while the antechamber was gradually turned over to the women.[61]

Employers were thus urged to break up spontaneous in-house sociability and to destroy the sort of *esprit de corps* and conviviality

[58] McBride, *Domestic Revolution*, p. 24; Pierre Guiral and Guy Thuillier, *La Vie quotidienne des domestiques en France au XIXe siècle*, pp. 81–85.

[59] Pariset, *Manuel*, pp. 185–186.

[60] Ibid., p. 126.

[61] Ibid., p. 18.

that their predecessors had tolerated or even encouraged. Under the Old Regime, masters had every interest in allowing solidarity to flourish, because the bonds between their servants could be put to use in public as signs of the master's power and of the prestige of the household. Nineteenth-century masters had no use for such solidarity, and felt threatened by their servants' clannishness.

Perhaps the most striking novelty in these handbooks is their marked emphasis on schedules and efficiency. The authors of earlier handbooks had denounced sloth as sinful and dangerous, but they couched the matter in broad ethical terms. By the later eighteenth century, notions of productivity had made a timid appearance in handbooks, but a few decades later the theme had become a central one. Jean-Charles Bailleul entitled one of the chapters in his handbook "Service at the Different Hours of the Day"; he concluded a daunting enumeration of tasks with the observation that "a good servant will be better regulated in his habits than the household clock."[62] Controlling the servants' time had become one of the cornerstones on which the master's authority rested. Madame Pariset believed as much, for she encouraged her readers to draw up schedules for their servants, insisting that the utmost vigilance and strictness be exercised in making sure that they were observed. A rigorous use of time, she wrote, will ensure that "order, peace, good morals, and happiness will reign in a household; without it, all is confusion, disorder, and hardship."[63] Others pointed out that a servant's idleness was the moral and economic equivalent of theft, for every hour misspent robbed the masters of time that was legitimately due to them.[64] In other words, a lazy servant was guilty of breaking his or her end of the covenant, and implicitly of subverting the masters' authority. An idle servant was such an appalling sight to masters that Madame Pariset suggested that

[62] Bailleul, *Moyens de former*, p. 37.
[63] Pariset, *Manuel*, p. 187.
[64] Celnart, *Manuel*, p. 19.

domestics be kept artificially busy when there was in reality no work to be done—copying out pages from some edifying book, for instance.[65] Of course, the easiest way of making sure that servants were constantly at work was to understaff one's household, which many of these employers did. An overworked servant cramming his or her duties into a tight schedule was much less of a threat to a nervous employer; such a servant would not have time to gossip, plot, steal, or eavesdrop—maybe not even time to think.

Postrevolutionary handbooks provided anxious masters and especially mistresses with rules of household management designed to keep servants under tight control. Domestics would be docile and manageable if they were confined to the household, separated from one another, and kept busy from dawn until late at night. But these handbooks also described some of the trappings and conventions of nineteenth-century service that served to maintain servants at a safe distance and mark them off clearly from their employers. Such, for instance, was the meaning of the new sartorial code that masters adopted for their servants in the nineteenth century. The once outlawed livery did reappear, but its wearing was now restricted to only a very few servants. While few masters still cared to dress their servants in liveries, most of them paid great attention to their servants' clothes and insisted that domestics wear uniforms that would make their status clear at a glance. The Abbé Grégoire, for one, professed outrage at the thought of the livery, a costume "aimed at creating castes by calling hatred or contempt upon certain categories of persons." Nonetheless, he continued, there was much to be said for insisting that servants wear clothes that would make them immediately recognizable to the public. Another writer, Charles Ozanam, encouraged the maidservant to adopt such sartorial distinctions herself, "so that strangers coming to the house for the first time

[65] Pariset, *Manuel*, p. 180.

will not take you for the lady of the house when you are only the maid."[66]

Though some employers did continue to array their servants in fancy attire, servants' costumes were much simpler and more uniform than in the previous century. Except on special occasions, men wore tones of black, white and grey, striped waistcoats, and gloves when serving at table. Women were dressed with equal simplicity, preferably in dark colors; when they appeared in public they were usually required to wear a white apron as an unmistakable sign of their condition. Minute details signaled a servant's status and occupation within the household. A chambermaid wore lace on her apron and cap, a housekeeper's cap was adorned with ribbon, and a cook's apron was made of linen instead of percale.[67] But the clothes of all servants within a given household were likely to be very similar, and very different from those of their masters. The symbolism of servants' clothes had evolved from a "vertical" code to a "horizontal" one: in the previous century, upper servants were clad in castoffs and liveries that signaled their bondage to wealthy employers, while lower servants simply wore the garments of the lower classes. By the early nineteenth century, all servants were dressed in roughly the same fashion, in drab uniforms that set them apart, as a group, from their masters.

Along with new clothes came new codes of behavior. Nineteenth-century masters were advised to insist upon marks of deference and a general formality of demeanor that would no doubt have baffled their eighteenth-century predecessors. Servants were never to keep their hats on or to sit down in the presence of their masters; they were to address their employers in the third person, to speak only when spoken to, and to append "Monsieur" or "Madame" to their every response; they were never to take part in any conversation carried on before them, never to smile at a

[66] Grégoire, *De la domesticité*, p. 189; Charles Ozanam, *Manuel des pieuses domestiques*, p. 186.

[67] Guiral and Thuillier, *Vie quotidienne*, pp. 46–50.

12. Nineteenth-century family with their maid: *Là Rentrée en Classe*,
by Letilly, 1837. (Phot. Bibl. nat. Paris)

joke, never to allow themselves the slightest sign of familiarity with their employers.[68]

This effort to maintain a physical as well as psychological distance between master and servant was sometimes justified on the grounds that servants were unclean. This idea had never been expressed in seventeenth- or eighteenth-century handbooks, and it speaks volumes about the new phobias of the nineteenth-century upper- and middle-classes. Bailleul pointed out to his readers that the hands of servants were always sweaty; he recommended that they wear gloves or use a towel when handling their employers' personal objects. With equal gravity he insisted that servants should touch drinking glasses as little as possible, for nothing, he said, was more repulsive than the sight of a servant's fingers upon a glass from which one was to drink.[69] Fears of dirt and contamination were yet another expression of the insecurities that plagued nineteenth-century employers and were translated into a constant preoccupation with maintaining a distance between master and servant.

This impulse toward physical segregation from servants was reflected in the new arrangement of living quarters in middle- and upper-class residences. The living quarters of servants were just as appalling in the nineteenth century as they had been in the eighteenth. In poorer households the maid slept in the kitchen, the dining room, in some dark alcove, or in a camp bed set up below the staircase. But most middle-class families inhabited apartment buildings, and when servants were not parked below stairs they were most commonly lodged in garrets just under the roof, in the miniscule rooms that made up the much decried

---

[68] Bailleul, *Moyens de former*, pp. 89–119; Celnart, *Manuel*, pp. 176–178.

[69] Bailleul, *Moyens de former*, pp. 56, 93; see also Ozanam, *Manuel*, pp. 148–149; for a penetrating discussion of similar fears and the rituals governing domestic life in nineteenth-century England, see Leonore Davidoff, "Mastered for Life: Servant and Wife in Victorian and Edwardian England," *Journal of Social History*, 7:406–428.

sixième étages.[70] In former times, many servants had bedded down outside their masters' doors, slept in their bedrooms, and even shared their beds with them. By the nineteenth century, a growing demand for privacy and the status anxieties of middle-class masters had made such arrangements unthinkable. Employers compensated for the narrowing of the social gap between their servants and themselves by putting as great a distance as possible between their own living quarters and those of their employees.

The norms that governed nineteenth-century domestic relations differed drastically from those that had prevailed a century earlier. Ideals and realities of domestic life had changed along with the identities, needs, and fears of new generations of masters. Under the Old Regime, the nobility set the tone for domestic relations. Aristocratic masters and those who emulated them needed the loyalty of their servants in order to impress the public with their own wealth and power. They were advised to treat their servants as children, to coax, cajole, and flog them into submission and gratitude. But they were also relatively unconcerned with the formalities of the relationship, and sufficiently imbued with a sense of their social superiority to allow servants free access to their living quarters and their private lives.

Some of the tensions and ambivalences that accompanied the protracted transition from the old paternalistic mode of domestic relations to the one that prevailed in the nineteenth century are reflected in Rousseau's description of master-servant relationships at Clarens. The masters portrayed in *La Nouvelle Héloïse* seem unable to decide between a secular version of traditional paternalism and a more cynical reliance on rules and monetary incentives. The former was not entirely plausible, and the latter not entirely acceptable. As a result, Rousseau's elaborate fantasy nearly crumbles under the weight of its own contradictions. But Rousseau was at his clearest and most forceful in his advocacy of specific

[70] Guiral and Thuillier, *Vie quotidienne*, pp. 37–44; McBride, *Domestic Revolution*, pp. 50–54.

principles of household management: servants should be confined to the household, separated from one another, and kept constantly busy under close supervision.

The authors of early nineteenth-century handbooks hardly mentioned the financial bond between master and servant. Whereas most of their counterparts under the Old Regime had deliberately ignored monetary incentives as inessential to the relationship, the later authors already seemed to take them for granted. But prescriptive literature suggests that employers were no longer able or anxious to establish moral and psychological ascendancy over their servants. Loyalty, when it was mentioned, was simply equated with the sort of hard and efficient work that demonstrated a servant's attachment to his or her master's material interests.[71] The emphasis, in these handbooks, was simply on rules and codes of behavior very similar to those advocated by Rousseau. Employers were advised to control their servants' behavior and to stifle any sign of independence or implicit challenge to their authority. They were to restrict their servants' mobility, to isolate them from one another, and to keep them occupied every minute of the day. At the same time, nineteenth-century masters insisted on elaborate rituals of deference, had their servants wear dull, inconspicuous costumes, and confined them below stairs or under the roof. They tried, in short, to accentuate symbolically the social distance between their employees and themselves when the gap was in fact much narrower than before. Unlike their predecessors, nineteenth-century masters needed to prove their social superiority not to the outside world, but to themselves.

The Revolution did not singlehandedly bring about this change in the ideals and realities of domestic service, but it did precipitate the transformation. Male service was decimated by economic crises and the emigration of many wealthy masters; social and political upheaval promoted the fortunes of families that had never before had access to servant holding. Above all, the Revolution speeded

---

[71] Bailleul, *Moyens de former*, p. 123.

up the demise of aristocratic service by dismantling the institutions that gave it legitimacy as a cultural model—the old aristocracy and the court. Like many of their predecessors, the legislators of the Revolution feared and resented the powerful and arrogant retainers of the rich; those fears surfaced in their systematic exclusion of servants from any participation in political life. In the early years of the Revolution, aristocratic service was discredited as a symbol of all that was rotten in the social and political fabric of the Old Regime. What was left of it had to be tamed and emasculated. It was left to new generations of masters and mistresses, many of them yet unsure of their own social standing, to devise a system of domestic relations that would keep servants at bay and under tight control.

Nineteenth-century masters wanted to see their servants as isolated and vulnerable creatures, which indeed most of them were. At the same time, employers were well aware that they no longer had any hold over the thoughts and emotions of their menials, and the idea that servants had secret inner lives of their own both fascinated and horrified them. The literature of the age contains recurrent figures of lonely, unhappy women whose lives of drudgery conceal dark secrets inaccessible to their masters. Such were Lamartine's Geneviève, the Goncourts' Germinie Lacerteux, and Flaubert's Felicité in the tale *A Simple Heart*. But the most powerful image of domestic service in nineteenth-century French literature was created by an acerbic critic of the bourgeoisie, Emile Zola.

In *Pot-Bouille*, Zola painted a chilling picture of the meanness and filth concealed behind the righteous appearances of a half-dozen Parisian bourgeois families residing in the same apartment building. Each family has its share of greed, violence, and adultery, and all of them do their best to maintain appearances of respectability. But every morning, the maids who work in the building, each one for a different family, lean out of their kitchen windows over the refuse in the back courtyard for their daily gossip session. Among them are the precocious fifteen-year-old

Louise, the sharp-tongued veteran Victoire, the impassive and venal Rachel, and a filthy and awkward provincial named Adèle. As they empty their slops into the courtyard below, they roar with laughter and exchange the most humiliating intimate stories of the physical and moral squalor in which their masters live.[72] Zola's symbolism may be heavy-handed, but the vision is hard to forget. Servants had always been the bad consciences of their masters. In an earlier age they were allowed to exorcise their masters' guilt in public by swearing and brawling on stage and in the street. Nineteenth-century masters, fearful of exposure, stripped their servants of lace and liveries and kept them confined to the home. But even after every effort had been made to stifle it, that conscience could not be silenced.

[72] Emile Zola, *Pot-Bouille*, pp. 120–121, 283, 300–307.

Conclusion

One of the chapters of Alexis de Tocqueville's *Democracy in America* compares the relations of masters and servants in "aristocracies" and democracies. Tocqueville observed that in democratic societies such as the young American nation, these relationships were characterized by aloofness and indifference on both sides. In aristocratic societies, despite the greater social distance between master and servant, "time ultimately binds them together. They are connected by a long series of common reminiscences, and however different they may be, they grow alike."[1] The will of the master, in such societies, is branded upon the mind and soul of the servant, rendering the latter incapable of distinguishing his interests and even his very identity from those of his employer: "The servant ultimately detaches his notion of interest from his own person; he deserts himself, as it were, or rather he transports himself into the character of his master and thus assumes an imaginary personality."[2]

This book has sought to describe and explain the characteristic features of domestic service in the "aristocratic" society that Tocqueville had in mind as he wrote these lines, France of the Old Regime. Its central purpose has been to determine the extent and meaning of what Tocqueville and others before him perceived as a loss of selfhood, as the servant's assumption of an "imaginary personality." The public espousal by servants of their masters'

[1] Alexis de Tocqueville, *Democracy in America*, trans. Henry Reeve, 2 vols. (New York, 1945), II:189.
[2] Ibid., II:190.

interests was indeed a normal feature of social life in the eighteenth century: those who resented it termed it "flattery" and those who promoted it called it loyalty.

The first chapters of this study have explained the existence of such bonds of loyalty with reference to the origins and outlook of the servants themselves. The poverty and general vulnerability of domestic workers, their origins as migrants, the isolation that was reinforced by the peculiarities of their occupation—all of these must be taken into account if one is to understand why they so often chose to cast in their lots with their masters. But most servants also knew or believed that their real future lay beyond the pale of service. I have argued that, paradoxically, such ultimate detachment from the occupation made servants more willing to comply temporarily with the dictates of their masters than workers or slaves who feel bound to their condition for life.

As for masters, they had every interest in expecting and creating such bonds. Eighteenth-century masters evolved in a world in which social power was contingent upon the ostentatious and wasteful display of wealth and on a certain theatrical aloofness from one's social inferiors. The use of "loyal" servants as status symbols and go-betweens was essential to the maintenance of rank and authority by the social elites.

None of this is meant to suggest that the identification of interests between master and servant derived from calculating rationality on the part of domestics or self-conscious manipulation on the part of their employers. Custom and inclination often played a large part in creating a bond between the two. Living conditions in seventeenth- and eighteenth-century households were such as to promote closeness between workers and employers who often shared rooms, beds, or secrets with each other.

Loyalty, *fidélité*, was the cornerstone of a certain ideal of service which I have called aristocratic. Its other features included the employment of large numbers of male servants, the wearing of liveries and other highly visible clothing, and the conspicuous idleness of servants. Although in many towns noblemen did employ more servants than did any other single category of the population, in strict numerical terms aristocratic service did not usually account for a majority of employers or servants. And yet, I have argued, this style of service was the socially dominant ideal. It was assiduously copied by commoners with social pretensions, like Monsieur Jourdain who, at the very beginning of Molière's play, loudly summons his lackeys and shows off their liveries to his dancing master. Even among very modest segments of the population, masters used their servants in the same way as did noblemen, sending them out on the street to settle scores on their behalf. Prescriptive literature and fiction offered the middling ranks of society no other model of servant holding and no other standards for master-servant relations. Never were the problems and ideals of middle-class masters addressed as a separate issue. Despite its continued predominance, this aristocratic ideal was slowly eroded in the eighteenth-century by economic, demographic, and especially cultural change. In postrevolutionary society it was replaced by a very different set of standards for domestic relations which one could term "bourgeois."

To anyone familiar with current debates on prerevolutionary French society, the argument that an "aristocratic" ideal was felled by the Revolution and replaced by a set of "bourgeois" standards may seem to go against the grain of current scholarship. It is now over twenty years since English and American scholars first began to challenge the orthodox interpretation of the French Revolution as the expression of a social struggle that pitted a rising bourgeoisie, bearing the torch of Enlightenment, against a decaying but still powerful aristocracy.[3] Where matters of culture are concerned, the current consensus is that no sharp line can be drawn between "aristocratic" and "bourgeois" culture. Wealthy commoners had always hankered after acceptance into

[3] The best recent summary, complete with references to the most significant contributions to the debate, can be found in William Doyle, *Origins of the French Revolution* (New York, 1980), part 1.

the ranks of the aristocracy, and they still did; blue-blooded noblemen could be just as critical of the old order as were members of the Third Estate. At the top of society, noblemen and commoners made up a single elite united in its manner of life, its infatuation with the new *philosophie*, and its hatred of royal and ministerial "despotism."[4] Although some historians still believe that the causes of the Revolution were primarily social,[5] other scholars are now suggesting that the major tensions leading up to the outburst of 1789 were "political" in the widest sense of the term, and pitted broad segments of society against the State and its agents.[6]

If that is the case, how are we to explain that domestic service, ostensibly a purely social phenomenon, was radically transformed by a primarily "political" revolution? The answer suggested here is that it may be fruitful to stop drawing such sharp distinctions between "social" and "political" categories, especially in the realms of culture and ideology. Domestic service was a social institution, but many of its features can be related to contemporary political culture—at least as that culture was perceived by critics. The loyalty demanded of servants was analogous to the ties that bound *créatures* to their protectors or courtiers to princes and kings; their allegiance to their masters' interests smacked of *privilège*, of private laws antithetical to the public good; their employers' use of them for display evoked the stilted pageantry of the court. The dismantling of aristocratic service under the Revolution can be seen as one aspect of the repudiation of a whole cultural system associated with the court and its politics. It is significant that the term "aristocratic" had both social and political connotations to eighteenth-century Frenchmen, that the sans-culottes, for in-

---

[4] Ibid., pp. 15–30.

[5] Most notably Colin Lucas, "Nobles, Bourgeois, and the Origins of the French Revolution," *Past and Present* 60 (August 1973):84–126.

[6] For instance Pierre Goubert, *L'Ancien Régime*, vol. 2, and François Furet, *Penser la Révolution Française*. This interpretation is of course inspired by Tocqueville's brilliant analysis in *The Old Regime and the French Revolution*.

stance, used the word *aristocrate* to designate both social and political enemies, be they Monarchists, Feuillants, Girondins, or simply the rich.[7]

The transformation of domestic service from a public to a private occupation and the erosion of the public bonds of loyalty between master and servant can thus be related, within the context of French history, to a broad sociopolitical shift which promoted the interests of an abstraction called "the Nation" over those of private individuals and their emissaries.[8] But the transformation in the relations between masters and servants that took place within the household is perhaps better understood as a transnational phenomenon, for similar changes were taking place simultaneously in other countries. The increasing physical and psychological segregation between master and servant within the domestic sphere was but one expression of the pangs of fear and self-consciousness that accompanied the birth of middle-class consciousness in Europe. Nineteenth-century masters had little use for the loyalty of their servants, but neither had they, psychologically, the means to secure it. It might have been for them that T. S. Eliot wrote J. Alfred Prufrock's famous confession:

> I have seen the moment of my greatness flicker,
> And I have seen the eternal Footman hold my coat,
>   and snicker,
> And in short, I was afraid.[9]

[7] Albert Soboul, *Les Sans-culottes parisiens en l'an II* (Paris, 1968), pp. 24–27.
[8] See Furet, *Penser la Révolution*, pp. 47–56.
[9] T. S. Eliot, *The Waste Land and Other Poems* (New York, 1934), pp. 6–7.

APPENDIXES

Social Origins of Servants in Aix and Paris

a. Occupations of Fathers of Female Servants, Aix

	1725–35		1755–65	
	Number	Percent	Number	Percent
Bourgeois or middle class	12	11	7	7.5
Artisans	21		28	
Other urban Servants	4		4	
	—		4	
		24		38.0
Laborers and farmers	68	65	51	54.5
Total sample	105	100%	94	100.0%

Source: A.D.A. Fonds de l'Hôpital Saint-Jacques, Expositions des Femmes Enceintes, XXH G 26, 28, 29, 32, 33

b. Occupations of Fathers of Male Servants, Paris, 1749

	Percent by Occupation	Subdivision of Total	
		Parisians	Immigrants
Servants	5.2	1	0.6
Unskilled workers	2.8	0.3	1.3
Journeymen	0.6	—	0.6
Skilled workers	14.6	0.3	12.9
Masters and merchants	10.4	1.3	8.7
Bourgeois	5.6	2	3.6
Nonprofessional commoners	6.6	—	6.6
Professionals	3.1	—	3.1
Private employees	1.7	—	1.7
Royal employees	2	0.6	0.6
Civil servants	2.8	—	2.8
Rural laborers	32.4	—	32.4
Other rural	12.2	—	12.2
Total	100.0%	92.6%	
		(7.4% unknown)	

Source: Daumard and Furet, *Structures et relations sociales à Paris*, pp. 60–63

Nominal Wages of Servants in Aix, 1710–1790
(in livres tournois per year)

	Unskilled*		Skilled**	
	Number of Indications	Average Wage	Number of Indications	Average Wage
		Female Wages		
1710–1719	13	24.5	—	—
1720–1729	16	33	—	—
1730–1739	18	26	—	—
1740–1749	30	43	7	77
1750–1759	15	50	8	62
1760–1769	27	48	3	75
1770–1779	29	50	5	72
1780–1790	10	55.5	9	83
		Male Wages		
1730–1739	—	—	5	91
1740–1749	6	87	—	—
1750–1759	19	84	8	156
1760–1769	12	82	9	171
1770–1779	9	89	13	212
1780–1790	13	118	7	251

* Maids, lackeys, chair carriers
** Chambermaids, governesses, valets, tutors, cooks

Sources: *Police records*. A.M.A. FF 63–73, FF 74, 75, 76, 87; *Archives of the Hôtel–Dieu of Marseille*. A.D.M. HVI G 103, 104, 106, 108
Livres de Raison. A.D.A. V B 19–21, V B 41, V B L12, A.D.M. IIIE 83, IIIE 84, XXIV H B73, B.M. Mss. 1645, 1647, 1651, 1652
Musée Arbaud. MQ 65, MQ 186

Wages of Servants in the Manneville Household in Caen,
1740–1775

(in livres tournois per year)

	Male Cooks	Upper Male Servants	Lackeys	Chamber-maids	Maids
1740–45	—	71	—	—	—
1746–50	150	83	50	70	24
1751–55	150	99	50	70	24
1756-60	150	84	48	60	36
1766–70	191	81	57	70	39
1771–75	225	100	75	78	46
Number of indications	*11*	*47*	*28*	*13*	*11*

Source: A.D.C. 2E 2810, Fonds Gosselin de Manneville, Registre de Gages des Domestiques

APPENDIX 4

Wealth at Marriage of Unskilled Workers, Servants,
Journeymen, and Master Artisans in Aix,
1769–1779

	Unskilled Workers	Servants	Journeymen	Master Artisans
Amount in livres				
to 150	5%	—	2%	3%
150–300	30%	35%	13%	11%
300–600	45%	27%	32%	26%
600–1200	15%	48%	38%	32%
1200–2400	4%	14%	11%	36%
2400 and over	1%	8%	4%	18%
Total number in sample	269	37	53	98

Source: A.D.M. IIC 236 (Contrôle des Actes)

SOURCES
AND BIBLIOGRAPHY

Sources and Bibliography

ARCHIVAL SOURCES

Fiscal Documents

A.D.C.   2C 22: Rôle de Taille, Bayeux, 1688
C 4538: Capitation 1768
C 4547: Capitation 1787

A.D.M.   IIC 236, IIC 1603, Enregistrement des Actes

A.D.M.   BB 14: Dénombrement de la population de Bayeux, 1774
1F 27: Dénombrement de l'an IV

A.M.A.   CC 13, Capitation 1701
CC 52-55, 57, 59: Capitations 1715–1719
CC 68, 69: Capitations 1755–1766

Notarial Records

A.D.A.   301E–309E
IVB 109–177: Insinuations, 1700–1790

A.D.M.   351E, 363E, 364E

Police Records

A.D.A.   IVB 1166–1189, IVB 1232–1275: Fonds de la Sénéchaussée d'Aix
208 U2, U14, U20, U29: Police Générale

Bibliography

A.D.C.   2B 855–883, 2B 1036-1062: Bailliage et Vicomté de
Bayeux
2L: Tribunaux Révolutionnaires
A.D.M.   IIB 1205–1245: Fonds de la Sénéchaussée de Marseille
A.M.A.   FF 63–76, FF 87–95: Délibérations du Bureau de Police
FF 98–99, LL 242: Ordonnances
FF 101–109: Procédures

Hospital Records

A.D.A.   XXH G 26–33: Hôpital Saint-Jacques, Expositions
des Femmes Enceintes
A.D.M.   IVG 103–108: Hôtel-Dieu de Marseille, Livres des
Filles

Account Books and Personal Papers

A.D.A.   XXIVH B 19–21: Audiffren
XXIVH B 41–43: Jean-Joseph de Bruges
XXIVH B 73: Melchior and Joseph Eyssautier
A.D.C.   2E 2808–2810: Gosselin de Manneville
2E 2862: Graindorge d'Orville
2E 6645: Simon de Franval
2E 6725: d'Hautefeuille
A.D.M.   IIIE 82: Arnaud de Nibles
IIIE 83: De Curbans
IIIE 84: Claude Joseph de Maliverny
B.M.   Mss. 1645–1648: Louis de Thomassin
Mss. 1651–1652: Charles-Alexandre de Mazenod
M.A.   MF 79: Pierre-César de Cadenet-Charleval
MQ 65: Baron de Sannes

346

Miscellaneous

Bibliothèque Nationale, Ms. 21 800: Police Générale

PUBLISHED PRIMARY SOURCES

Les Amours, intrigues et caballes des domestiques des grandes maisons de ce temps. Paris, 1633.

L'Art d'être heureux sur la terre mis à la portée du peuple de toutes les nations. Paris, 1785.

Audiger. See Franklin, Alfred.

Avis à la livrée par un homme qui la porte. Paris, 1789.

Avis salutaires aux pères et mères qui veulent se sauver par l'éducation chrétienne qu'ils doivent à leurs enfants. Marseille, 1698.

Bailleul, Jean-Charles. *Moyens de former un bon domestique*. Paris, 1812.

Barbier, Edmond. *Chronique de la régence et du règne de Louis XV*. 8 vols. Paris, 1866.

Bayle-Mouillard. See Celnart.

Berthélé, Joseph, ed. *Montpellier en 1768 et 1836, d'après deux documents inédits*. Montpellier, 1909.

Besnard, François-Yves. *Mémoires d'un nonagénaire*. 2 vols. Paris, 1880.

Blanchard, Antoine. *Essai d'exhortation pour les états différens des malades*. 2 vols. Paris, 1736.

Bléton, Jean-François. *Des Devoirs des serviteurs, des maîtres, des enfants, des parents et de tous les hommes envers Dieu, l'Eglise et l'Etat*. Lyon, 1830.

Brillon, Pierre-Jacques. *Dictionnaire des arrêts, ou jurisprudence universelle*. 6 vols. Paris, 1727.

Busson, Jean-Charles. *Etude sur les rapports des domestiques et des maîtres et sur les moyens d'améliorer ces rapports*. Besançon, 1844.

Cailhava l'Estendoux, Jean-François. *De l'Art de la comédie.* 2 vols. Paris, 1786.

Castel de Saint-Pierre, Charles. *Avantages de l'éducation des collèges sur l'éducation domestique.* Paris, 1740.

Celnart, Madame (Elizabeth Bayle-Mouillard). *Manuel complet des domestiques, ou l'art de former des bons serviteurs.* Paris, 1836.

Collet, Abbé Pierre. *Instructions et prières à l'usage des domestiques et des personnes travaillant en ville.* Paris, 1758.

————. *Traîté des devoirs des gens du monde et surtout des chefs de famille.* Paris, 1764.

Conty, Armand de Bourbon, Prince de. *Mémoires de Monseigneur le Prince de Conty touchant les obligations d'un gouverneur de province et la conduite de sa maison.* Paris, 1669.

Denisart, Jean-Baptiste. *Collection de décisions nouvelles et de notes relatives à la jurisprudence actuelle.* 4 vols. Paris, 1771.

Devoirs généraux des domestiques de l'un et l'autre sexe envers Dieu et leurs maîtres et maîtresses. Paris, 1713.

Les Domestiques chrétiens ou la morale en action des domestiques. Paris, 1828.

Dubois, Pierre, ed. *La Vie pénible et laborieuse de Jean-Joseph Esmieu, marchand-colporteur en Provence sous la Révolution Française.* Toulon, 1967.

Duguet, Jacques-Joseph. *Conduite d'une dame chrétienne pour vivre saintement dans le monde.* Paris, 1725.

L'Etat de servitude, ou la misère des domestiques. Paris, 1711.

Expilly, Jean-Joseph. *Dictionnaire géographique, historique, et politique des Gaules et de la France.* 6 vols. Paris, 1762–1770.

Fénelon, François de la Mothe. *De l'Education des filles.* Paris, 1881.

Fleury, Claude. See Franklin, Alfred.

Fouin, Louis. *De l'Etat des domestiques en France et des moyens propres à les moraliser.* Paris, 1837.

Franklin, Alfred. *La Vie de Paris sous Louis XIV: Tenue de maison et domesticité.* Paris, 1898. Includes reprints of Audiger, *La*

Maison réglée (1692) and Claude Fleury, *Les Devoirs des maîtres et des domestiques* (1688).

Fréminville, Edmé de Poix de. *Dictionnaire ou traîté de la police générale des villes, bourgs, paroisses et seigneuries de la campagne.* Paris, 1758.

Genlis, Comtesse Stephanie de. *Manuel de la jeune femme, ou guide complet de la maîtresse de maison.* Paris, 1829.

Gourville, Jean de. *Mémoires de Monsieur de Gourville concernant les affaires auxquelles il a été employé par la cour depuis 1642 jusqu'en 1698.* 2 vols. Paris, 1724.

Grégoire, Abbé Henri. *De la Domesticité chez les peuples anciens et modernes.* Paris, 1814.

Isambert, François-André et al. *Recueil général des anciennes lois françaises depuis 420 jusqu'à la Révolution.* 29 vols. Paris, 1821–1833.

Lambert, Anne-Thérèse de. *Avis d'une mère à son fils et à sa fille.* Paris, 1728.

Leblanc, Abbé Jean. *Lettres de Monsieur l'Abbé Leblanc.* 2 vols. Amsterdam, 1751.

Legrain. "Souvenirs de Legrain, valet de chambre de Mirabeau." *Nouvelle Revue rétrospective* 1. Paris, 1901.

Liancourt, Duchesse de. *Règlement donné par une dame de qualité à M*** sa petite-fille pour sa conduite et celle de sa maison.* 1698; reprint ed., Paris, 1728.

Lordelot, Bénigne. *Les Devoirs de la vie domestique par un père de famille.* Paris, 1706.

Marana, Jean-Paul. *Lettre d'un sicilien à un de ses amis.* Paris, 1883.

Mercier, Louis-Sébastien. *Le Tableau de Paris.* 12 vols. Amsterdam 1782–88.

Merlin, Philippe-Antoine. *Répertoire universel et raisonné de jurisprudence.* 4 vols. Paris, 1812.

Messance. *Recherches sur la population des généralités d'Auvergne, de Lyon, de Rouen, et de quelques provinces et villes du royaume.* Paris, 1766.

Moheau. *Recherches et considérations sur la population de France.* Paris, 1778.

Muralt, Béat-Louis. *Lettre sur les anglois, les françois, et les voiages.* Paris, 1728.

Ozanam, Charles. *Manuel des pieuses domestiques.* Paris, 1847.

Pariset, Madame. *Manuel de la maîtresse de maison, ou lettres sur l'économie domestique.* Paris, 1821.

Quesnay, François. *François Quesnay et la physiocratie.* Vol. 2. Paris, 1958.

Recueil de pièces rares et facétieuses anciennes et modernes. Paris, 1873.

Réimpression de l'Ancien Moniteur. 31 vols. Paris, 1863–1870.

Rousseau, Jean-Jacques. *Les Confessions.* 2 vols. Paris, 1952.

———. *Politics and the Arts: Letter to Monsieur d'Alembert on the Theatre.* Trans. Allan Bloom. Ithaca, N.Y., 1968.

Siéyès, Emmanuel. *Qu'est-ce-que le Tiers-Etat? Précédé de l'Essai sur les privilèges.* Paris, 1888.

de Staal de Launay, Marguerite. *Mémoires de Madame de Staal de Launay.* Paris, n.d.

Tallemant des Réaux. *Historiettes.* 2 vols. Paris, 1960.

Toussaint de Saint-Luc. *Le Bon laquais, ou vie de Jacques Cochois, dit Jasmin.* Paris, 1739.

Turmeau de La Morandière, Denis. *Police sur les mendians, les vagabonds, les joueurs de profession, les intrigants, les filles prostituées, les domestiques hors de maison depuis long-temps, et les gens sans aveu.* Paris, 1764.

Varet, Alexandre. *De l'Education chrétienne des enfants selon les maximes de l'Ecriture sainte.* Paris, 1666.

Vauban, Sébastien le Prestre de. *Projet d'une dixme royale.* Paris, 1708.

Vauvenargues, Luc de Clapiers de. *Oeuvres complètes.* 2 vols. Paris, 1968.

Viollet de Wagnon, Jacques. *L'Auteur laquais, ou réponses aux objections qui ont été faites au corps de ce nom sur la vie de Jacques Cochois, dit Jasmin.* Avignon, 1750.

WORKS OF FICTION

Chasles, Robert. *Les Illustres Françoises*. 2 vols. Paris, 1967.

Diderot, Denis. *Jacques le Fataliste*. Paris, 1973.

――――. *Oeuvres complètes*. 20 vols. Paris, 1875–1877.

――――. *Paradoxe sur le comédien précédé des entretiens sur le fils naturel*. Paris, 1967.

Fielding, Henry. *Tom Jones*. New York, 1950.

La Bruyère, Jean de. *Les Caractères*. Paris, 1932.

Lamartine, Alphonse de. *Geneviève, histoire d'une servante*. Paris, 1947.

Lesage, Alain-René. *Gil Blas de Santillane*. 2 vols. Paris, 1973.

Marivaux, Pierre Carlet de. *Le Paysan parvenu*. Paris, 1965.

――――. *Théâtre complet*. 2 vols. Paris, 1968.

――――. *La Vie de Marianne*. Lausanne, 1961.

Montesquieu, Charles de. *Lettres persanes*. Paris, 1964.

Mouhy, Charles de Fieux de. *Mémoires d'une fille de qualité qui ne s'est point retirée du monde*. 4 vols. Amsterdam, 1747.

――――. *La Mouche, ou les espiègleries et aventures galantes de Bigand*. 2 vols. Paris, 1777.

Regnard, Jean-François. *Théâtre*. 2 vols. Paris, 1876.

Restif de La Bretonne, Nicolas-Edmé. *Les Contemporaines*. Paris, Charpentier ed., n.d.

Rousseau, Jean-Jacques. *Emile ou de l'éducation*. Paris, 1964.

――――. *Julie ou la nouvelle Héloïse*. Paris, 1967.

Sorel, Charles. *Histoire comique de Francion*. 2 vols. Paris, 1924.

Suite des Illustres Françoises. Lille, 1780.

Voltaire, François Marie Arouet de. *Oeuvres complètes*. 52 vols. Paris, 1877–1885.

Zola, Emile. *Pot-Bouille*. Paris, 1957.

SECONDARY WORKS

Abbiateci, André et al. *Crimes et criminalité en France aux 17e et 18e siècles*. Paris, 1967.

Bibliography

Auerbach, Erich. "La Cour et la ville." In *Scenes from the Drama of European Literature*. New York, 1959.

Auger, Madeleine. *Condition juridique et économique du personnel domestique féminin*. Paris, 1935.

d'Avenel Georges. *Histoire économique de la propriété, des salaires, et de tous les prix en général*. 4 vols. Paris, 1898.

Babeau, Albert. *Les Artisans et les domestiques d'autrefois*. Paris, 1898.

Berlanstein, Lenard. *The Barristers of Toulouse in the Eighteenth Century*. Baltimore, 1975.

Berman, Marshall. *The Politics of Authenticity: Radical Individualism and the Emergence of Modern Society*. New York, 1972.

Blanc, François-Paul. "Les Enfants abandonnés à Marseille au XVIIIe siècle." Thèse de Droit, Aix-en-Provence, 1972.

Blanchard, Raoul. *Les Alpes occidentales*. 6 vols. Paris, 1945.

Bloch, Marc. *La Société féodale*. 2 vols. Paris, 1940.

Bluche, François. *Les Magistrats du Parlement de Paris au XVIIIe siècle*. Besançon, 1960.

Blunt, Anthony. *Art and Architecture in France, 1500–1700*. London, 1973.

Brooks, Peter. *The Novel of Worldliness: Crébillon, Marivaux, Laclos, Stendhal*. Princeton, 1969.

Carrière, Jacqueline. *La Population d'Aix-en-Provence à la fin du XVIIe siècle*. Aix-en-Provence, 1958.

Castan, Yves. *Honnêteté et relations sociales en Languedoc, 1715–1780*. Paris, 1974.

Chartier, Roger; Compère, M.; and Julia, D. *L'Education en France du XVIe au XVIIIe siècle*. Paris, 1976.

Chatelain, Abel. "Migrations et domesticité féminine urbaine en France, 18e–20e siècles." *Revue d'histoire économique et sociale* 47 (1969): 506–528.

Chevalier, Louis. *Classes laborieuses et classes dangereuses*. Paris, 1958.

Cipolla, Carlo. *Before the Industrial Revolution*. London, 1976.

Cobb, Richard. *The Police and the People*. Oxford, 1970.

Corvisier, André. "Service militaire et mobilité géographique au dix-huitième siècle." *Annales de démographie historique* (1970), pp. 185–204.

Coste, Jean-Paul. *La Ville d'Aix-en-Provence en 1695: Structure urbaine et société.* 2 vols. Aix-en-Provence, 1970.

Cunnington, Phillis. *The Costume of Household Servants from the Middle Ages to 1900.* London, 1974.

Cusenier, Marcel. *Les Domestiques en France.* Paris, 1912.

Darnton, Robert. *The Business of Enlightenment: A Publishing History of the Encyclopédie, 1775–1800.* Cambridge, Mass., 1979.

Daumard, Adeline, and Furet, François. *Structures et relations sociales à Paris au milieu du XVIIIe siècle.* Paris, 1961.

Davidoff, Leonore. "Mastered for Life: Servant and Wife in Victorian and Edwardian England." *Journal of Social History* 7 (Summer 1974):406–408.

Davis, Natalie. *Society and Culture in Early Modern France.* Stanford, 1975.

Depaw, Jacques. "Illicit Sexual Activity and Society in Eighteenth-Century Nantes." Trans. Elborg Forster. In Robert Forster and Orest Ranum, eds., *Family and Society.* Baltimore, 1976.

Douglas, Mary. *Purity and Danger.* London, 1966.

Duby, Georges, and Wallon, A., eds. *Histoire de la France rurale.* 3 vols. Paris, 1973.

Elias, Norbert. *La Civilisation des moeurs.* Paris, 1973.

———. *La Société de cour.* Paris, 1974.

El Kordi, Mohammed. *Bayeux aux 17e et 18e siècles.* Paris, 1970.

Emelina, Jean. *Les Valets et les servantes dans le théâtre comique en France de 1610 à 1700.* Grenoble, 1975.

———. *Les Valets et les servantes dans le théâtre de Molière.* Aix-en-Provence, 1958.

Eyglunent, Annie. "Délinquance, criminalité, et troubles sociaux dans la Sénéchaussée de Digne." Mémoire de Maîtrise, Univ. de Provence, 1969.

Fairchilds, Cissie. "Female Sexual Attitudes and the Rise of Illegitimacy: A Case Study." *Journal of Interdisciplinary History* 8 (Spring 1978):627–663.

————. "Masters and Servants in Eighteenth-Century Toulouse." *Journal of Social History* 12 (Spring 1979):368–393.

————. *Poverty and Charity in Aix-en-Provence, 1640–1789*. Baltimore, 1976.

Farge, Arlette. *Vivre dans la rue à Paris au XVIIIe siècle*. Paris, 1979.

————. *Le Vol d'aliments à Paris au XVIIIe siècle*. Paris, 1974.

Flandrin, Jean-Louis. *Familles: Parenté, maison, sexualité dans l'ancienne société*. Paris, 1976.

Fourcade, Olivier. *De la Condition sociale des domestiques*. Paris, 1898.

Fox-Genovese, Elizabeth. *The Origins of Physiocracy*. Ithaca, 1976.

Fradin, Bernard. "Domestiques d'établissement et domestiques de maison à Lyon au XVIIIe siècle." Mémoire de Maîtrise, Univ. de Lyon, 1976.

Furet, François. *Penser la Révolution Française*. Paris, 1978.

Furet, François, and Ozouf, Jacques, eds. *Lire et Ecrire: L'Alphabétisation des français de Calvin à Jules Ferry*. Paris, 1977.

Gaiffe, Felix. *Le Drame en France au XVIIIe siècle*. 1910; rept. ed., Paris, 1970.

Garden, Maurice. *Lyon et les lyonnais au XVIIIe siècle*. Paris, 1970.

Geertz, Clifford. *Negara: The Theatre-State in Nineteenth-Century Bali*. Princeton, 1980.

Genovese, Eugene. *Roll, Jordan, Roll: The World the Slaves Made*. New York, 1972.

Geremek, Bronislaw. "Criminalité, vagabondage, paupérisme: La Marginalité à l'aube des temps modernes." *Revue d'histoire moderne et contemporaine* 21 (July–September 1974):337–375.

Gillis, John. "Servants, Sexual Relations, and the Risks of Illegitimacy in London, 1801–1900." *Feminist Studies* 5 (February 1979):142–173.

Girouard, Mark. *Life in the English Country House*. New Haven and London, 1978.

Goffman, Erving. *Asylums: Essays on the Social Situation of Inmates and Other Patients*. New York, 1961.

Goubert, Pierre. *L'Ancien Régime*. 2 vols. Paris, 1969 and 1973.

Greer, Donald. *The Incidence of Emigration during the French Revolution*. Cambridge, Mass., 1951.

———. *The Incidence of Terror during the French Revolution*. Cambridge, Mass. 1935.

Grissolange, Bérénice. "Aix-en-Provence sous la Révolution: Structures sociales et familiales." Mémoire de Maîtrise, Univ. de Provence, 1974.

Guillaume, Pierre, and Poussou, Jean-Pierre. *Démographie historique*. Paris, 1970.

Guiral, Pierre, and Thuillier, Guy. *La Vie quotidienne des domestiques en France au XIXe siècle*. Paris, 1978.

Gutton, Jean-Pierre. *Domestiques et serviteurs dans la France de l'Ancien Régime*. Paris, 1981.

———. *La Société et les pauvres en Europe, 16e–18e siècles*. Paris, 1974.

Hay, Douglas et al. *Albion's Fatal Tree: Crime and Society in Eighteenth-Century England*. New York, 1975.

Hecht, J. Jean. *The Domestic Servant Class in Eighteenth-Century England*. London, 1956.

Hom, Léon. *De la Situation juridique des gens de service*. Paris, 1901.

Hommeril, Philippe. "La Criminalité dans le Calvados de 1792 à 1799." Mémoire de Maîtrise, Univ. de Caen, 1973.

Horn, Pamela. *The Rise and Fall of the Victorian Servant*. Dublin, 1975.

Hufton, Olwen. *Bayeux in the Late Eighteenth Century: A Social Study*. Oxford, 1967.

———. *The Poor of Eighteenth-Century France*. Oxford, 1974.

———. "Women and the Family Economy in Eighteenth-Century France." *French Historical Studies* 9 (Spring 1975):1–22.

Kaplow, Jeffry. *The Names of Kings: The Parisian Laboring Poor in the Eighteenth Century*. New York, 1972.

Katz, Paul. *Situation économîque et sociale des domestiques en France, en Allemagne, et en Suisse depuis le Moyen-Age jusqu'à nos jours.* Montpellier, 1941.

Katzman, David. *Seven Days a Week: Women and Domestic Service in Industrializing America.* New York, 1978.

Kreiss, Paul. "The Valet in French Comedy, 1670–1730." 3 vols. Ph.D. diss., Northwestern Univ. 1968.

Labrousse, Camille Ernest et al. *Histoire économique et sociale de la France.* Vol. 2. Paris, 1970.

Lagrave, Henri. *Le Théâtre et le public à Paris de 1715 à 1750.* Paris, 1972.

Laslett, Peter. *Family Life and Illicit Love in Earlier Generations.* Cambridge, Eng., 1977.

―――. *Household and Family in Past Times. Cambridge*, Eng., 1972.

Léon, Pierre. *Structures économiques et problèmes sociaux du monde rural dans la France du sud-est.* Paris, 1966.

Le Roy Ladurie, Emmanuel. *Les Paysans de Languedoc.* 2 vols. Paris, 1966.

Levasseur, Emile. *Histoire des classes ouvrières et de l'industrie en France avant 1789.* 2 vols. Paris, 1901.

Lottin, Alain. "Naissances illégitimes et filles-mères à Lille." *Revue d'histoire moderne et contemporaine* 17 (April 1970):278–322.

Lough, John. *Paris Theatre Audiences in the Seventeenth and Eighteenth Centuries.* London, 1957.

McBride, Theresa. *The Domestic Revolution: The Modernisation of Household Service in England and France, 1820–1920.* London, 1976.

Marion, Marcel. *Dictionnaire des institutions de la France aux XVIIe et XVIIIe siècles.* Paris, 1923.

Martin-Fugier, Anne. *La Place des bonnes: La domesticité féminine à Paris en 1900.* Paris, 1979.

Mazuy, François. *Essai historique sur les moeurs et les coutumes des marseillais au XIX siècle.* Marseille, 1854.

Mousnier, Roland. *Les Institutions de la France sous la monarchie absolue.* 2 vols. Paris, 1974.

Muheim, Henri. "Une Source exceptionnelle: Le recensement de la population lyonnaise en 1709, les domestiques dans la société." In *Actes du 89e congrès des sociétés savantes,* pp. 207–217. Lyon, 1964.

Pariset, François, ed. *Bordeaux au XVIIIe siècle.* Bordeaux, 1968.

Peristiany, J. G., ed. *Honor and Shame: The Values of Mediterranean Society.* London, 1966.

Perrot, Jean-Claude. *Genèse d'une ville moderne: Caen au XVIIIe siècle.* 2 vols. Lille, 1974.

Personnaz, André. *Le Louage des domestiques.* Paris, 1909.

Phan, Marie-Claude. "Les Déclarations de Grossesse en France: Essai institutionnel." *Revue d'histoire moderne et contemporaine* 22 (January–March 1975):61–88.

Poussou, Jean-Pierre. "Les Mouvements migratoires en France de la fin du XVe siècle au debut du XIXe siècle." *Annales de démographie historique* (1970), pp. 11–78.

Ranum, Orest. "Courtesy, Absolutism, and the Rise of the French State, 1630–1660." *Journal of Modern History* 52 (September 1980):426–451.

Reinhard, Maurice, ed. *Contributions à l'histoire démographique de la Révolution Française.* 3 vols. Paris, 1962, 1965, 1970.

Renault du Motey, Henri. *L'Esclavage à Rome, le servage au Moyen-Âge, la domesticité dans les temps modernes.* Douai, 1881.

Reynaud-Lefaucheur, Thérèse. "Les Femmes dans la population marseillaise en 1793." Mémoire de Maîtrise, Univ. de Provence, 1975.

Ribaric-Demers, Maria. *Le Valet et la soubrette de Molière à la Révolution.* Paris, 1970.

Richard, Henri. *Du Louage des services domestiques en droit français.* Angers, 1906.

Rigault, Claude. *Les Domestiques dans le théâtre de Marivaux.* Paris, 1968.

Rossiaud, Jacques, "Prostitution, jeunesse et société dans les villes du sud-est au XVe siecle." *Annales: Economies, sociétés, civilisations* 31 (March–April 1976): 289–325.

Rouget, Françoise; Sauty M.; and Patouillard, D. "La Population de Marseille en 1793: Approche sociologique." Mémoire de Maîtrise, Univ. de Provence, 1971.

Roux-Alpheran, A. *Les Rues d'Aix, ou recherches historiques sur l'ancienne capitale de la Provence.* 2 vols. Aix-en-Provence, 1846–1848.

Rudé, George. *The Crowd in the French Revolution.* London, 1959.

Sauty, Robert. *De la Condition juridique des domestiques.* Paris, 1911.

Scott, Joan, and Tilly, Louise. *Women, Work, and Family.* New York, 1978.

————. "Women's Work and the Family Economy in Nineteenth-Century Europe." *Comparative Studies in Society and History* 17 (January 1975):36–64.

Sennett, Richard. *The Fall of Public Man.* New York, 1977.

Sentou, Jean. *Fortunes et groupes sociaux à Toulouse sous la Révolution: Essai d'histoire statistique.* Toulouse, 1969.

Sewell, William H., Jr. *Work and Revolution in France: The Language of Labor from the Old Regime to 1848.* Cambridge, Eng., 1980.

Shorter, Edward. *The Making of the Modern Family.* New York, 1975.

Siméoni, Michèle, and Siméoni, Joseph. "L'Alphabétisation à Aix au XVIIIe siècle." Mémoire de Maîtrise, Univ. de Provence, 1975.

Slater, Miriam. "The Weightiest Business: Marriage in an Upper Gentry Family in Seventeenth-Century England." *Past and Present* 72 (August 1976):25–64.

Starobinski, Jean. *Jean-Jacques Rousseau: La Transparence et l'obstacle.* Paris, 1957.

Stone, Lawrence. *The Family, Sex, and Marriage in England, 1500–1800.* New York, 1977.

Thompson, Edward P. "Patrician Society, Plebeian Culture." *Journal of Social History* 7 (Spring 1974):382–405.

Trumbach, Randolph. *The Rise of the Egalitarian Family.* New York, 1978.

Turner, Victor. *The Ritual Process: Structure and Anti-Structure.* Chicago, 1969.

Veblen, Thorstein. *The Theory of the Leisure Class.* New York 1934.

Vétû, Paul. *De la Domesticité en France et dans l'ancienne Rome.* Dijon, 1868.

La Ville au XVIIIe siècle. Colloque du Centre Aixois d'Etudes et de Recherches sur le XVIIIe Siècle. Aix-en-Provence, 1975.

Vovelle, Michel. *Piété baroque et déchristianisation en Provence au XVIIIe siècle.* Paris, 1973.

Vovelle, Michel et al. *Histoire d'Aix-en-Provence.* Aix-en-Provence, 1977.

Wills, Antoinette. "Criminal Life and Criminal Justice during the French Revolution: The Six Provisional Criminal Courts of Paris, 1791–1792." Ph.D. diss., Univ. of Washington, 1975.

Index

Library of Congress Cataloging in Publication Data

Maza, Sarah C., 1953-
Servants and masters in eighteenth-century France.
Bibliography: p.   Includes index.
1. Domestics—France—History—18th century.
2. Master and servant—France—History—18th century.
I. Title.
HD8039.D52F85 1983   305.4'364   83-42566
ISBN 0-691-05394-4

Sarah C. Maza is Assistant Professor of History at
Northwestern University, Evanston, Illinois.